Althusser

and His Contemporaries

POST-CONTEMPORARY INTERVENTIONS

Series Editors: Fredric Jameson, Michael Hardt, and Roberto Dainotto

Althusser

and His Contemporaries

PHILOSOPHY'S PERPETUAL WAR

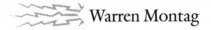 Warren Montag

Duke University Press   Durham and London   2013

© 2013 Duke University Press
All rights reserved
Printed in the United States of America on acid-free paper ∞
Designed by Courtney Leigh Baker
Typeset in Galliard by Tseng Information Systems, Inc.
Library of Congress Cataloging-in-Publication Data
Montag, Warren.
Althusser and his contemporaries : philosophy's perpetual war /
Warren Montag.
pages cm — (Post-contemporary interventions)
Includes bibliographical references and index.
ISBN 978-0-8223-5386-7 (cloth : alk. paper)
ISBN 978-0-8223-5400-0 (pbk. : alk. paper)
1. Althusser, Louis, 1918–1990. 2. Structuralism.
3. Poststructuralism. I. Title. II. Series:
Post-contemporary interventions.
B2430.A474M66 2013
194 — dc23
2012048670

Para Dolores, Elisa y Jacobo

אין אנדענק פון שמואל יאסף מאנטאג

Contents

Acknowledgments

Étienne Balibar and Pierre Macherey have encouraged and challenged me in innumerable ways, opening up paths that I am still exploring. I couldn't have written a book like this without their help and generosity. I also want to acknowledge one of this work's absent causes. In the summer of 1983, a few months before his unexpected death, I spent a week with Michel Pêcheux translating "Discourse: Structure or Event" page by page as he wrote it. I remember every word of the extraordinary conversations we had, and they helped shape my view of Althusser and of his philosophical moment.

I discovered Althusser with G. M. Goshgarian many years ago, and, fortunately, we continue to argue about his texts even today. I have benefited in many ways from his help and expertise. Gregory Elliot, whose work transformed the study of Althusser in English, has been a great friend and inspiration.

My comrades and friends who make up the editorial collective of *Décalages* have provided the kind of community in which thought flourishes: Aurelio Sainz Pezonaga, Juan Pedro Garcia, Filippo Del Lucchese, Vittorio Morfino, Giorgos Fourtounis, Jason E. Smith, and Matt Bonal. I want to express my gratitude to the founders of *Rethinking Marxism*, especially Jack Amariglio, David Ruccio, Antonio Callari, and Rick Wolff, who have been supportive of my work from the beginning.

I also want to acknowledge the following people without whom the book would not have been what it is: Nancy Armstrong, Yann Moulier Boutang, Sebastian Budgen, Alex Callinicos, Michel de Certeau (1925–1986), Won Choi, Dan Fineman, Alain Gigandet, Michael Hardt, Spencer Jackson, Mateusz Janik, James Kavanagh, William Lewis, Jacques Lezra, François Matheron, David McInerney, Pierre-François Moreau, Antonio Negri, Jason Read, Elisabeth Roudinesco, Juan Domingo Sanchez, Hasana Sharp, Michael Sprinker (1950–1999), Ted Stolze, Peter Thomas, André Tosel, and Maria Turchetto.

Agne Jomantaite provided invaluable help in preparing the manuscript. I also thank Alexandra Vittes and Molly Quinn for their work.

Finally, I thank Courtney Berger and Christine Choi from Duke University Press for their help and guidance.

Earlier portions of chapter 8 originally appeared as "The Soul Is the Prison of the Body: Althusser and Foucault, 1970–1975," in *Yale French Studies* 88 (1995): 53–77, and chapter 9 was originally published as "The Late Althusser: Materialism of the Encounter or Philosophy of Nothing?" in *Culture, Theory, and Critique* 51, no. 2 (2010): 157–70. Reprinted by permission of the publisher, Taylor and Francis.

For foreign language sources where there is no published English translation all translations are my own.

Introduction

WHY READ ALTHUSSER TODAY?

*The essays submitted to you had to take the position of recognizing
openly that struggle is at the heart of every philosophy.*

LOUIS ALTHUSSER,

"Is It Simple to Be a Marxist in Philosophy?"

To pose the question, "Why read Althusser today?" is to admit at the out-set that his status as a philosopher remains unclear in a way that is not true of his contemporaries and friends, Foucault and Derrida. And, indeed, de-spite the persistent hostility to the latter in the Anglophone world, Althus-ser alone could boast that more had been written against him than about him by the end of the twentieth century: an impressive number of books in various languages have the phrase "against Althusser" in the title.[1] Whether to denounce him as a Stalinist, a structuralist, or both, most of his critics, despite their often incompatible theoretical and political positions, unwit-tingly collaborated to produce an overwhelmingly negative judgment of his work. Others, willing at least to grant Althusser a place in the history of thought, chronicled the rise and fall of an "Althusserianism" confined to a moment that has come and gone and outside of which it can have no signifi-cance or effect.[2] Perhaps even more noteworthy is the fact that an impres-sive range of public intellectuals and specialists even now feel compelled to demonstrate that Althusser's work is without life or meaning.

The fact that his death in 1990, followed very quickly by the publication of his widely read autobiography, *The Future Lasts Forever*, brought Althus-ser to the attention of a new generation guided by theoretical passions and imperatives different in certain respects from that of the 1960s and 1970s made the task of denouncing him appear all the more urgent. His autobiog-raphy greatly facilitated this task even for those who possessed little famil-iarity either with his texts or the philosophical works to which everything Althusser wrote referred directly or indirectly. Following the line of least resistance, such critics could cite the tragic "Case of Althusser," madman and murderer, as he himself explained it, using his own words to prove the imposture or simply the failure of his work, effectively taking the side of Althusser against himself. And yet, such figures, from Mark Lilla (who wrote a review of Althusser's autobiography entitled "Marx and Murder") to Christopher Hitchens ("by 1980 Althusser had been exposed as the utter fraud he later confessed himself to be") to Tony Judt (who exhibited a particular anxiety about Althusser, to whom he devotes an entire chapter of his widely reviewed and highly acclaimed *Reappraisals: Reflections on the Forgotten Twentieth Century*), all in some sense testify to the "spectral" qualities of Althusser's major texts, the spirit of which is never quite laid to rest and survived even his own always ambivalent and contradictory attempts to negate, deny, and undo what he had written.[3] Needless to say, the effect of the repeated efforts (including his own) to finish with Althusser once and for all is to defer the desired end and thus paradoxically keep his oeuvre alive. They are also a testimony to the extraordinary power of his work.

But we must not mistake its power for its profundity, as if its true meaning lay hidden beneath a textual surface stubbornly resistant to interpretation, awaiting the ideal reader to disclose its secrets. For Althusser the very act of writing divested thought of any interior as well as any illusion that writing issues from an interior. Writing and, perhaps even more, publication—Althusser more than once wanted to recall his books the instant they were published—were, as Mallarmé said in a phrase that never ceased to inspire Althusser, like a throw of the dice that cannot abolish chance. Althusser wrote that it is not philosophers' "intentions that count. What count are the real effects of their philosophies."[4] And the effects of Althusser's philosophy are striking indeed: it produced as its result not only the reiterated denunciations by the figures cited above, but it moved both Jacques Rancière and E. P. Thompson, two very notable and accomplished thinkers, not otherwise so inclined, to undertake impressive book-length critical readings in the 1970s whose arguments are often eclipsed by a passion, and even violence, whose intensity is striking.[5] While they would appear to have little in common but an antipathy to Althusser, they, starting from very different cultural, political, and theoretical perspectives, finally arrived at remarkably similar critiques of his work—the terms of which are nearly identical. The threat must have seemed great indeed to have united Rancière and Thompson in a ferocious no-holds-barred assault on Althusser (who, significantly, did not respond to either critique). Even this assault, however, must be regarded as an effect, not the only effect to be sure, but an effect nevertheless, of Althusser's work.

Rancière's text, significantly the first book in what has become a distinguished philosophical oeuvre, is written from the point of view of a former student, if not disciple, of a master who promised to deliver a philosophy capable of changing the world rather than merely interpreting it. Events, particularly the events of 1968, showed, however, that the immense theoretical revolution to which Althusser declared allegiance was an elaborate ruse, the ruse of domination masquerading as its own critique: "the Marxism we learned in the Althusserian school was a philosophy of order, whose every principle divided us from the movement of revolt that was shaking the bourgeois order."[6] And, according to Rancière, no principle was more decisive in deterring his young students from joining the movement of revolt than Althusser's critique of humanism and his theory of the interpellation of the individual as subject. Althusser, he testifies, "wanted to make us believe that the critique of the subject was itself the 'Marxist theoretical revolution.' As if philosophy had not for two centuries had a field day with the liquidation of the subject."

Thompson, who was aware of Rancière's book but does not appear to have been influenced by it (he refers to him in a single footnote as a "lively" expression of "the Maoist freak-out," one among the many "heresies" to which Althusser's dogmatic cult gave rise), will go even further: not only has Althusser reduced human experience, feeling, and decision to anonymous structures so abstracted from what is genuinely human that they resemble Platonic forms, but he has argued that the entire dimension of subjectivity is nothing more than the means by which a mode of production secures its own reproduction. From Thompson's perspective, the notion that individuals are interpellated as subjects is literally unthinkable. Althusser's most widely read text is, writes Thompson, "perhaps the ugliest thing he has ever done, the crisis of the idealist delirium. I will spare myself the tedium of criticism, since in its naivety, its refusal of all relevant evidence, and its absurd idealist inventions, it exposes itself."[7] For both Rancière and Thompson, Althusser's power is fundamentally a power of seduction and deception; their task as they see it is to break the spell with which he has held so many in thrall.

I will not here try to respond to these critiques; I simply want to note their rhetorical as well as rational force and the excess of aggression that often make reading them uncomfortable. From Althusser's perspective, such responses showed more clearly than any examination of his texts that he had struck a nerve, one of philosophy's "sensitive points" that certain thinkers before him had "touched" and that he, like them, had activated philosophy's defenses.[8] He often referred to Marx, Freud, and Nietzsche (about whom Althusser had finally little to say) in this regard, but above all to Machiavelli and Spinoza. This, however, did not mean that Althusser embraced the ideal of a philosophical martyrdom, according to which the enmity of his peers would be the surest sign of his philosophy's veracity. On the contrary, Althusser's constant recourse to Machiavelli and Spinoza not only taught him to resist the lure of martyrdom's fictive triumph but also taught that there is no virtue in weakness but only in power, that the armed prophet triumphs, that is, inscribes his prophecy in reality, while the unarmed prophet comes to ruin. But what is it to arm oneself in philosophy or to make one's philosophical positions effective? It was from these two thinkers that Althusser learned that strategy was as necessary in philosophy as in politics.

Strategy for Althusser, however, was not a matter of rhetoric, of persuading others through noble fictions or impressive sounding but ultimately meaningless strings of words to believe ideas whose truth he could not demonstrate. Perhaps alone among his contemporaries, Althusser, who had adopted Napoleon's military maxim, "on s'engage et puis on voit," (meaning, first we engage the enemy and then see what does and doesn't work), produced, following the publication of each of his major texts, a reflection on what he had begun to call by the mid-1960s the theoretical conjuncture, that is, the specific historical and philosophical context into which each of his works was introduced and whose relations it did or did not succeed in modifying. Thus, in June 1966, slightly more than six months after *For Marx* and *Reading Capital* (and the explosive reactions to them in France and around the world), Althusser delivered an address to an audience that included Derrida, among others, entitled "The Philosophical Conjuncture and Marxist Theoretical Research," in which he described the very rich philosophical scene of that time as a field where conflicting philosophies are locked in a battle characterized by a multiplicity of forces arrayed in ever shifting alliances that required constant tactical adjustments.[9] Nearly ten years later, reflecting upon the body of work he had so far produced (for the purposes of an academic *soutenance* or defense), Althusser concluded that, if anything, he had failed to acknowledge the degree to which the history of philosophy, including and especially French philosophy of the 1960s, was a perpetual war whose stakes, whose very rationality, remained incarnate in relations of force: "ideas only have a historical existence if they are taken up by and incorporated into the materiality of social relations." The relations between ideas are "relations of force that make it so that some ideas are in power, while others remain subordinated to them."[10] How does one shift the balance of forces in philosophy given that it was never a matter of all or nothing? In part, Althusser showed that to neutralize or at least diminish the hold of the ideas that are in power required an operation whose success would be measured not by the validity of one's arguments alone (which, after all, may fall on deaf ears or hardened hearts) but by a demonstrable change in what is actually said and thought, by a breeching and a freeing up that permits something new to emerge.

But here Althusser's meditations on theoretical practice take a surprising turn: What does it mean concretely to engage with other philosophies on a field of conflict? Let us begin with the phrase "other philosophies." Althusser did not regard the history of philosophy as a succession of closed systems, each of which could be identified with an author who would serve as its center and principle of unity, of which Marxism or materialism would be one among others, relating to them, addressing them, criticizing them from the outside in a philosophical version of siege warfare or a war of position. If we can speak of philosophical adversaries, "the adversary is not a united body: the philosophical battlefield is thus not the reproduction of the simple rationalist opposition of truth and error in the form of opposing 'systems.' There is not on the one side the homogeneous camp of 'the good,' and on the other the camp of 'the bad.'"[11] In fact, Althusser repeatedly argued that the most effective attacks on Marxism came from within rather than from without, based not on the importation into Marxism of foreign theories such as functionalism or rational choice theory but on citations from Marx, Engels, and Lenin. If this were true, then the most effective defenses of Marxism might require a detour outside of it, to apparently foreign and even apparently anti-Marxist philosophies whose concepts might play an indispensable role in neutralizing these attacks or even in making Marx's thought intelligible. In this sense, the distinction between Marxist and non-Marxist or idealist and materialist systems of thought is thus rendered null and void. The perpetual war of tendencies rages within as well as between these systems.

It was precisely with respect to Hegel, otherwise thought to be "the main enemy" from Althusser's perspective, that he argued that to read *en matérialiste* or in a materialist way is thus not to accept or reject a philosophical doctrine in toto as if it were homogeneous but instead "to trace lines of demarcation within it," to make visible and palpable the presence of conflicting forces within even the most apparently coherent text and to heighten and intensify its contradictions.[12] To do so is to take the side of a text against itself, one of its sides against the other or others, to discern the lines of force that constitute it. If all this sounds excessively Marxist, the attribute that would be precisely conferred upon Althusser, as distinct from most of his contemporaries, and the archaic status that would render him irrelevant to the present, let us recall that in 1967 Derrida, undoubtedly influenced by his friend and colleague, would describe his own philosophical activity in remarkably similar terms. A grammatology, a science of the letter, of writing in its material existence, could only begin to undo (or more precisely, to deconstruct) the age-old domination of the philosophy of the logos and of ontotheology by first thinking through the struggle it was compelled to wage:

> The movements of deconstruction do not address [or perhaps "shake"—Derrida uses the verb "solliciter"] structures from the outside. They are only possible and effective, they only aim their blows by inhabiting these structures. By inhabiting them in a certain way, for one inhabits always and especially when one does not suspect it. Operating necessarily from the interior, borrowing from the former structure all the strategic and economic resources of subversion, borrowing them structurally, that is, without being able to isolate their elements and atoms, the enterprise of deconstruction is always in a certain way led astray by its own labor.[13]

To imagine that it is possible to wage a struggle from the outside when there exists no outside, except an outside already inscribed within a given field as its outside, is thus to take up a position always inscribed within as a function of the order one would overturn. In this sense, one must operate necessarily from the interior, and the manner in which one inhabits this interior determines whether one can undermine and destabilize the conceptual order. To imagine the possibility of simply stepping outside or, as Althusser put it, of finding an empty corner of the forest, is to be condemned to repeat the very discourse with which one would break. Thus for Althusser, it was not a matter of choice: to realize his philosophical positions was to occupy a place in the already full world of philosophy and to occupy this place was to engage with and within the already existing philosophies to make them move or move over. This is precisely what is so valuable in Althusser: the record of his thought is simultaneously a record of the way he inhabited or occupied a specific philosophical conjuncture, not only engaging with his contemporaries but intervening within them "to make them speak," disengaging them from themselves, discovering their specific quantity of force. Waging a philosophical struggle, in other words, made him an incomparable reader: to read Althusser is thus to read him reading, sometimes incisively, but just as often struggling to grasp not the meaning of a text or body of work but precisely the contradictions around which it was constituted.

Further, since there can be no philosophy that would not itself embody the very conflicts in which it seeks to intervene, insofar as philosophies attempt to master these conflicts by interiorizing them only to find themselves afflicted by what they cannot digest, Althusser's position comes very close to Hegel's. Every philosophy is the realization of a contradiction that it necessarily lacks the means to resolve. Thus, it is not enough to read others, that is, to make visible their contradictions; one must constantly attempt after the fact to grasp the conflictuality proper to one's own thought, an attempt that produces new contradictions requiring new interventions ad infinitum.

Accordingly, if we take Althusser at his word, the power of his work, measured by the force of the reactions to it, cannot be explained by reference to the way in which it transcends its historical moment but precisely by what in it is most historical. Outside of the vicious circle of mimicry and rejection, a small but growing number of works have sought precisely to situate Althusser historically, without ceding to the temptation to declare the end of Althusser and any interest he might have for the present moment.[14] Some of the most valuable of these have placed his work in the context of Marxism, a heterogeneous and still developing context to be sure, and like any other, defined by conflicts and divergences. Such an approach to Althusser is hardly surprising: the vast majority of Althusser's direct references (especially in the work published during his lifetime) to predecessors and contemporaries are to Marxists (Marx, Engels, Plekhanov, Lenin, Stalin, Mao, Gramsci, and Garaudy, among others), and the polemics in which he engaged nearly all involved his fellow Communists and Marxists, who mostly took him to task for incorrectly or even abusively interpreting the works of Marx and Lenin. Gregory Elliot's *Althusser: the Detour of*

Theory and, more recently, William Lewis's *Louis Althusser and the Traditions of French Marxism*, together with G. M. Goshgarian's introductions to the English translations of Althusser's posthumously published texts (as well as François Matheron's careful and thorough situating of the French originals), consider Althusser's major works as the interventions that Althusser himself always insisted they were. Elliot, Lewis, and Goshgarian locate the texts in the debates within and around the French Communist Party in the 1960s and 1970s and read them as simultaneously commenting on Marx and advocating specific positions within the international Communist movement, as well as within the world of French (and to some extent European) communism and Maoism. This work is absolutely necessary: it is no more possible to understand Althusser's texts without reference to the political controversies of his period than it is to comprehend the works of Hobbes and Locke without a detailed knowledge of the political and social struggles of seventeenth-century England.

I want, however, to pose a different question, even if it can only be addressed on the basis of the foregoing studies: How do we begin to understand what Althusser himself called his "theoretical conjuncture"? For decades scholars in the Anglophone world have tended to view the major French philosophers of the sixties and the seventies as essentially separate from and often opposed to one another, each endeavoring to think, even if about remarkably similar questions, in a way that was fundamentally incompatible with their contemporaries. There was accordingly little room for conjunction of any kind. Foucault, Derrida, and Deleuze of course all cultivated such a view, which in turn permitted the rise internationally of groups of Foucauldians, Derridians, Deleuzeans, as well as Althusserians, who sought to show how and why their philosopher was unique among his contemporaries, necessitating the magnification of differences and the suppression of similarities. Each was supplied with a genealogy (often with the philosopher's explicit or tacit approval) that showed the way in which an individual philosopher belonged not to the historical present but to a tradition: Foucault to French epistemology, Derrida to phenomenology and Heidegger, Deleuze to Bergsonianism, and, of course, Althusser to Marxism. In Althusser's case, the effect was particularly unfortunate: those students of French philosophical theory not interested in Marxism believed they could safely ignore him, while Marxists, even those lacking any interest or competence in the questions Althusser discussed in his works, felt obliged to read and refute him, producing a mass of irrelevant "critiques."[15]

Althusser's death altered all this forever; not only the reception of his own work but our understanding of French thought in the 1960s and 1970s has irrevocably changed. Shortly after his death an archive was established in which the manuscripts found in his possession or which he had given to others, together with as many letters as could be collected from his correspondents, would be cataloged and prepared for publication. The results have been significant. First, there was the discovery that Althusser published only a small part of what he actually produced. A number of full-length manuscripts were found, in addition to dozens of more or less finished essays. Nearly three thousand pages of material from different periods of his career have now been published in French, not all of which have appeared in English.

The posthumous publications not only necessitate a thorough reevaluation of Althusser's project but, taken together with other materials in the archive (unpublished manuscripts in various stages of completion, lecture notes, letters, and marginalia), demonstrate very clearly that Althusser regarded the task of understanding the theoretical conjuncture as one of his highest priorities. He read and studied the work of the contemporaries named above and exhorted his students to do the same. The record of his seminars shows that at the very same moment that he and his young followers produced *Reading Capital*, they devoted courses to the study of structuralism and psychoanalysis, reading such contemporaries as Foucault, Derrida, Deleuze, and Lacan with the same rigor with which they approached the texts of Marx, generating symptomatic readings of their illustrious contemporaries. In fact, a number of documents show Althusser's appraisal of the theoretical conjuncture clearly identified a number of his most prominent non-Marxist contemporaries (especially Lacan, Foucault, Derrida, and Deleuze) as "objective allies" in the struggle against idealism, while many of the official philosophers of Marxism (particularly those engaged in the task of defining a Marxist humanism) were, whatever their subjective commitments, among the most effective partisans of idealism and spiritualism.

But it is the content of these encounters that is perhaps most surprising. While a few texts from the last decade of Althusser's life show his interest in developing what he called an "aleatory materialism," the contents of the archive reveal that by the early sixties at the latest Althusser sought to conceptualize a philosophy of the encounter.[16] In opposition to the mechanistic determinism attributed to him by Thompson and others, Althusser worked to overcome the opposition between chance and necessity by defining historical necessity as the product of chance encounters between absolutely singular entities. In place of the Stalinist establishing "the laws of historical development" or the structuralist revealing order and unity beneath the appearance of disorder and diversity, there thus emerges an entirely unexpected Althusser, heir to the aleatory thought of Epicurus and Lucretius, as well as Spinoza's absolute nominalism. What is perhaps most surprising about this current in Althusser's thought is that, even if it was made explicit only at the end of his life, it was present, although nearly unnoticed, throughout his work, beginning with the essays that make up *For Marx*. We should not make the mistake, though, of treating this underground current as the hidden truth of Althusser's work that readers up to this point have simply failed to see. The persistent "misreadings" of Althusser are indices of the theoretical conflicts that animate it: many of these conflicts are based on countervailing tendencies that coexist with and in their antagonism, neutralize, or at least render invisible the philosophy of the encounter.

We may thus begin to see the extent to which Althusser shared common philosophical concerns with some of his most notable contemporaries and why he would take interest in their work. I want to explore the ways in which, as we have noted, Althusser read or, more precisely, intervened in their work, drawing lines of demarcation to set free those elements that might lead to the "recommencement" of a materialism of the encounter, the only possible materialism from Althusser's perspective. Not very long ago, the commentary on Althusser focused on the theme of agency, on the opposition of science and ideology, on the meaning of his "antihumanism," or on his critique of "historicism." I do not intend here to supply new answers to the old questions. Instead, I want to examine the way that the encounters in which Althusser's participation was decisive, encounters that constituted the specificity of this extraordinary period in French thought, can be understood as having occurred around three nodal points, sites of intensive overdetermination, which are also nodes in a network of discourses both internal and external to Althusser.

STRUCTURE

Was Althusser's a philosophy of order, as Rancière insisted?[17] It is true that Althusser acutely felt the need to move beyond a merely descriptive approach to history, which proved incapable of establishing casual relations in that such an approach essentially nullified political practice. At the same time, however, he explicitly sought to escape theories of the hidden order of history, associated in his time with Hegel and certain "mechanistic" forms of Marxism. The concept of structure as it emerged in his time appeared precisely to open the possibility of theorizing the determinate *disorder* of history, irreducible either to randomness or to a final order of which it was merely the ruse or function. He and his colleagues carefully analyzed the concept of structure as it functioned in the work of their contemporaries in order to differentiate within it a materialist element. Althusser opened the way to a notion of structure as singularity and as a form of causality entirely immanent in its effects, even if his thought was suspended in part by the events of 1968 and in part by the impasses proper to it (if the two can be separated), deferred to the time, perhaps our own, when new encounters would allow it to resume.

SUBJECT

Is Althusser the thinker of the death of the subject or its liquidation? If Althusser in some sense tried to escape every philosophy of order, it was certainly not through the alternative traditionally offered by philosophy: the individual subject is the author of his or her thoughts and deeds and therefore capable of choosing to rebel. Of course, if the possibility of revolt or resistance finally resides in the realm of subjectivity, is it not the case that Althusser must have recourse to some version of the political subject, if he is not to be simply the theoretician of and apologist for an immutable order? Further, does he himself not speak of intervention and taking sides in philosophy, both of which, as Badiou reminds us, imply a subjective dimension in which choices are made and decisions taken?[18] To address these questions whose very persistence makes it impossible to dismiss them as the effect of a collective misreading, I will take them as already inscribed in Althusser's texts, specifically in the long process of theoretical reflection and conflict that culminated in the theory of the interpellation of the individual as subject. It was in and through this process that Althusser was compelled to examine psychoanalysis (especially Lacan), and this process is where he both genuinely encountered Spinoza and was able to wrest from his texts certain powerful ideas. Perhaps the key to understanding his theory of the interpellated subject was what he termed "the material existence of ideology"[19]: from lived experience to discourse to ideological state apparatuses, he confronted the aporias of his theory, even if he finally succeeded only in displacing them.

How can we theorize the possibility of a transformation of, if not an end to, the regime of subjection? The notion that the historical present is the site of conflicting forces whose configuration is always unstable has given way to an orientation to an event radically outside the apparatuses of domination that will arrive from beyond the present. Indeed, from this point of view the present itself is intelligible only on the basis of its own incompleteness, the empty place of a future no longer determined by the contradictions of the present but radically external to it and incomprehensible in its terms. Althusser declared early on that the question of destiny, of what we may hope for, was essentially a religious question and that to be a Marxist in philosophy was to refuse all notions of origin or end. As is well known, however, the concept of eschatology reemerged in the eighties and nineties, seemingly divested of its religious forms. I argue that the late Althusser did not entirely escape the effects of a certain eschatological thought, which can be discerned in his work on aleatory materialism. However, one of his earliest essays, "On the International of Decent Feelings" (1946), offers an extraordinary critique of the eschatologies that were rampant after 1945, a critique that offers everything necessary to confront the surprising turns in Althusser's last work.

If we apply to Althusser the same protocol of reading that he applied to Marx, we must understand his work as constituted by contradiction and antagonism, and it becomes intelligible on this basis alone. To read Althusser in this way is to draw lines of demarcation within his texts, thus making their conflicts visible. The question to be answered is this: What are the contradictions that haunt Althusser's texts, the ways in which it, by virtue of its very development, diverges from itself? It is only by cutting these oblique paths through Althusser's work, the path of structure, the path of the subject, and the path of origin/end, that we may identify its power, not only the power to terrify but the power to fracture what appears to be solid in order to open a way forward.

PART I

Structure

The Theoretical Conjuncture
Structure, Structurality, Structuralism

Few questions in the area broadly designated as "theory" would seem less likely to arouse interest than the question of "structure" in Althusser's work and, to situate this question historically, Althusser's relation to structuralism. For those who know Althusser's texts well, the question recalls the critiques and commentaries of more than twenty years ago, which, whatever their merits, today appear dated. The passions that drove them have cooled considerably; many of his critics have adopted theoretical positions that they once would have criticized far more severely than even the most objectionable that they claimed to find in Althusser. To be blunt, for anyone who shares Althusser's theoretical antihumanism or who has simply read his work carefully, the vast majority, however important they may be for an understanding of the Anglo-American or French Marxist culture of the 1960s and 1970s, have nothing to tell us about Althusser.

For a wider audience, however, the question holds little interest precisely because it is not a question at all. After all, may we not read in dozens of handbooks, encyclopedias, anthologies, and historical accounts that Althusser was a nearly perfect specimen of that now-extinct species, the structuralist, and that his Marxism was, as one often cited account puts it, "a structural Marxism," that is, a Marxism that sought to legitimize itself in the eyes of an audience steeped in linguistics and anthropology by using the terms and concepts in vogue at the time?[1] Did not Althusser employ the noun "structure" and the adjective "structural" in his best-known works, all of which were written during the high point of the structuralist enterprise? This view, however, is historicist in precisely the terms Althusser singled out for criticism: it assigns a meaning to Althusser's philosophy only by confining it to a period within which it alone possesses significance. Because this period has seen its "rise and fall" and now remains irrevocably past, we can contemplate its charms only from the perspective of our maturity. For it is well known (at least in the Anglophone world), according to a theoretical model that bears a stronger resemblance to Kuhn's notion of successive paradigms than to the notion of historical progress understood by Hegel or Marx, that structuralism, soon after 1968, was replaced by poststructuralism, which in turn begat postmodernism. From this perspective, Althusser's work, its significance and importance, lies outside of and prior to the historical present, being part of a moment the supersession of which constitutes the very meaning of the present.

Interestingly, recent developments have made it possible to argue a position diametrically opposed to that outlined above. The posthumous publication of volumes of material by Althusser, from a period that ranges from 1947 to the 1980s, has produced ample evidence to corroborate his exculpatory statement in *Essays in Self-Criticism*: "we were never structuralists" (a statement previously regarded as a disingenuous attempt to dissociate his work from the worldview whose demise would otherwise render it irrelevant).[2] First, there have come to light very severe critiques of "structuralist ideology," the severest of which is reserved for Lévi-Strauss, whose "formalism" and "functionalism" Althusser dissects in some detail.[3] He would go so far as to denounce what he himself called "structural Marxism" as mere ideology in 1967 (referring to Lucien Sebag's *Marxisme et structuralism*, a work unfamiliar to English language critics of Althusser, but which had some importance in France in the mid-sixties).[4]

Even more importantly, however, the posthumous publications brought to light a previously unknown strain in Althusser's thought, a strain he called as early as 1966, "a theory of the encounter," whose presence is visible from the early sixties on.[5] With his specification of the materialism of the encounter, it became possible, if not inevitable, to see in such works as "Contradiction and Overdetermination" (1962) and "Lenin and Philosophy" (1968) a philosophy of the conjuncture, according to which "history is a process without a subject or goals" and therefore the site of an infinity of encounters between heterogeneous forces the outcome of which could never be predicted.[6] It was an Althusser inspired by Epicurus and Lucretius (both of whose works he read very closely in the original languages), as well as Machiavelli, Spinoza, and Nietzsche, for whom structure might be thought to be a reduction of real complexity and heterogeneity to an imaginary order.[7]

Finally, there have emerged a number of texts in various stages of completion on philosophy itself, the forms of its material and historical existence, as well as the manner in which it is practiced. These works make explicit Althusser's conception of philosophy as the site of a perpetual war (a point made in detail in *Philosophy and the Spontaneous Philosophy of the Scientists*, a book-length work first published in French in 1974 but almost universally ignored by Althusser's commentators) in which, as in all wars according to Hobbes (a familiar reference point for Althusser), "force and fraud are the cardinal virtues."[8] These works also specify Althusser's sense of the theoretical conjuncture, the notion that philosophy at any given moment consisted of a disposition of forces that his interventions (like those of every philosopher—with or without their knowledge or consent) aimed to modify.

Althusser's analysis of his own theoretical conjuncture and the important if not dominant role of structuralism within it did not take the form of a coherent text or group of texts. At best, he presented brief, highly schematic outlines to his circle; the analysis that guided his intervention (and everything he wrote he considered an intervention) remained immanent in his work, existing in practical, but not theoretical, states. It must therefore be reconstructed from a few published pieces (notably on Lacan and now on Lévi-Strauss), fragments of published texts, unpublished manuscripts, lecture notes, and correspondence. Why undertake such a dubious task at all? I would argue that Althusser's conception of philosophy exists not as an ideal space, free from the pressures of power and interest, where competing claims would be adjudicated by reason, but as a constellation of conflicting forces, of ideas held in place by relations of force, in which no truth triumphs except the truth armed against its adversaries, gave his analysis a necessary exactitude and rigor. The disciple of Machiavelli and Lenin could settle for nothing less than an exact inventory of forces in play and an identification of friends as well as enemies. In theoretical terms, this translates into a very careful and informed survey of philosophical works, reading them "to the letter" and noting their effects on the theoretical conjuncture of which they are a part and their effects on the relations of dominance and subordination between the ideas that constitute it.

Such an approach to Althusser's reading of structuralist works may be effective, however, only if it is carried out with the following proviso: that we not regard Althusser as a rational actor in a game of strategy, as the absolute master of his words and deeds (even if not of their consequences, which can be "unintended"). To see Althusser as master of his work would, of course, contradict in the most flagrant way everything he himself wrote about subjects and texts. It was he who wrote that the "golden rule of materialism is not to judge a being by its self-consciousness."[9] It was Althusser who judged Freud's greatness to be his decentering of the human subject by attributing the unconscious primacy over consciousness. Even more, it was Althusser who, following Hegel, insisted that the history of philosophy could only be understood on the basis of its constitutive contradictions, contradictions that, for Althusser, were always overdetermined. From his point of view, even the most rigorously argued philosophical text was necessarily a constellation of oversights, discrepancies, and disparities, requiring a reading attuned to the symptoms of the conflicts that animated it unawares. These ideas are well known, too well known to require further discussion; if they possess any validity at all, however, they must be as applicable to Althusser's texts as any others. Indeed, we would do well to heed Étienne Balibar's observation:

> The letter of Althusser's texts is certainly very different from the self-interpretations (including his self-criticisms) that the author himself proposed. It is reasonable to expect that other readers, who are serious and accurate but who were not part of (if not untouched by) the intellectual adventure of the author, will be in a better position to clarify "what Althusser really thought" and to discuss how his work can possibly be transformed and carried on further today. What Althusser "thought" is of course not what he "wanted to think." It is what he actually wrote, with all the contradictions and aporias of the written text, which we may call its "unconscious": neither a subjective key to be unraveled, not a mystical secret behind the door but an objective meaning to be produced by means of a symptomatic reading.[10]

Following Balibar's analysis, we might say that Althusser's struggle against structuralism was above all a struggle internal to his own work against the tendency to follow the slope of least resistance in defining and defending Marx's discovery.

Having said all that, our inquiry into Althusser's analysis of and relation to structuralism must begin by posing as a problem what is often taken as self-evident: the meaning and function of the term *structuralism*. To insist on problematizing what can be very easily defined and historically located might at first seem perverse, an example of a corrosive skepticism, often attributed to Althusser and his contemporaries, that appears in the guise of a demand for rigor, when in fact it seeks only to undo and negate knowledge. Are there not dozens, even hundreds, of books alone devoted to this topic (the Library of Congress as of 2010 listed nine hundred books on structuralism)? That there exists a generally shared sense of what structuralism is or was cannot be denied. Scholars in the humanities and social sciences know the name of Saussure and can recite the list of conceptual pairs (the famous "binary oppositions") around which, it is generally agreed, all structuralist activity was unfailingly organized: the signifier and the signified, the synchronic and the diachronic, and perhaps, more recently, structure and agency. Of course, one can cite more elaborate versions of this narrative that vary according to academic discipline. Thus, in literary and cultural studies, structuralism is identified with formalism, an emphasis on the formal order of texts or other "signifying practices," the systems or codes that govern even the minutest details of a given work and whose function is independent of any historical determination. The best accounts of structuralism from this perspective construct a genealogy of structuralism that shows the way in which the immediate forbears of the movement, Russian formalism (Propp, Eichenbaum, and Shklovsky), the Prague school (Murakowsky), and the descendants of Saussure. In certain branches of the social sciences, this heritage is disavowed in favor of a more peculiarly French lineage: structuralism springs fully formed from the body of Durkheim's functionalism even if it later borrowed terminology from linguistics. In both cases, the most sophisticated accounts will speak of the foundational role of the "linguistic model" (the idea that a finite set of elements are combined according to a set of rules of which the human actors are for the most part unconscious) in the analysis of social phenomena. These descriptions of structuralism, taken in their totality and despite all the inconsistencies and incompatibilities that this totality exhibits, do not take the form of mere opinion; they comprise a sanctified knowledge, encoded in the rituals that determine one's progress through academia. It will not be easy, effectively at least, to call these narratives into question or even to think about them in a new way.[11]

Such a task might begin merely by examining the historical boundaries of structuralism as it existed in France.[12] When did it begin and when did it end, if indeed it has? It certainly did not begin in the 1960s. Two major conferences on the topic of structure, the proceedings of which were published, took place in 1959.[13] Lévi-Strauss's *Structural Anthropology* as well as Georges Dumezil's *L'idéologie tripartie des Indo-Européens* both appeared in 1958 (while Lacan's "linguistic turn" took place even earlier), and the former consisted of essays that had been published several years earlier, occasioning lively debates. In fact, the essays themselves were responses to critiques directed at Lévi-Strauss's even earlier *Elementary Structures of Kinship*, published in 1947 and whose influence on Lacan is incontestable. This text might well qualify as a starting point, given that it was perhaps the first attempt to apply in a comprehensive way the linguistic model to a social reality other than language, were it not for the fact that the term *structuralism* in its broader sense as a program for the study of all sorts of social phenomena had already been proposed by members of the Prague circle in the 1930s.[14] To make matters even more complicated, for these early structuralists, as well as for Lévi-Strauss himself in the 1950s, Saussure was far less important and cited a figure than Nicolas Troubetzkoy, whose name is completely absent from many accounts of structuralism. In fact, Troubetzkoy saw his work on phonology, especially in its antipsychologism and antisubjectivism, as a rejection of Saussure, who was regarded as a continuation of earlier "psychologistic" theories of language.[15] Indeed, Roman Jakobson asserts that Husserl's early *Logical Investigations* (1900–1901) provided the inspiration for Troubetzkoy's revolution in phonology and the linguistic model more broadly.[16] Thus, simply by following the chain of references in certain important structuralist works, we find ourselves in unfamiliar territory bereft of the usual reference points.

Another index of the problem of specifying structuralism is the difficulty simply of determining which authors can be described as structuralists. While some, such as Lévi-Strauss, seem unambiguously to fit virtually any description of a structuralist, what is one to say about such figures as Barthes, Lacan, or Foucault, all of whom were designated in such venues as *Magazine Littéraire* as structuralists in the mid-sixties (and, it should be noted, did nothing at the time to dispute the designation)? It is possible to respond that these authors (whose contemporary partisans fiercely resist their definition as structuralists) at most had a structuralist period: it would be hard to deny that Barthes's *Fashion System*, published in 1967, is a textbook application of the linguistic model to fashion, while *The Pleasure of the Text* written a few years later abandons this model almost entirely. The case of Foucault is even more complicated: he himself repeatedly labeled his *The Birth of the Clinic*, published in 1963, as "a structural study" ("une étude structurale") (although the phrase disappears from the edition of 1972, the edition on which the English translation is based) whose aim was to "treat semantic elements . . . as functional segments . . . forming a system"[17] (a phrase again omitted from the second edition published in 1972). A review of the debates surrounding the appearance of *Les mots et les choses* reveals that both his adversaries and his defenders, in France at least, regarded him as part of a structuralist movement. Deleuze, a philosopher seldom associated with structuralism, wrote a very positive overview of structuralism at the end of 1967, at the very moment he was writing the supposedly post-structuralist work *Difference and Repetition*.[18] The point here is neither to criticize the dominant periodizations in order to propose another that would correspond more exactly to the supposed discontinuities actually discoverable in the writing of the period, nor to draw new boundaries, narrower or more restrictive. I raise these problems in order to suggest we know far less about this period than we think we do, and the received ideas concerning structuralism cannot bear up under scrutiny.

It may well be that the conjuncture we now inhabit has selected something previously invisible both in Althusser and in the works of his contemporaries, freeing us unpredictably and unforeseeably from the interpretive grid that history imposes on us unawares. As a measure of that distance that it is possible and even necessary to take from our previous understanding of structuralism, we might well take advantage of some materials that the passage of time has made available to us. Althusser's correspondence (part of which has been published), unpublished texts, lecture notes, and so on from the period 1961–68 show Althusser's vivid interest in the emergent movement of structuralism. These materials also show an unmistakable shift in attitude between 1962 and 1966. Althusser's first reported encounters with Barthes, for example, provoke lyrical outpourings; within a very few years, his assessment would be profoundly negative. Suffice it to say that whatever hopes he had once entertained that structuralism marked the advent of a new era, a rupture in the human sciences, were profoundly diminished by 1966, although criticisms of structuralism began to surface in the published work as early as 1963 and are found in abundance in Althusser's contribution to *Reading Capital* (1965). The encounter between Althusser and structuralism was a complex one: neither entirely external nor internal to the field he sought to understand, his vantage point might well prove to be a privileged one from which structuralism can be seen in a new light, a light that makes visible the fissures and stresses that have so far escaped the attention of those who have thus far sought to study it. Thus, to examine this encounter will be not simply to read Althusser in a new way but the entire field of structuralism as well, a field whose boundaries will certainly be readjusted in the process.

Toward a Prehistory of Structuralism
From Montesquieu to Dilthey

There is no more accurate a gauge of the importance with which Althusser regarded the structuralist movement than the fact that he organized an entire year's seminar on it. His seminar at the École Normale Supérieure in the academic year 1962–63, attended by some of his most well known pupils (Balibar, Macherey, Rancière, and Pêcheux, among others), was devoted to the topic of "The Origins of Structuralism."[1] The fact that the seminar was held some years before the high point of structuralism (François Dosse argues with justification that 1966 was the "watershed year for structuralism") certainly reflected Althusser's sense of the urgency, of taking stock of what he would soon refer to as the "theoretical conjuncture," to understand the forces and impulses of which his own work would inescapably bear the imprint.[2] It also, however, and perhaps even more importantly, reflected his excitement at contemporary developments in the sciences, social sciences, and in philosophy—his sense that his own work was part of a larger movement.

Indeed, his voluminous correspondence with Franca Madonia, the Italian translator of Althusser and Lévi-Strauss during the crucial years 1961–68, reveals the eagerness with which Althusser devoured the monuments of structuralism. In November 1962 he reports the extraordinary nature of his encounter with Foucault's *Histoire de la folie à l'âge classique*:

> I am in the midst of reading, what might be called reading, quickly and deeply, reacting to every sign at each instant, taking notes so that no idea escapes me—the little devils sometimes move more quickly than my pen—a capital book. Capital because it has created quite a stir, capital to the highest degree for theoretical reasons, capital be-

cause it was written by one of my former students . . . capital because I am without doubt (due in part to this last circumstance and also to other reasons connected to the themes running through my head at this moment) practically the only person able to write something meaningful and important on it. I'm referring to a book by Michel Foucault entitled *Histoire de la folie à l'âge classique*.[3]

In February 1963 he recounts staying up most of the preceding night reading Jean-Pierre Vernant's *Les origines de la pensée grecque*, which he refers to as "an interesting little book on Greece that I might recommend if you have any interest in that country (it is Greece between the Mycenean and Athenian periods, an excellent analysis of the structures of this period . . . I'm shocking you with my structures!)."[4] On May 8, 1963, he writes that Barthes had sent him the newly published *Sur Racine* the day before and that he spent most of the night reading it. He intends to write Barthes immediately:

> Finally [there is] a breath of fresh air among the debris and dust of academic criticism! Finally someone to say that the famous Racinian "psychology," that the famous and so violent, so pure, so ferocious Racinian passions "do not exist!" Someone to say that it is above all literature and written for that, put on the page for that, with the required decor, the initial conventions, the essential relations apart from which there is only effect, illustration, phenomena. That it is a game within the rules of the game that precede the game and what does it matter that Racine himself did not know the rules! The fact is that he respected them and that knowing that he respected them we can extract them naked from the decor of seas of sun of nights of women and of kings who throughout their infinite discourses do nothing other than comment on the code.[5]

Earlier in the same year, Althusser had described a lecture by Barthes on structuralism, which provoked a lively discussion afterward: "we (I) and my men kept quiet: not a bad idea! We let the great theoretical void that summarized the situation prevail in all its purity on every front and on everyone's lips."[6]

The written record of the seminar is also important in another way: nearly everything about the structuralism with which it is occupied, from the definition of the movement to its historical antecedents, is at variance with what one typically finds in virtually any of the innumerable anthologies and summaries devoted to the topic. The space of this difference opens the possibility of thinking in a new way about structuralism, its sources and boundaries, and of reading its texts differently. The schedule of the seminar drawn up by Althusser includes presentations on figures we would expect to see: Jacques Rancière and Michel Pêcheux on Lacan and Althusser himself on Lévi-Strauss ("à la recherche de ses ancêtres putatifs," in search of his supposed ancestors) and Foucault's *Folie et déraison* ("structuralisme et histoire idéologique selon Foucault").[7] And while the inclusion of Foucault's manifestly historical treatise in a course on structuralism may surprise some readers today, Foucault was typically viewed as a part of the structuralist movement, a view that he himself was at some pains to cultivate, especially in the years immediately following the publication of his first major work.

Less in keeping with notions of structuralism either then or now, the seminar included an examination of the work of the historian of the biological sciences Georges Canguilhem by Pierre Macherey. The conjugation of both Canguilhem and Foucault and thus, as we shall see in greater detail, the tradition of *épistemologie* (a rigorously historical approach to the history of the sciences, associated with Bachelard, Koyre, Cavaillès, as well as Canguilhem and Foucault) with the work of Lacan and Lévi-Strauss is significant. Not only did it give rise to a current of thought that crystalized around the journal *Cahiers pour l'analyse* (which arguably had its origins in Althusser's seminar), but it calls into question the facile definition of structuralism as an ahistorical formalism or functionalism. Althusser's sense of structuralism as part of a broader movement can be seen in a letter from October 1962, shortly before the seminar began:

> [There will be] a gigantic course in which I will take up a certain number of themes that are (currently) essential to me: the theme of the origin of philosophy for Nietzsche (and on this topic, the theme of all the objects rejected by a civilization in its own constitution); the theme of the archaeology of a science (how the field of objects with which a science makes, through rupture, its own field is constituted); finally, the theme of the relations between structuralist thought and Marxism (on a number of essential points: in particular, what I am most concerned with, the point of the essence of superstructures).[8]

It is quite clear that structuralism as Althusser conceived it in 1962 was not a doctrine unified around a shared set of propositions but a field of inquiry still in formation and therefore open and dynamic.

But perhaps the most powerful *Entfremdungseffekt* of all, the effect that will definitively distance us from the accepted view of structuralism, is delivered by the content of the seminar's inaugural lecture in which Althusser attempts to trace historically the path that led to the founding moments of structuralism. The path, as Althusser retraces it, is far from familiar: he sets out, not from Troubetzkoy or Saussure, or even Marx and Freud, but "from Montesquieu to Dilthey."[9] Taken as a whole, the text of the prospectus of the seminar presents us with a puzzle: the linguistic model, the primacy of the synchronic over the diachronic, while undoubtedly evoked by the inclusion of Lacan and Lévi-Strauss, are displaced from the center of structuralist thought or refigured as one component of a larger complex, although one whose nature may not be immediately clear to those acquainted with the prevailing view of structuralism.

If the itinerary of Althusser's inaugural lecture can be reconciled only with difficulty with what we know about structuralism, it is much more easily related both to his own work of the preceding decade and to the themes and controversies in philosophy and the social sciences in France during the fifties. In fact, when we turn to Althusser's *Montesquieu: Politics and History* published in 1959, and thus several years before the seminar took place, it is possible to read the work not simply as textual analysis (even one in which Althusser performs a symptomatic reading) but also, as might be expected from the author, as the taking of a position through Montesquieu in the theoretical conflicts of the time. Althusser's identification in 1962 of Montesquieu as the founding moment of structuralism's prehistory makes visible the way in which his analysis of some of Montesquieu's key concepts, notably those of law, spirit, nature, and principle, is simultaneously a meditation on what he will later explicitly identify as the central problems of structuralism. Montesquieu, according to Althusser, wished in his treatment of history to avoid both a narrative of facts, whose diversity can only be described but never explained, and a narrative of essences in which all that does not correspond to the norm is declared unintelligible. Instead, Montesquieu sought to discover the necessity that governs all that exists, even in its diversity, "a necessity whose empire is so strict that it embraces not only bizarre institutions, which last, but even the accident that produces victory or defeat in a battle and is contained in a momentary encounter." This necessity is to be grasped through a new concept of law, a Newtonian concept to be precise, that will make it "possible to draw from human institutions themselves the wherewithal to think their diversity in a uniformity and their changes in a constancy: the law of their diversification and the law of their development."[10] Such a law would be the law of laws, or the spirit of the laws: not the laws made by humans, which they may or merely should obey but often do not, but the laws that govern human beings even when they violate "their" laws and that determines this very violation. If this were not enough to relate Althusser's Montesquieu to the central concerns of, say, Lévi-Strauss's *Structural Anthropology*, published only one year earlier in 1958, Althusser will argue that the very effectivity of this law of laws is that human beings follow it "without knowing it," that is, to use a phrase essential to Lévi-Strauss's structuralism, they are "unconscious laws."[11]

But, as is the case with the structuralists to whom Althusser would later turn his attention, we must judge Montesquieu not only by what he proposes but by what he accomplishes, not by "his word but by his work." As Althusser argues, Montesquieu seeks, following Spinoza, not to judge but to explain, not to compare history to a moral norm outside of it only to find it wanting but to investigate the concatenation of causes and effects without theological or moral prejudice. But such a position alone would not suffice to make Montesquieu's a truly immanent analysis; he must also refuse any recourse to transcendental terms even in his explanation, any temptation to reduce the real diversity and complexity of history to a principle, whether theological or anthropological, outside of and prior to its heterogeneity, even, as Althusser puts it (referring to the phenomenological tradition in order to show its complicity with a certain idealism) any "intuition of essences." Here Althusser's language closely resembles that which he will later use in analyzing structuralism: Does *The Spirit of Laws* in its discussion of the three types of government in history lapse into a "formalism" of "pure atemporal models?"[12]

To answer this question Althusser will carry out in practice what he will describe theoretically only later: he draws a line of demarcation through Montesquieu's text, making visible the antagonism proper to the latter's philosophical endeavor. He reminds us that Montesquieu is often viewed as a "formalist" because he speaks of the "nature" of the three types of government and because this nature is itself, as the title of his great work indicates, derived from "a few words of pure constitutional law." Such a reading is a careless one, though, according to Althusser; it neglects that fact "the nature of a government is formal for Montesquieu himself, so long as it is separated from its principle," that is, the concrete conditions of its existence.

There can be no nature without a principle; nature always exists in a realized form, a totality in which nature and principle are irrevocably united. As Hegel noted, it was Montesquieu who introduced the notion of the state as totality, not as an ideal to be aimed at but rather as an explanatory principle. The spirit of the laws is that inner unity of which laws and customs, norms and facts are equally the expression: "it becomes the fundamental category which makes it possible to think, no longer the reality of an ideal state, but the concrete and hitherto unintelligible diversity. History is no longer that infinite space in which are haphazardly scattered the innumerable works of caprice and accident, to the discouragement of the understanding. . . . This space has a structure."[13]

But Montesquieu, it appears, cannot escape the problem of a separation between essence and its expression, between the model and its realization. For if the nature of a government is inseparable from and even in an important sense subordinate to the principle insofar as the actions determine this nature, what determines the principle itself, the passion of virtue in democracies, honor in monarchies, and fear in despotic states? What determines the transformation of virtue into avarice, the typical form of degradation of a democratic state? The manners and morals of a nation, its corporeal and practical life, of which the principle of a government is an expression. Thus we arrive at the fatal ambiguity that sets *The Spirit of Laws* against itself: either we divorce the principles from their real causes, which are not only plural (customs, religion, climate, population, etc.) but which, to the extent they are rooted in an infinite nature that exhibits its own history, prove utterly indifferent to that of humankind, and thus arrive at static models whose transformation remains unintelligible, or the possibility of historical explanation fades in the face of an infinity of causes.

It was Hegel, according to Althusser, who was Montesquieu's immediate descendant, resolving the contradictions that disrupted *The Spirit of the Laws* with a rigorously "spiritual" conception of the whole or totality. In the *Philosophy of Mind* (1830), Hegel commends Montesquieu for having introduced the concept of spirit (*esprit*) into philosophy, a concept that by "bringing together what the intellect has separated . . . becomes a brilliant form of the rational, for the essential character of the rational is to bring together what is separated."[14] Similarly, in the *Philosophy of Right*, Hegel credits Montesquieu with "always treating the part in its relation to the whole," particularly, "the dependence of laws on the specific character of the state."[15] Hegel, or at least Hegel according to the Althusser of this period, as he is portrayed in the essays contemporaneous with the seminar on structuralism, not only appropriated the notion of whole or totality from Montesquieu but confronted and overcame, in an imaginary form, of course, its difficulties. The Hegel of "Contradiction and Overdetermination," written a few months before the beginning of the seminar, is well known: if not a caricature of Hegel, even a brilliant and eloquent caricature, it is the Hegel of the famous programmatic statements in the preface to the *Phenomenology of Spirit*, that is, precisely Hegel taken at his word rather than at his work. In "On the Materialist Dialectic," a response to the critiques of "Contradiction and Overdetermination" written toward the end of the academic year and thus just as the seminar on structuralism was concluding, Althusser reconstructs, in a passage of remarkable density, the dialectic according to the preface to the *Phenomenology*, a dialectic whose "motor force" is an "ideological concept," negativity: "In a text as beautiful as the night, the *Phenomenology* celebrates '*the labor of the negative*' in beings and works, the Spirit's sojourn even in death, the universal trouble of negativity dismembering the corpse of Being to give birth to the glorious body of that infinity of nothingness become being, the Spirit—and every philosopher trembles in his soul as if he was in the presence of the Mysteries."[16]

Hegel overcame the ambiguities of Montesquieu's "dialectic of history" by means of a negation, the specific form of which was a "reduction" (which he "derived" from Montesquieu) of "all the elements that make up the concrete life of a historical epoch (economic, social, political, and legal institutions, customs, ethics, art, religion, philosophy and even historical *events*: wars, battles, defeats and so on) to *one* principle of internal unity."[17] Althusser, using the exact terms he used to describe Montesquieu's method, argues that Hegel's dialectic reduces "'the infinite diversity' of a given society to a 'simple internal principle' with the difference that Hegel's reduction, at least in theory, leaves no remainder, not even, at the extreme, nature itself which can be conceived as the merely contingent externalization of Spirit."[18] It is worth noting that Deleuze cites these passages from *For Marx* in his discussion of Hegel (in *Difference and Repetition*) as the thinker of the identical against difference for whom there is only an "infinite circulation of the identical by means of negativity."[19]

Althusser's objective during this period was, as is well known, not to "read" Hegel but Marx, to read Marx's relation to Hegel or even to the Hegel-in-Marx, the Hegelian survivals that haunted Marx's materialist dialectic. Although this activity earned him the reputation of an anti-Hegelian, we now know that Althusser's relation to Hegel was far more complicated. Althusser possessed an intimate knowledge of Hegel, a fact that could be gleaned even from the texts of 1962–63 alone, in which his summary of the Hegelian dialectic is so extraordinarily dense that few critics saw the need to dispute (or were even capable of disputing) his presentation of Hegel.[20] His *Mémoire* "On Content in the Thought of G. W. F. Hegel," which he wrote in 1947 but was only published after his death, clearly reveals that he had read Hegel's major texts "to the letter" as he liked to say.[21] Further, he published two short pieces on Hegel in the same period: "Man, that Night" a review of Kojève's *Introduction to the Reading of Hegel* (1947) and "The Return to Hegel: the Last Word in Academic Revisionism" (published anonymously in 1950), a critique of the Hegel revival in France in the immediate postwar period, especially Hyppolite's work. François Matheron is right to argue that Althusser's attitude toward Hegel changes considerably between 1947 and 1950 and that his critique of French Hegelianism includes a critique of concepts whose utility he apparently endorsed at the time of the *Mémoire*, such as alienation.[22] We should be careful, however, not to take this period as an epistemological break in the sense that Althusser ultimately rejected: a break reducible to a before and an after. After all, Althusser would himself "return" to Hegel by 1968 in "On Marx's Relation to Hegel," an essay whose arguments not only are directly relevant to the questions raised by structuralism but perhaps more importantly are derived from (or at least coincide with) his work from the period 1947–50.[23]

Althusser's critique of the two leading interpreters of Hegel, Alexandre Kojeve and Jean Hyppolite, focuses on what he calls their "existentialism," that is, their tendency (in different ways) to turn the *Phenomenology* into a drama of the human, of man, a succession of "robinsonades": the struggle for recognition, the master-slave dialectic, or even the dilemma of the unhappy consciousness defined what at the time was called "the human condition." Althusser argued that Kojève grasped "substance as subject" (founded on an anthropology, according to which man is the principle of negativity) but failed to grasp the sense in which subject is always substance, already expressed in objective form.[24] The terms of this critique are striking indeed: substance and subject. They recall an opposition that will be central to Althusser's thought: Hegel and Spinoza. It is noteworthy that Althusser at the very beginning of his academic career has already begun to identify with one of Hegel's most important predecessors and adversaries, the thinker of substance as "a process without a subject" in which humanity is merely one part among others, determined by the same necessity that determines all that exists.[25] Althusser was already speaking the language of Spinoza and producing a "Spinozist" reading of Hegel. Even when Althusser summarizes Hegel in order to reject him in the publications of the early 1960s and seeks to identify the specific difference that defines the materialist dialectic, there is not the slightest trace of an anthropology of any kind in his summary. There is no special place for humanity in his account of spirit's long return to itself: alienation, as Althusser will write in 1968, is not, for Hegel, peculiar to human history. Hegel shares this "theoretical antihumanism" with Althusser's Montesquieu: what is most important in human history (which for both can only be understood as part of a larger nonhuman history) is what happens behind the backs of human beings, without their being aware, even if what happens is an "unintended consequence" of intentional human action.

Finally, though, Hegel cannot escape from the consequences of his "solution" to the pluralism that inescapably threatens the intelligibility of Montesquieu's totality. The very negativity that ceaselessly converts difference into identity and reduces diversity to simplicity leads Hegel's dialectic into an impasse in which he will find himself in distinguished company. It is this impasse that, according to Althusser, makes Hegelian philosophy directly relevant to some of the most notorious dilemmas of structuralism. The nature of the Hegelian "spiritual" totality is such that its "parts are so many 'total parts,' each expressing the others, and each expressing the social totality that contains them," and "in which each element of the whole . . . is never anything more than the presence of the concept itself at a historically given moment."[26] Accordingly,

> the structure of historical existence is such that all the elements of the whole always co-exist in one and the same time, one and the same present, and are therefore contemporaneous with one another in one and the same present. This means that the structure of the historical existence of the Hegelian social totality allows what I propose to call an "essential section" (coup d'essence), i.e., an intellectual operation in which a vertical break is made at any moment in historical time, a break in the present such that all the elements of the whole are in an immediate relationship with one another, a relationship that immediately expresses their internal essence.[27]

History, according to such a conception, becomes a continuous succession of totalities whose separation into distinct periods becomes the primary task of the historian.

It is not difficult to see the way in which, for Althusser, Hegel's concept of historical time was "still alive." Some of the most famous structuralist works, works being written as Althusser spoke these lines in the seminar on *Capital* (he refers directly to those of Lévi-Strauss), which, far from having surpassed Hegel as their authors believed, merely repeated his theses on history in a new scientific lexicon among whose master-concepts diachrony and synchrony reigned supreme. According to Althusser, the distinction between diachrony and synchrony "is based on a conception of historical time as continuous, homogeneous and contemporaneous with itself. The synchronic is contemporaneity with itself, the co-presence of essence with its determinations, the present being readable as a structure in an 'essential section' because the present is the very existence of the essential structure. . . . It follows that the diachronic is merely the development of this present in the sequence of a temporal continuity in which the 'events' to which 'history' in the strict sense can be reduced (Lévi-Strauss) are merely successive contingent presents in the time continuum."[28]

This passage is crucial in several respects. Althusser rejects the very problematic that defined structuralist activity, especially in the social sciences. His critique of historicism, which the above passage precedes in *Reading Capital*, can then in no way be a privileging of the synchronic over the diachronic, any more than his critique of structuralism would resemble that of a Marxist like Lucien Goldmann, whose work Althusser knew well, who viewed himself as a partisan of the diachronic against the synchronic.[29] Instead, the two terms together formed a unit that was nothing less than the living form of a certain Hegelianism. Taking the side of the diachronic, seen as the necessity of change, in no way challenged the spiritual nature of the totalities whose succession it sought to grasp; on the contrary, the labor of the negative continued to convert difference into identity by negating the negativity of difference and in this way gave every epoch or period a unified Zeitgeist or worldview "expressed" in all its parts, which would be surpassed by another equally unified totality. Thus, behind the scientific pretensions of the various social sciences of the time, despite their invocation of the linguistic model and their use of quantitative techniques, a certain spiritualism, whose objective was the denial of difference and the imaginary reduction of the irreducibly material, continued to work.

The critique of Hegel here is more, however, than an unpleasant and unexpected revelation about the ancestry of structuralism and its inheritance. It is also a critique of the actual forms of this living on of Hegelianism, but, and this is essential, one that takes its distance from all other critiques (or at least the most influential) of this very Hegelianism. We may now understand why Dilthey, whose name appears no more than two or three times in Althusser's published corpus, would figure as the terminal point in the prehistory of structuralism. In 1959 at a conference on the topic of genesis and structure, the two concepts whose opposition appeared to define the philosophical conflict in France in the 1950s, Derrida presented a paper (one of his earliest publications) on "Genesis and Structure in Phenomenology" in which Husserl's critique of Dilthey is presented not as escaping the dilemma of genesis or structure, diachrony or synchrony, but as providing a foundation (perhaps the foundation) from which such antinomies could be criticized. This was no ordinary conference (in fact, it was one of two major colloquia devoted to structuralism in France in 1959): the proceedings, published in 1964 as *Entretiens sur les notions de genèse et de structure* include essays by a group as remarkable for its diversity as for its notoriety.[30] The participants included Lucien Goldmann, Jean Piaget, Ernst Bloch, Leszek Kolakowski, Serge Mallet, Georges Lapassade, Jean-Pierre Vernant, and Nicolas Abraham. The discussions that followed the presentations were transcribed and included in the text of the proceedings. A number of the presentations sought to reconcile genesis and structure as complementary elements equally necessary to rational historical and scientific inquiry. Derrida's paper (which would be included in an amended version in *Writing and Difference*) was distinguished from the others in its attempt to interrogate these concepts, together with their supposed opposition or complementarity, critically. In a very important sense, Derrida's text is an intervention, an attempt from within the problematic of Husserl's phenomenology to call into question the two nominally opposing forms in which it was actualized in France: on the one hand, a philosophy of consciousness and, on the other, a formalism.

In Derrida's "Genesis and Structure," Husserl's philosophical itinerary is marked by the failure, repeated at each stage of his work, "to reconcile the structuralist demand (which leads to a comprehensive description of a totality, of a form or a function organized according to an internal legality in which elements have meaning only in the solidarity of their correlation or their opposition), with the genetic demand (that is, the search for the origin and foundation of the structure)." Such an endeavor, however, was predicated on a critique of the existing attempts to think these concepts, whether separately or as a unity. According to Derrida, "Husserl's first phenomenological works were developed approximately at the same time as the first structuralist projects, or at least those that declared structure to be their theme, for it would not be difficult to show that a certain structuralism has always been philosophy's most spontaneous gesture." Among the most important of the "first philosophies of structure" was Diltheyism, which combined a conception of an originless static system with a notion of "abusive transitions" from one static realm to another. Derrida will put it in a way that makes its relevance to Althusser obvious: "the structuralism of the *Weltanschauungsphilosophie* is a historicism."[31]

Its structuralism is moreover grounded in its notion of the historical totality as "a finite totality all of whose manifestations and cultural productions are structurally solidary, coherent, governed by the same function, by the same finite unity of a subjective totality."[32] It was precisely the idea of a subjective totality that made historicism a tempting alternative (and therefore a dangerous adversary) to the depthless "naturalism" that converted even spiritual, intellectual realities into reified empirically determinable facts like any others. Dilthey recognized that human history or *geistige* history necessitated a different kind of knowledge. Rather than simply represented, like the facts and even events of the natural world, the human, social past had to be relived, its originating intention reactivated through an active empathy with an other spirit or mind (Dilthey's conception of *verstehen*).[33] What remains radically absent from historicist inquiry and what renders it despite itself, and despite Dilthey's protestations privately to Husserl, as a relativism and a skepticism, is the transcendental element to which the phenomenological reduction would return it, the *Ur-struktur*, the structure of all structures.[34] It is an Ur-struktur not only because it is the structure of all structures but because it makes possible the thinking of its own origin, the structural a priori of all historicity, genesis, and becoming. However, is there not still a prior level, the level from which it is possible to ask what is structure in general, the structure of which both the transcendental and empirical structures would be examples (and here Derrida argues that the same reduction can and must be carried out in relation to genesis, which must possess a general form for the distinction between transcendental and empirical genesis to be meaningful)? But on the basis of what or from where can this question be asked: Is there a transcendental of the transcendental? If Husserl refrained from asking these questions, according to Derrida, it was not from either neglect or dogmatism but from a recognition that at the origin is a kind of absence, a "transcendental I" that cannot determine the meaning of nonsense or comprehend its own death.[35] Thus, for Derrida, structure remains open: no system can be closed upon itself, its elements understood only in relation to each other, governed by the rules that define their very closure. By calling the possibility of closure into question, Derrida inescapably problematizes the oppositions of genesis and structure and of synchrony and diachrony.

In certain respects there is a convergence between Althusser and Derrida around the critique of the philosophical pairs that furnished the model of inquiry for a number of disciplines. Is their critique the same? The answer to this question may be found in the recorded remarks by a member of Derrida's audience in the discussion that followed his presentation. Father Stanislas Breton, the Catholic philosopher who admired Spinoza and could speak intelligently about Lenin and who would later become one of Althusser's closest friends, asked a question of Derrida that Althusser himself would pose in his notes on Derrida's texts a few years later, a question that concerned the very concepts, "sous rature" and "*différance*," that he would publicly praise: "my last remark concerns a duality in structure; it can be interpreted in a horizontal or vertical sense. In a horizontal sense it is a system of correlations; but in Husserl, it is understood that these correlations always require a vertical point of anchorage. The transcendental ego is precisely this point of anchorage, that vertical to which all structures appeal. Do you accept this duality of structure such as it is lived in phenomenology?"[36] This question, to which no answer was recorded, is precisely the one Althusser would pose with very few modifications to Derrida's work of the 1960s.

3

Settling Accounts with Phenomenology
Husserl and His Critics

Husserl's critique of Dilthey first appeared in *Philosophie als strenge Wissenschaft* (*Philosophy as a Rigorous Science*) in 1911.[1] The problem underlying Dilthey's *Lebensphilosophie*, and the notion of *Weltanschauung* in particular, undoubtedly made him relevant to the origins of structuralism as understood by Althusser. His aim was to think the unity of each specific epoch, the unity of its "spiritual" (*geistige*) content, as well as the unity of the objectified forms in which this content was expressed. For Hegel, according to Dilthey, these epochs are intelligible only insofar as they are all moments in the development of spirit, which thus constitutes the telos, the arche-telos, that confers meaning upon them. Dilthey's history is also a succession of epochs but without any origin or end. On the contrary, the intelligibility of a historical epoch can de derived from it alone, in precisely that inner unity to which all external manifestations can be reduced. If Dilthey thereby escapes one Hegel, he nevertheless runs headlong into another: Althusser's Hegel, the Hegel whose (fortunate) failure to realize the teleology of spirit he hoped to establish resulted in the first and perhaps most coherent presentation of the synchronic-diachronic opposition, making visible the impasse to which such an opposition must lead.

It is not surprising then that Husserl's critique of Dilthey might superficially resemble Althusser's critique of Hegel (and, by extension, Lévi-Strauss). Husserl's discussion is brief and even more schematic than Althusser's: Dilthey's historicism results in relativism and skepticism. It is relativist in that each epoch has its truth, its spirit whether subjective or objective. There is no means by which to judge or rank epochs, to establish progress or regression, given that we exist in our own epoch with its truth. It is skeptical in that we cannot know whether one religion or philosophy possesses any more validity than any other or even whether our knowledge of it is accurate, in that we cannot escape the structures of our own epoch and are powerless not to impose them on the objects of historical knowledge. In his haste to reject every form of transcendence, Dilthey has sacrificed the possibility of an objective, universal historical knowledge. No historical epoch can be known except from the vantage point of another historical epoch.

Husserl's critique of Dilthey takes place in the context of his sense of the impasse of philosophy at the beginning of the twentieth century. To a great extent philosophy has lost the will to scientificity that characterized and determined its most important moments: the Socratic-Platonic, the Cartesian, the Kantian. With what Husserl calls Hegel's romanticism there began a weakening and adulteration of "the impulse toward the constitution of a rigorous philosophical science." Hegel's philosophy, which Husserl insists must be understood as a reaction to the "naturalism" of the eighteenth century, became its inverse, that is, "a scepticism which invalidated all absolute ideality and subjectivity." Dilthey's Weltanschauung philosophy is "a result of the transformation of Hegel's metaphysical philosophy of history into a skeptical historicism."[2] The aim of establishing philosophy as a science lives on but paradoxically only in the modern forms of naturalism (positivism and pragmatism) least capable of providing a foundation of objectivity—in that the phenomena of consciousness become mere facts to be known like any other—disengaged from the essence that, given the privileged place of consciousness, is the ground of any possible objectivity.

In the case of historicism, as noted above, its greatest strength, that precisely which it has to contribute to knowledge, is the source of the fatal contradiction by which it subverts the possibility of any objective knowledge, a subversion that must extend to its own activity. In its attempt to reconstruct the "structure" ("Struktur," the term used both by Dilthey and Husserl) of an epoch, the unity of all human or geistige phenomena found in a particular period, such that every one is an expression of every other one, a universal identity, an overcoming of difference, historicism does not require any labor of the negative to produce this "expressive totality." Each historical totality thus described is so internally coherent (each of its elements expressing all other elements) and so self-contained (one cannot speak of the endurance of the same element in different historical totalities given that the identity of any particular element, despite the fact we may use the same name to refer to it, is determined by the totality of which it is a part and thus can only become something other in each period) that not only can we not explain how one self-identical totality is transformed into another different but equally self-identical totality, but nothing can thus endure through these separate worlds. To follow the doctrine of historicism strictly, Husserl argues, one would be compelled to admit that even the principle of noncontradiction would have to be surrendered to a historicism so absolute that its own statements would have to be recognized not as valid in and of themselves but as expressions of the "life" of an epoch both reducible and limited to the totality it forms and of necessity invalid beyond it. Thus, according to Husserl, historicism, despite itself, relies on certain absolute validities. The task of philosophy, he will argue, is to establish the foundation of the objectivity to which even the most skeptical claims must allude. Philosophy is a "science of origins," whose object must be consciousness in its essence, prior to its phenomenal expressions, a science capable of thinking the possibility of ideas that may never be historically thought.[3]

In 1955 Althusser published "Sur l'objectivité de l'histoire," an essay cast in the form of a letter to Paul Ricoeur in response to the latter's very critical review of Raymond Aron's *Introduction à la philosophie de l'histoire*.[4] Althusser's account of the differences between the two philosophers resembles in certain important respects the Dilthey-Husserl controversy, especially as it was represented by Husserl.[5] Althusser begins his essay by summarizing Ricoeur's critique of Aron's rejection of the possibility of "a universally valid science of history." To ask whether such a science is possible, implying that it does not exist and nullifying the knowledge heretofore produced, rather than to ask what is the foundation of the knowledge that we already possess, of the theory that is already at work and producing results, is to reproduce Kant's exclusion of metaphysics as the possible object of a science. Posed this way, an answer cannot be "'found in science itself' but only 'outside of science' in the nature of the 'historical object' which to be sure is not derived from the actual results of historical research but by a philosophy of history that operates at the level of the a priori." Kant, Althusser writes, "showed that it is meaningless to speak of an object outside of the very conditions of objectivity. The ideal form in which he conceived these conditions is not, for the moment, important. The fact is that he conceived them and on the basis of the existing sciences." In opposition, Aron seeks to restore to the past precisely the truth that escapes historical narrative: the equivocity, the inexhaustibility, the complexity of history (all familiar philosophical and even theological notions designed to render an object unknowable). In the face of such a reality, the historian can but "make a choice (in which he finds both his greatness and his consolation), he chooses the meaning of his past, he takes as an a priori a theory which is that of his people or class when it is not merely that of his own character."[6] Given the inaccessibility of the past (which derives, in part, from its irreducible alterity) and the inescapability of the present (precisely Dilthey's dilemma according to Husserl), there can be no objective knowledge of history according to Aron.

But while Althusser rejects in Aron exactly what Ricoeur singles out for a critique, he takes great pains to demonstrate that he does so for very different reasons. It would not be quite accurate to say that Ricoeur rejects the subjectivism of Aron's approach; on the contrary, his entire analysis rests on a distinction between good and bad subjectivity that suggests that he "has in fact given in to some of the same temptations and simplistic arguments that [he] so accurately condemns in Aron." For Ricoeur, the objectivity of history is determined by the subjectivity of the historian, whether he is motivated by an authentic "intention of objectivity," the choice to "comprehend rationally." The result, argues Althusser, is a "purely internal conception of objectivity." But what historian does not imagine that he or she has chosen objectivity? To call this choice transcendental rather than merely empirical, implying that it is the precondition of research only begs the question. Here Althusser interestingly plays Husserl (whose account of the origins of geometry he earlier labeled "formalist") against Ricoeur: "In fact, if we follow Husserl on this point, we will see that he does not define Galilean physics by a simple 'intention of objectivity,' but that he gives precisely to this objectivity a structure corresponding to a general theory of the physical object, 'which can be determined mathematically.'" Ricoeur's subjectivist orientation allows him to mistake for historical knowledge the reliving, the reexperiencing of a past across the distance of time, a "representification of the real itself in its Immediacy," in "its unique flavor like the Madeleine on Proust's tongue." Ricoeur's conception of science must still be founded on immediate experience, motivated by a "nostalgia for perception" that cannot reconcile "the sun of the peasant and that of the astronomer and cannot help feel that there is one sun too many, a sun of luminous, warm days, and a relation between energy and mass."[7] Althusser dismisses this antimony (in which subjectivism and formalism coexist in perfect harmony) as a dilemma only for those who see science as the double of immediate experience rather than as the knowledge of the concrete, which among other things will make its transformation possible.

The interest of this early essay by Althusser lies in the fact that it sketches out a critique of both sides of the debates that raged in French philosophy in the 1950s: consciousness or structure, or in Althusser's terms, subjectivism or formalism, both of which positions could be, and often were, defended with citations from Husserl. This critique, although couched in Marxist terms, was in fact drawn from two thinkers whose influence on Althusser was enormous: Jean Cavaillès and Georges Canguilhem. It is Cavaillès in particular who figures most centrally in Althusser's examination of the alternatives around which French philosophy, especially insofar as it addressed the problem of scientific knowledge, appeared to be structured. His most influential work was his last, *Sur la logique et l'histoire de la science*, written in prison in occupied France in 1943.[8] Cavaillès, an indefatigable militant in the Resistance who had been captured several times only to escape, was finally executed by the Germans in 1943, shortly after completing the manuscript (although the copy entrusted to his sister lacked both references and a title). The first edition of the work was published in 1946 under the auspices of Cavaillès's close friends, Canguilhem and Charles Ehresmann. The circumstances of the text's composition, which made Cavaillès the tragic hero of what would become the antihumanist current, should not be allowed to overshadow the remarkable text itself, which has often been referred to but seldom explicated.[9] It is a dense work that makes few concessions to the reader and presupposes a high degree of familiarity with the totality of Husserl's work, as well as with the logical positivism of the Vienna circle, two traditions that often ignored each other and whose partisans typically claimed not to be able to make sense of the other's philosophical idiom. *Sur la logique* is divided into three sections, a critique of "philosophies of consciousness," which takes Kant (and to a lesser extent Bolzano) as its primary example, a critique of the "logicism" of the Vienna school (particularly Carnap), and a critical examination of Husserlian phenomenology, and culminates in a call for a new philosophy for, if not of, science, a philosophy of the concept.

While Kant, in the section on transcendental analytic in the *Critique of Pure Reason*, announces that logic insofar as it constitutes a set of necessary rules must be completely separated from psychology, which is concerned with the merely contingent rules that govern how we actually think, he nevertheless treats logic as an action of ordering and unification that presupposes a concrete consciousness as the origin of these actions. In fact, for Kant, even if there is a certain structure of consciousness, it is still in consciousness, with the result that "there is nothing prior to consciousness."

The act of knowledge is nothing more then than the knowledge of the act itself, a moment of "internal self-illumination." To know itself, however, it must extract the necessary and the a priori from the contingent and the empirical, which thus do not belong to consciousness but to "something else," something other. Because this other is not consciousness, "it accordingly eludes all attempts to grasp it, and the suspicion arises that this pseudo empirical is only consciousness once again, denying itself in a game in which it is the first to be deceived."[10]

A theory of scientific knowledge, then, in seeking to avoid subordination either to the absolute necessity of consciousness or to the contingency of the "historical existent," turns toward formalism, and "insofar as it identifies itself with the system of all possible formalisms, it absorbs rather than canonizes the totality of formalizable demonstrations and so the totality of science." The goal here is a "universal syntax," which governs the formulation of any scientific utterance, the logic of all possible scientific discoveries in which the law of iteration operates. Its very validity, however, depends upon the theory's being self-sufficient, in no way dependent on a reality outside of itself, part of which may not yet be known: everything is knowable in principle. But this syntax accounts only for the form of discoveries, not their content: we cannot derive the semantic dimension from the syntactical, as the problem of the relationship between mathematics and physics shows. Unless physics is to become a logic, it must have some reference to "the world" or to "an object," which of necessity lies outside of the combinatory and which indeed justifies the selection of certain elements over others. Formalism, ultimately "requires an ontology, a theory of objects that finally fixes the relative position of the authentic meanings and of the independent beings which either claim to found them or to which they are not related."[11]

Phenomenology represents an attempt to construct the synthesis of formalism and the philosophy of consciousness. The gesture of the ἐποχή (epoché) establishes a correlation between noetic acts and noetic contents and thus allows a reduction of the apparently irreducible moments of the act for philosophies of consciousness and the object for formalism. For Cavaillès, however, Husserl's solution to the opposition of philosophies of consciousness and logicism is itself founded on the ultimate primacy of consciousness. The very correlation between consciousness and its objects (the intentionality of consciousness) overcomes the problem of the heteronomy of objects by making objects one of the poles of consciousness. This movement in turn solves the problem of the object in formalism by accepting the incompleteness of formal systems, as well as solving the problem of the relations between systems (there is no system of all possible systems that would not itself be part of another system) by seeing these problems as solvable only through a reduction to a transcendental consciousness. But Cavaillès directs his most forceful critique precisely toward this recourse to the transcendental or to the "absolute" as the solution to the contradictions of consciousness and logicism. Because for phenomenology "the motive of research and the foundation of objectivities are precisely the relation to a creative subjectivity," it follows that "if this subjectivity is in its turn subject to norms, a new transcendental investigation would be needed in order to relate its norms to a higher subjectivity, since no content but rather consciousness alone has the authority to posit itself in itself. If transcendental logic really founds logic, there is no absolute logic (that is governing the absolute subjective activity). If there is an absolute logic, it can draw its authority only from itself and then it is not transcendental."[12]

It is only in the concluding pages of the work that Cavaillès suggests a way out of the impasses of transcendentalism, performing a genuinely symptomatic or deconstructive reading, with the aid of Spinoza, of the very notion of consciousness in phenomenology. In an analysis of Husserl's *Origins of Geometry*, which Derrida would take great pains to refute in his introduction to the French translation of 1962, Cavaillès argues that Husserl's quest for the origin of geometry, the first science of ideal objects in a human practice directed toward the transformation of things in the world, in fact deprives this science of precisely its originality, that is, its singularity, confusing it with what it is not.[13] Husserl must deny the radicality of the rupture that marks the inauguration of a science, projecting into the past, before the beginning, a prior moment of which it would be the continuation. For every science this moment is the same; it is the origin that guarantees the continuity and unity of the progress that follows it: consciousness or that which always is but never has an origin; Cavaillès states it in this manner, "if there is a consciousness of progress, there is no progress of consciousness." In opposition, Cavaillès will argue that in the history of a science "what comes after is more than what existed before, not because it contains it or even because it prolongs it, but because it departs from it and carries in its content the mark of its superiority, unique every time, with more consciousness in it—and not the same consciousness." There is then no consciousness standing outside of and prior to history, which might thus always be the same. There is no consciousness in general, only an infinite plurality of singular consciousnesses (Cavaillès uses the Spinozist phrase "singular essences"), none of which functions as the cause, even the immanent cause of its ideas: each "dwells in the immediacy of the idea, lost in it and losing itself with it."[14] If a given consciousness (for we can no longer speak of consciousness in general) is indistinguishable from the idea and disappears with it, there is only one conclusion to be drawn. The final lines of *Sur la logique* possessed, for Althusser and his students, among others, the mobilizing force of a political slogan and would be cited by Georges Canguilhem in his defense of Foucault's *Les mots et les choses* against the anti-antihumanists of the time: "It is not a philosophy of consciousness but a philosophy of the concept which can provide a theory of science. The generating necessity is not that of an activity, but the necessity of a dialectic."[15]

The notion of a philosophy of the concept was central to the seminar of 1962–63 and was treated at some length in one of the few presentations that was more or less directly to take a published form: Pierre Macherey's "Georges Canguilhem's Philosophy of Science: Epistemology and History of Science," published the following year in *La Pensée*, a theoretical journal associated with the French Communist Party (Parti communiste français [PCF]) with an introduction by Althusser.[16] What place might the philosophy of the concept have in a seminar on structuralism? Macherey's essay, together with Althusser's brief but very interesting preface, demonstrates their identification with a tradition that refused both formalism and logicism and any philosophy of the subject as ways of understanding the history of science or history per se in favor of what Macherey called "a properly dialectical and materialist approach."[17] Canguilhem was not a well-known figure beyond a relatively narrow and specialized audience, even if this audience included some of France's most prominent intellectuals.[18] He was something of a philosopher's philosopher, the nature of whose work (not simply its difficulty but the breadth of scientific knowledge it required of its readers) proved too "technical" for philosophers and too "philosophical" for specialists in the life sciences. Indeed, Macherey's essay was, according to Althusser's foreword, "the first systematic overview" of Canguilhem's work. What distinguished this work from others in the fields of epistemology (the philosophy of science) and the history of science (Althusser speaks of its "radical novelty") is that Canguilhem refuses to separate these fields but instead seeks to understand their profound unity. Not content to describe a "logic of scientific discovery" adequate to science in general on the one hand and a narrative of successive discoveries on the other, Canguilhem demands "a scrupulous respect for the reality of real science." This simple attention to the details of the practice of a specific science leads to an acknowledgment of the fact that "things don't happen in science the way we and in particular philosophers thought they did. Incontestable advances in a given science often do not occur according to the norms of an epistemological legality; for all that, however, they remain incontestable, having been validated repeatedly."[19] Such a logic of scientific discovery is nothing more than an ideal of how a science ought to advance but may not (every such norm has its exceptions), although it has an extra-scientific, that is, political, utility: it can declare certain disciplines, fields, and theories a priori unscientific.

A scrupulous attention to the reality of scientific practice will result not simply in the destruction of any logical protocol external to this practice, it also revolutionizes the very notion of the history of science. To write the history of a science, not as it should be but as it is, is to abandon any notion of this history as continuous progress based on "problem solving," leading in turn to a paradigm shift. On the contrary, as Althusser jocularly puts it, "reality has a bit more imagination." In contrast to the reassuring simplicity of the "idealist schema," in the actually existing history of the sciences, "there are imaginary responses which leave the real problem they evade without a true response; there are sciences which are called sciences and are only the scientific imposture of a social ideology; there are non-scientific ideologies which, in paradoxical encounters, give birth to true discoveries—just as one sees fire leap from the impact of foreign bodies." Such a conception of the history of the sciences must itself be the product of (and here Althusser repeats the phrase) an "encounter," a "specific theoretical conjuncture" characterized by the paradoxical convergence of "Marx-Lenin, Husserl, Hegel—indeed paradoxically but really for those who know those 'ruses' of history, of Nietzsche—without forgetting everything that proves valuable today in the linguistic model." It is a conception of history so disconcerting to those familiar with more traditional accounts of scientific method and progress that Althusser anticipates some will be tempted to classify it as "a variety of irrationalism." To do so, he tells us, would be a "serious error," the consequences of which would be grave. For in giving us a new epistemology based on the real history of scientific practice, Canguilhem has produced a truly rational conception of science, one that has "reached the shores of materialism and the dialectic."[20]

The key text for Macherey's essay is not Canguilhem's *The Normal and the Pathological* (the second revised and extended version of which would only appear in 1966, two years after Macherey's text) but *La formation du concept de réflexe aux XVIIe et XVIIIe siècles*, first published in 1955. For Canguilhem the history of a science (and Macherey cautions us not to associate history with progress or development, with a cumulative, linear time, given that the imposition of such a notion on the real history of a science can only lead to a distortion of the actual events that have constituted it) can best be described as the "birth and adventure of concepts." Why concepts instead of theories, especially when the former appear identifiable with mere words or even images, while the latter implies a group of logically coherent propositions (which, in the sciences, would be based on observation and experimentation)? Macherey finds that "Canguilhem substitutes the filiation of concepts for the chain of theories. In this way every internal criterion, which could only be given by a scientific theory, will be rejected. Canguilhem's goal is thus to give to the idea of a history of science all its value, by seeking to identify, behind the science that conceals its history, the real history that governs and constitutes science. . . . It might be said that this is the effort to think science in its real body, the concept, instead of its ideal legality." The formation of concepts is better understood by "logic of biology than by a formal philosophical logic," that is, a logic of emergence, drift, and mutation.[21] It may be the case (although such a fact is a priori inadmissible for the "history of science as it is done"), as it was for the concept of reflex according to Canguilhem, that a concept may first appear in a theoretical context other than the one it logically implies. It may be that the concept thus precedes its theory and makes it possible, transported from the context in which it emerged and endowed with completely different meaning, a phenomenon that Canguilhem referred to as the "theoretical polyvalence of concepts" (a phrase readers of Foucault will undoubtedly recognize).[22] To make matters even more complicated, the relation between the concept and the language that must be its element is heteronomous: a word is not a concept, and the absence of a word is not necessarily indication of the absence of a concept.[23]

It is the notion of the "theoretical polyvalence of concepts" that allows us to see the importance of Canguilhem for Althusser's critique of structuralism. Despite Althusser's rejection of the opposition of synchrony and diachrony, which he viewed as a version of Hegelianism, his notion of the epistemological break has often been seen as a mere sign of the discontinuity that separates a science from its ideological prehistory. Such a notion would not distinguish Althusser from the Kuhnian theory of a paradigm shift between Aristotelian and Galilean physics, or even from the Husserl of the *Origins of Geometry*, for whom there is a "dislocation" between the concrete practice of the land surveyor and Pythagorean and Euclidean abstraction. In the latter case, this very dislocation allows us to posit a "passage" between the divided worlds of the concrete life and science which retraces, in the form of an ideal objectivity, "the concrete forms and gestures of an earlier practice."[24] Here, even Derrida's insistence that the origin of geometry according to Husserl is a case of that movement of difference and deferral that he named *différance*, in that the significance of geometry is realized only in the necessary supplement that is radically absent from the origin, only reaffirms a kind of continuity (mediated to be sure) between the concrete and the abstract, between the material and the ideal. It is for this reason that Althusser insisted that "the concepts of origin, 'original ground,' genesis and mediation should be regarded as suspect a priori."[25] There is no continuity, not even the continuity deferred across difference, a notion that is revealed to be compatible, if not complicit, with a kind of logicism. The notion of the theoretical polyvalence of concepts renders the notion of origin meaningless; it ceases to have any explanatory power. The transcendental even if it is present only in its absence can only establish a norm outside and beyond the real history of science, a truth to which it must be reduced.

But it is not primarily Derrida against whom Althusser is arguing in this passage; it is rather the detour through Husserl by which some of the most compelling and intelligent Marxist philosophers, precisely those not content to apply the categories of dialectical materialism as enumerated in the manuals that circulated through the Communist movement, turned to Husserl as a way of enriching Marxism. For these thinkers, especially in the 1940s and 1950s, Husserl provided the antidote to both the individualism and spiritualism that Marxists saw in existentialism and the romanticism of Heidegger's philosophy of being. Merleau-Ponty had in some respects opened this path by showing the way in which phenomenology might be compatible with a certain materialism. Others, including Communists, such as Althusser's colleague and friend Jean-Toussaint Desanti and, above all, Tran Duc Thao, a Vietnamese Communist and longtime resident of France, whose work *Phenomenology and Dialectical Materialism* has not been sufficiently appreciated, and those writing from an independent Marxist perspective, such as Claude Lefort and Jean-Francois Lyotard (especially in *La phénomenologie*, the first edition of which appeared in 1954, an important text sympathetic to Thao's argument), worked from the position that Thao summarizes in a brief phrase: "Marxism necessarily emerges as the only conceivable solution to the problems posed by phenomenology."[26] Such a position was of course possible only if one refused merely to condemn Husserl and instead entered into his work in order to "identify the internal contradictions of the Husserlian oeuvre itself."[27] Precisely because both Thao and Lyotard explicitly sought not to uncover and present the meaning of Husserl's texts, assuming, within each period of Husserl's thought at least, a coherence, but rather to describe the coexistence of contradictory meanings in a textual disarray that was never definitively overcome, their readings appeared superior to earlier efforts to criticize (however sympathetically) Husserl, such as Sartre's *Transcendence of the Ego* (1937).

Significantly, the materialist kernel that Thao claims to abstract from Husserl takes as its logical starting point the very remarks on the origin of mathematics from Husserl's last phase that Althusser pointedly criticizes in the passage from *Reading Capital* cited above (and which form the central focus of Derrida's introduction to *L'origine de la géométrie*, which is, interestingly, critical not so much of Thao's positions—Derrida has often expressed admiration for *Phenomenology and Dialectical Materialism*—as of his critique of Husserl).[28] The concept of the transcendental (which Thao declares finally to be "superfluous" in Husserl) has obscured "the exceptional importance that Husserl has constantly accorded to the 'thing' (*Ding*). Intersubjective communities and the spiritual entities constituted in them are definitively founded on natural psychic realities which, in turn, are founded on physical realities." Unlike the Heidegger of *Being and Time* who, according to Thao, defines being-in-the-world not as "an objective circumstance imposed by the reality of things, but as an ontological structure that belongs to the nature of human existence," itself freed from objective necessity by death (freedom-toward-death), Husserl declares "natural reality" to be the "basis of all other realities" and the "phenomenology of material nature" to occupy "a privileged position."[29] Such a phenomenology, however, would not be a "naturalism" that denies any constitutive role for consciousness, anymore than it would produce a skepticism incapable of conceiving anything other than consciousness. Phenomenological reduction, according this time to Lyotard, resolves the antimony of subject and object: "the truth of science is not founded on God as in Descartes or on a priori conditions of possibility as in Kant" but on the immediate lived experience in which "man and world are found to be originarily in accord."[30]

If this originary inseparability of consciousness and world becomes, for the philosophical-political current under consideration, the principle of a materialism, it is, as Thao takes great pains to show, not a mechanistic materialism and not a materialism of an abstract, inert, or indeterminate matter. Instead (and it is on this point that Husserl's fragment on the origins of geometry takes on its full importance), the matter or nature that is the object of our knowledge is not simply the product of or determined by sense experience, for this experience is itself framed and determined by material existence: "the notion of consciousness takes into full account the enigma of consciousness inasmuch as the object that is worked on takes on its meaning for man as human product. The realization of meaning is precisely nothing but the symbolic transposition of material operations of production into a system of intentional operations in which the subject appropriates the object ideally, in reproducing it in his own consciousness." Thus, geometry as ideal objectivity is not a reflection of or founded in the lived experience of space; its foundation is the "human praxis" of the appropriation of nature in the course of agricultural production, "the creative materiality of the laboring masses" whose power and destiny give geometry its truth.[31]

Even this foundation, however, would constitute an origin of geometry or science in precisely the terms that Althusser, applying Canguilhem's notion of the filiation and polyvalence of concepts, finds meaningless, an imposition of a transcendental term on the real history of a science whose function is precisely to furnish an essential identity that will persist beyond the mutations and variations of that history. For Husserl, the question of determining the origin of geometry is crucial: out of a "first creative act" arises "its persisting manner of being: it is not only a mobile forward process from one set of acquisitions to another but a continuous synthesis in which all acquisitions maintain their validity, all make up a totality such that, at every present stage, the total acquisition is, so to speak, the total premise for the acquisitions of the new level."[32] For Althusser, the fact that Thao takes the "first creative act" to be that of the laboring masses engaged in productive activity rather than that of an originary consciousness, and thus material rather than ideal, changes nothing. Thao remains captive of a "philosophy of the origin" that requires and does not hesitate to produce an external guarantee of the objectivity of a science that is simultaneously its principle and its truth, that which founds that persistence, mobility, and iterability (the different forms in which Husserl tries to conceptualize the essential continuity of mathematics). In invoking an origin that to be sure does not contain the "total meaning" but only the element of ideal objectivity that founds and insures the continuity and compatibility, that is, the fundamental identity of geometry throughout its history, Husserl turns our attention away from the real complexity of the history of a given science, which inescapably exhibits multiple "origins" or beginnings, stops, starts, restarts, and recommencements that recast an entire field back to its origins. From the point of view of the reality of scientific practice, we can no longer speak of *the* origin in what Althusser calls its "idealist" sense: "the present, actual, eternal constituent essence that produces from the heart of its constituent depth, all the phenomena of history."[33] To trace the "adventures of the concept," whose real history may not in any way correspond to a logical sequence, will require a philosophy that does not seek the truth of a science outside of or prior to it in an origin or foundation of truth.

The critique of every philosophy of the origin, of course, recalls the importance of Cavaillès and Canguilhem for Althusser, as outlined above; it also, however, signals the presence of another, perhaps more surprising, philosophical reference: Hegel, nominally the main enemy in the struggle to grasp the specificity of Marxism, but he, on this front at least, proves an ally, as Althusser would later make explicit. In a response in 1967 to critics entitled "La querelle de l'humanisme" ("The Humanist Controversy"), part of which was delivered at Jean Hyppolite's seminar on Hegel in February 1968 and later published in the French edition of *Lenin and Philosophy* (1972) as "On the Relation Between Marx and Hegel," Althusser would argue that "in Hegel, there is no origin, nor (what is only its phenomenon) any beginning."[34] Interestingly, Lyotard, in his overview of phenomenology, made a similar argument in order, however, to show that in the *Science of Logic*, Hegel, insofar as he establishes a "dialectical identification of being and concept," simply "leaps over" the problem of "originarity."[35] In contrast to the notion of an antepredicative world outside of and prior to any act of knowing, the belief or faith (Glaube) that must precede any predication, Hegel refuses any notion of a transcendental or "ineffable" realm beyond knowledge. Absolute knowledge is an end already other than itself in a process that has always already begun and thus has no real beginning. Further, for

Hegel, the separation of self (*moi*) and world, insurmountable for Husserl, is only a moment, determinate and fleeting, in the long return of spirit to itself. In its avoidance of origins and specifically the origin of knowledge in an act of human consciousness, Hegel's philosophy can only appear "metaphysical, speculative and inauthentic."[36]

But does not this refusal of origins place Althusser on the side of structure against consciousness, to employ the terms most commentators have used to describe the primary theoretical conflict of the period? Is it not for this very reason that so many commentators have ranked Althusser among the structuralists? The answer to this question may be somewhat surprising. In "On Feuerbach," written in 1967 and only published posthumously, Althusser argues that Feuerbach is the unrecognized or disavowed father both of Husserl's phenomenology and of Dilthey's historicism. This common filiation allows Althusser to categorize both philosophies as "hermeneutic" in that they take the human world as a world of "meaning" rather than mere fact, which is a priori distinct from and opposed to that of the natural world: meaning is the product of the mind that knows it and is thus known from within. Althusser argues that it is a "strategic" imperative to subject every notion of origin or genesis (which Feuerbach bequeathed to his descendants and which has been faithfully handed down from generation to generation) to a "radical critique." To "elaborate a non-genetic theory of historical emergence" will require, however, not simply a break with this tradition but with "any structural-functional theory" as well. If this double imperative is surprising, Althusser will go even further: when it comes to the concept of ideology, "the structural interpretation is fundamentally indistinguishable from the hermeneutic."[37]

Before we dismiss this statement as either a deliberate provocation or a crude amalgamation of philosophical orientations that decades of commentary have assured us exist in complete opposition, we might recall that on this precise point Althusser has another quite illustrious "companion in heresy": Michel Foucault. In his introduction to the English edition of Canguilhem's *The Normal and the Pathological*, published in 1978, Foucault attempted to situate Canguilhem in the landscape of French philosophy in the postwar period, a task that required an overview of the type Foucault usually avoided in his distrust of superficial generalities and artificial coherences, making the piece particularly interesting. Of all the antagonisms that divided the world of French philosophy in the 1950s and 1960s, Foucault argues, Marxism and anti-Marxism, psychoanalysis and its critics (and we might well add structuralism and antistructuralism), the line dividing "the two modalities according to which phenomenology was taken up in France" traversed all these other oppositions in a way whose importance has not been recognized.[38] This particular dividing line allows us to see in Marxism not a relatively homogeneous field whose differences would be but variants of a few central postulates but instead the site of an irreducible theoretical heterogeneity in which, at least for a time, phenomenology played a central organizing role.

While there is no doubt that Althusser shared Foucault's perspective, the two philosophers differed in quite striking ways about the precise nature of this theoretical dominance and the forms that it took. For Foucault, phenomenology was the fundamental ground and horizon of thought in this period: the major philosophical positions that one might adopt or at least align oneself with were internal to phenomenology. He alludes to the conclusion of Cavaillès's *Sur la logique* in describing the two modalities: on the one hand, "a philosophy of experience, of meaning, of the subject" (associated with Sartre and Merleau-Ponty) and on the other, "a philosophy of knowledge (savoir), rationality, and of the concept" (associated with Cavaillès, Bachelard, and Canguilhem). Each tendency had its founding text (both derived from opposed readings of Husserl's *Cartesian Meditations*): for "the philosophy of the subject," Sartre's *Transcendence of the Ego* (1937), and for "the theory of science," Cavaillès's "two theses on the axiomatic method and the formation of set theory" (1938). The latter is characterized by a return "to the founding principle's of Husserl's thought: those of formalism and intuitionism."[39]

What is immediately striking about Foucault's formulation is its amalgamation of what Althusser regarded as two incompatible positions into a single opposition to the philosophy of consciousness. For Foucault, the tradition issuing out of Husserl's early critique of psychologism, which he describes, citing Cavaillès's theses, as formalism, culminates in the philosophy of the concept. For Althusser, in contrast, Cavaillès's *Sur la logique* represents a new position in relation to the earlier works, one in which both the philosophy of consciousness, discussed in the first chapter of the work, and formalism, discussed in the second, are rejected in the third and final chapter as forms of transcendentalism that cannot grasp "singular essences." It is the statement of a third position that immediately reorganizes the theoretical field by making visible a certain complicity between what were thought to be inalterably opposed philosophies, and, in doing so, this position resides outside the framework of phenomenology (with the assistance of Hegel and, even more, Spinoza). The difference between these views of the "theoretical conjuncture" is extremely important; in particular it will determine how one will understand structuralism.

4

Lévi-Strauss
Ancestors and Descendants, Causes and Effects

To examine Althusser's thesis concerning the relation between philosophies of consciousness and formalism, we might take as an index of the problem the example of the linguistic model, which was mentioned earlier in connection with the theoretical conjuncture that made possible the development of Canguilhem's philosophy. While the formalism of this model is certainly not the same as the mathematical formalism to which Foucault refers, neither is it entirely unrelated to it; in any case the linguistic model has been understood to be opposed to any philosophy of consciousness. The focal point of Althusser's treatment of the linguistic model was Lévi-Strauss, for whom structural linguistics and semiology functioned as models for a scientific analysis of social phenomena.[1] In the lecture notes for his presentation to the seminar of 1962–63, "Lévi-Strauss à la recherche de ses ancêtres putatifs," Althusser not only rejects Lévi-Strauss's account of the history of structural anthropology and of his place in that history as "false," but he proposes to "determine its principle of selectivity." According to Lévi-Strauss's construction of his theoretical past, the work of "Durkheim, Mauss, Boas, Radcliffe-Brown, etc." illuminated by notions of structure developed in such diverse fields as "*Gestalt* psychology, linguistics, mathematics, [and] biology" formed the problematic within which his work took shape. Althusser, however, is less interested in official chronologies and genealogies than in identifying the "forgotten ancestors" whose patrimony weighs all the more heavily for being unrecognized and unthought.[2] Of these, Althusser tells us, one in particular emerges as essential: Hegel.

For those familiar with the debates around Lévi-Strauss's work, from Claude Lefort's "L'échange et la lutte des hommes," published in *Les Temps*

Modernes in 1951, to Lévi-Strauss's own critique of Sartre's *Critique of Dialectical Reason* in *La pensée sauvage* in 1962, Althusser's identification of Hegel as Lévi-Strauss's forgotten forebearer might well, at least at first, appear absurd.[3] But, let us recall, this is not even the full extent of Althusser's argument: in the notes for "Lévi-Strauss à la recherche de ses ancêtres putatifs" from 1962, as well as the passages from "On Feuerbach" (1967) quoted at the end of chapter 3, the confrontation between Lévi-Strauss and his phenomenological critics is not a real confrontation at all but merely a local conflict between two possible theoretical variants of a single problematic. But before we turn to the reading of Lévi-Strauss's texts by Althusser, a reading that remains to be reconstructed from a single, short (posthumously published) essay written in 1966, the notes of the lecture referred to above, and Althusser's reading notes and a few scattered references, it might prove valuable to return to the historical origins of structuralism and, in particular, the history of the linguistic model with Althusser's argument in mind.

Of all the figures associated with the emergence of structuralism and the linguistic model, none is more closely connected to each of the important moments of the history than Roman Jakobson, the trajectory of whose life is the itinerary of structuralism itself: from Moscow to Prague to Paris and New York. Lévi-Strauss himself has asserted that his own views were to a large degree shaped by his attending Jakobson's lectures during the exile of the war years in New York. It is all the more significant then that his account of the origins of structural linguistics confirms Althusser's otherwise surprising assertions about the theoretical filiations of this movement. In an overview of twentieth-century linguistics, delivered as a series of lectures at the end of the 1960s, Jakobson argued that the "structural linguistics" that emerged in Prague in the late twenties and thirties, and whose proponents already saw it at that time as a model for inquiry for the human sciences in general, had its sources in "phenomenology in its Husserlian and Hegelian versions."[4]

In particular, Jakobson cites Husserl's *Logical Investigations* (the early "formalist" Husserl, if we follow Foucault's account in the introduction to Canguilhem's *The Normal and the Pathological*), which announces as its objective "the idea of a *universal grammar* conceived by the rationalists of the seventeenth and eighteenth century."[5] Husserl's description of the project of a universal grammar is in fact an exact description of the linguistic model that Lévi-Strauss, by his own admission, would borrow with little modification from Jakobson's account of Trubetzkoy's phonology, which, in turn, had its origins in Husserl's following statement:

> Even in the sphere of grammar there are fixed standards, *a priori* norms that may not be transgressed. As in the proper sphere of logic, the *a priori* element separates itself off from the empirical and practically logical, so in the grammatical sphere the so-called purely grammatical, the a priori element or "idealized form of speech" as it is well called, separates itself off from the empirical element. In both cases, the empirical element is in fact determined by universal, yet merely factual traits of human nature, partly by chance peculiarities of race, nationality and national history, or by the peculiarities of the individual and his life experience.[6]

The task of a phenomenological investigation, then, is to "lay bare an ideal framework which each actual language will fill up and clothe differently."[7]

We are thus as far from the existentialism of a Sartre as any of the structuralist works he denounced. To make this distance even more apparent, we should recall that perhaps even more important than Husserl's rehabilitation of the idea of a pure grammar was the critique of psychologism with which he opens the *Logical Investigations*. Against the argument that logic is a technology used by the mind in which it originates, thus the study of the laws of thought (a psychology) or the laws of the human mind (an anthropology), Husserl proposes the project of a pure logic. The question is not the contingency of how we think or have thought but rather the necessity that governs the very possibility of thinking at all, the a priori that makes thought possible. That this "formalist" or structuralist moment in Husserl was succeeded by a reassertion of the rights of the cogito and of consciousness as the necessary foundation of even the a priori itself did not prevent Husserl's early work from producing effects in domains other than that of philosophy in the strict sense, which remained impervious to his later critique of his own early "logicism," preserving what would be constituted retroactively as his structuralism.

Among the documents Jakobson cites in his account of the mutation of an element of phenomenology into structuralism is one of the earliest declarations of a "structuralist perspective." In the eighth and final volume of the *Travaux du Cercle Linguistique de Prague* (1939), dedicated to the memory of the recently deceased "M. le Prince Trubetzkoy," there appeared an essay entitled "Perspectives du structuralism" by Hendrik J. Pos, a former student of Husserl and a member of the Prague circle.[8] Pos, a nearly forgotten figure, was named by Lyotard in *La phénomenologie* (1954) as representing, along with Heidegger, Fink, Merleau-Ponty, and Lévinas, one of the major lines along which Husserl's thought developed.[9] Pos's document is nothing less than a manifesto that draws from Trubetskoy's *Elements of Phonology* a series of conclusions, both methodological and substantive, valid for all the social or human sciences. Significantly, many of these same conclusions would be repeated by Lévi-Strauss nearly twenty years later in *Structural Anthropology*.

Pos begins his assessment of Trubetskoy's originality by underscoring his critique of the "nominalism" that dominated phonetics through the 1920s. According to the nominalist approach, knowledge sought to represent a reality constituted of infinitely varied individual facts. The activity of phonetics before Trubetskoy consisted of recording all the sounds uttered by all the speaking subjects; this activity by its very nature could have no end and from it only inductive generalizations could be drawn concerning the resemblances of all the sounds thus far recorded. Nominalism had broken with the psychologism that saw sounds as expressions of the intentions of speaking subjects and had thus restored it to its specificity, but it had done so "at the cost of an unperceived change of object."[10] Without any reference to speaking subjects, sounds became individual noises dissociated from language, their form understood at the expense of their function.

The structuralist revolution, according to Pos, would consist in establishing regularities, the system anterior to "the phonic phenomena," understanding the latter as "directly derived from the activity of the speaking subject." Thus, at the origins of structuralism is Husserl, and not simply the logicist Husserl of 1900 but the author of *Cartesian Meditations*, the champion of the cogito. Pos's statement is surprising to say the least: the phonological system becomes intelligible only when we recognize the speaking subject as the origin of language (recall that Husserl defined philosophy as "the science of origins"). Does structuralism then begin with the subject? Not exactly: sounds don't, strictly speaking, originate in the individual subject. Phonemes presuppose a speaker and a listener, one who produces the sound and the one for whom the sound is produced and whose comprehension is necessary to the function of language. Any inquiry into the speaking subject that "discovers the common and identical by which subjects understand each other, makes known a reality that surpasses the isolated world of the individual subject, a reality that could not be known by remaining at the point of view of the individual subject."[11] For Pos, this is precisely the importance of phonology for the human sciences in general:

> From this perspective, phonology has a precious contribution to make to the science of intersubjective reality. Thanks to the discovery of the ideal system of phonemes, one can see the possibility of enlarging the domain of the reality that precedes any separation between individuals. . . . An exhaustive analysis of intersubjective understanding would show how language along with other social, moral and cultural values constitutes the vehicle and the expression of a spiritual reality that envelops individuals, that signifies a source of enrichment and communion for them without detracting from the individuality of each.[12]

The reality that precedes and exceeds individuals, the system of sound elements common to all speaking subjects, takes the form of an unconscious finality or teleology, which is itself an "organ in the grand organism of human society."[13]

Pos's emphasis on the primacy not just of the intersubjective over the individual subject, whose autonomy then becomes largely illusory, but on the systematic, rule-governed nature of this intersubjective realm in which individual subjects obey laws, which precede and envelop them unconsciously, is not restricted to the domain of phonology or even linguistics in general. On the contrary, such a model will of necessity be valid for all genuinely cultural forms, that is, precisely the forms proper to the intersubjective life of which language is the most immediate, inescapable, and concrete expression. If Pos appears to have adopted a position diametrically opposed to the more familiar reading of Husserl associated with Sartre, he was far from alone in his opposition. It is true that Sartre might draw from the *Cartesian Meditations* the notion that the "problem of the other," that is, the problem of perceiving the other not as object but as alter ego, was the central drama of human existence. According to this view, intersubjectivity was not a given but an achievement, in fact, an ethical imperative. Readers are familiar with the frontal assault on this construction of the cogito that concludes Lacan's famous essay on the mirror stage. It should be noted, however, that some years earlier, Merleau-Ponty argued that Sartre's philosophy culminated in the "absurdity of a solipsism of the many," counterposing an "originary relation of comprehension" prior to the division of self and other, "in the absence of which the feeling of solitude and the concept of solipsism themselves would have no meaning for us."[14] Initially, Merleau-Ponty cited, as did Lacan, Henri Wallon's *Les origines du caractère chez l'enfant*.[15] Wallon's text was seen as proof of an original transitivism in which an "incontinent sociability" until a certain age prevents a clear separation between one's own feelings and those of others and which persists as an element even into adulthood, the condition of there existing "a single, intersubjective world."[16] Later, he would follow Pos and posit language as the primary site and mechanism of this intersubjective world. Accordingly, while quite critical of the "objectivism" of French social theory at the beginning of the 1950s, with its tendency to discount the lived experience of social subjects, Merleau-Ponty would, by the decade's end, have come to terms with the linguistic model as a model for inquiry even in extremely quantitative forms.

But if phenomenology's relation to Lévi-Strauss's work in particular and to the emergence of structuralism more generally appears only obliquely—relevant at all, in fact, only insofar as it is the immanent cause of the revolution in linguistics that produced phonology—Lévi-Strauss openly avows the kinship, if not exactly the influence, of another tradition equally concerned with preserving the rights and privileges of consciousness and the human subject (however much it disdained these terms). Claude Lefort's severe critique of Lévi-Strauss's *Elementary Structures of Kinship* is only the most lucid of a significant number of attacks on the "mathematical formalism" that was thought to characterize the latter's investigation of the exchange of women in so-called primitive societies. While Lévi-Strauss declares his intention "to transcend empirical observation and discover deeper realities," by "deeper realities" complains Lefort, he does not mean "the lived meaning" of exchange, its origins in human subjectivity: "Lévi-Strauss has turned away from a phenomenological analysis. The deepest reality according to him is mathematical reality."[17] Following Durkheim, he has effaced the specificity of the human, treating the facts of human existence as if they were facts of physical nature, thereby neglecting the reality of the consciousness that precedes, causes, and later interprets what are not mere events, but actions. In particular, asks Lefort (based on precisely the reading of Hegel that Althusser had rejected from the beginning of his career), how can we understand exchange in the absence of a conception of the struggle between consciousnesses for recognition (here, of course, he lapses into a notion of the primacy of individual consciousnesses over any collective entity, despite arguing exactly the opposite earlier in the essay).

Responding to Lefort and others in *Structural Anthropology* (1958), Lévi-Strauss vehemently rejected the notion that he ignored the concrete reality of human existence, replacing it with the abstractions that his mathematical model required. After all, he argued, are there not other developments in the human sciences that, despite the rigorously formal nature of their methods, do not take as their starting point "abstract notions, but concrete individuals and groups"?[18] Further, are not these new studies extremely interested in and, in fact, dependent on theories of the most subtle and fleeting of "subjective" phenomena? It is one of history's little paradoxes that while a horde of English-language critics of structuralism in the 1980s protested that structuralist methods only described but did not explain the facts of human action because they failed to trace the origins of such actions to the internal motivations of "real men" or actors, Lévi-Strauss would cite game theory itself, specifically the founding work of Morgenstern and von Neumann, *The Theory of Games and Economic Behavior*, in defense of structuralism.[19] Of course, this is a paradox only because many of the critics of structuralism were not terribly familiar with the actual texts in which structuralist theories were expressed, nor were they aware of the genealogy of structuralism, which turns out not to be at all what was expected. But this kinship, as unwelcome as its revelation may be, is expressed in another way: it is now rational choice theory itself that stands accused, in an uncanny repetition of the French debates of the 1950s, of a reductive formalism that ignores the concrete complexity of human existence.

The connection between game theory and Lévi-Strauss's structuralism, a connection that is repeatedly stressed by Lévi-Strauss in the most important chapter in *Structural Anthropology* ("The Notion of Structure in Ethnology") and supported with lengthy citations, has been all but ignored by recent commentators. Althusser and the group of young philosophers around him, in contrast, were quite interested in this connection. Lévi-Strauss himself thus showed the way in which his ethnology, for all its mathematical finery, was not only compatible with a philosophical anthropology, a theory of the human subject, but it presupposed such a theory in its central presentation of society as the effect of systems of communication or exchange. It is not difficult to see the allure of von Neumann and Morgenstern's work for Lévi-Strauss: just as his analysis of kinship systems and rules governing the exchange of women "penetrated the door of the romantic," where it had once been assumed that a myriad of undefinable and ungraspable "sentiments" governed individuals' choice of husband or wife, so game theory sidestepped the problem of individual psychology (which was assumed to make the measurement of utility, and thus a quantitative account of economic behavior, impossible) in determining "a complete set of rules of behavior in all conceivable situations," rules for both "a social economy and for games." The set of rules is complete indeed: no individual, no matter how ignorant of the state of affairs determining the probability of his attaining his preference, no matter how mistaken in his calculations, can violate these rules. There exists a rule for every conceivable situation in which an individual is engaged in "maximizing behavior" and historical, social influences do nothing to "change the formal properties of the process of maximizing." The authors aim at nothing less than a total theory capable of "analyzing decisions, the information on the basis of which they are undertaken and the interrelatedness of such sets of information (at the various moves) with each other."[20] The vague, "metaphysical" distinction between rationality and irrationality is replaced by an always measurable ratio of preference to information, and corresponding to every possible ratio is a course of action that necessarily follows from it according to the axioms that govern economic behavior. Von Neumann and Morgenstern have thus established nothing less than a universal combinatory, a universal synchronic (or "static," to use their term) system or rather the theory of that combinatory whose existence had been noted some time before: the world market, whose harmony and equilibrium are perpetually repeated as a consequence of every action of every utility maximizer (the operative definition of the human individual) who inhabits it.

Is not this axiomatization of human behavior, which appears to reduce "real men" to a set of functions and submits the most purposive human action to the implacable logic of a combinatory, itself a kind of antihumanism? Are not human beings no more than "bearers of structures" (to use Marx's phrase, the mere repetition of which by Althusser would cause no end of scandal), structures that are not even historical and material but merely logical? Further, is this not a return, in the guise of a mathematical description of certain psychological or subjective states, to the most reductive kind of objectivism, one that cannot distinguish between natural and human phenomena? The response to all these questions must be emphatically negative. The coherence of *The Theory of Games and Economic Behavior* rests on the presupposition of the most classical kind of humanism, as defined by Althusser in his essay "Marxism and Humanism" (1964): it attributes to man a universal essence that is expressed in each and every individual. As Pierre Raymond has remarked of the calculation of probabilities in the human sciences: "for probability to be applied to these different facts, individuals must be made uniform (and not singularized), treated as an effect without cause, isolated and abstract, while at the same time the necessary element of a collectivity in isolation from which it cannot be understood."[21] Further, the theory is a hermeneutic theory that does not consider human action as if it were a natural event but seeks what is behind the action, the subjective internal state (the decision, the preference) whose meaning it expresses.

But to understand fully in what way and to what extent it is possible to justify Althusser's rather provocative assertion that Lévi-Strauss's structuralism (and structuralism more generally) "is thus in the last instance a hermeneutic" and that "the concept of structure is its theoretical fig-leaf," we must turn to the centerpiece of Althusser's critique of structuralism: his analysis of Lévi-Strauss.[22] It is necessary to remark at the outset of this discussion that Althusser did not initially approach Lévi-Strauss as an adversary or as part of opposing theoretical and political camp. On the contrary, as his correspondence shows, in preparing for the seminar of 1962–63, Althusser read Lévi-Strauss's work (above all, *Structural Anthropology*, which he continued to regard, in opposition to *The Savage Mind*, as the key text) in order "to take from it what I need to nourish the concepts in me waiting to be delivered," and he has no doubt that he will be able "to disentangle its imposture from its fecundity."[23] For Althusser, in the lecture notes of 1962, Lévi-Strauss's misrecognition of his theoretical genealogy did not prevent him from adding to and thus transforming the philosophical archive to which his work, without his realizing it, belonged. In particular, his notion of structure as stated in chapter fifteen of *Structural Anthropology* marks a certain advance over the related notions that preceded it, notions whose function was to denote the unity of apparently diverse phenomena: Plato's Idea, the *Gestalt*, and Hegel's totality. Lévi-Strauss's conception of structure differed from these attempts to theorize the unity of a given field, precisely in that it "did not suppress the specific character of the phenomena" whose unity it nevertheless described.[24] This is what Althusser hoped the concept of structure would allow him to theorize, a paradoxical unity of the diverse without reduction or negation; it is what Montesquieu, who could not finally escape the opposition between the abstract and the concrete, came close to grasping, only to retreat; that to which Hegel in his "flight forward into theory" provided an imaginary and spiritual "solution."

Lévi-Strauss's refusal to transcend or overcome the difference between the various instances of the social whole, his "relegating of the totality to a secondary position" is what, in Althusser's eyes, both "distanced him from Hegel" and "brought him close to Marx and Freud."[25] In this way Lévi-Strauss was also very close to Althusser, who, earlier that year (that is, in the summer of 1962) had written "Contradiction and Overdetermination," criticizing the use of a Hegelian notion of a single central contradiction (in the case of capitalism, the contradiction between labor and capital) as the essence or truth in relation to which all else in a given society must be understood as phenomenal expressions: "overdetermination is inevitable and thinkable as soon as the real existence of the forms of the superstructure and of the national and international conjuncture has been recognized—an existence that is largely specific and autonomous and therefore irreducible to a pure phenomenon."[26]

The phenomena whose specific existence Lévi-Strauss's method refused to suppress, according to Althusser, were the levels (*niveaux*) of which every society necessarily consists. There exist three fundamental levels on which systems of communication (or exchange) are organized, which ensure the survival and reproduction of the individuals who make up a given society: the system of the communication of women, the system of the communication of goods, and the system of the communication of messages. These systems, as social realities, are independent of each other. Each has an autonomous existence: none is the expression of any other, nor do all express some transcendental level. But, as in the case cited by Lévi-Strauss, while heavy molecules of two thick liquids separated by a nearly impermeable barrier and electrons emitted by a cathodic tube are two absolutely different and autonomous phenomena, their movements are governed by the same physical laws, a fact that allows us to compare them. In the same way, culture consists of "rules applicable to all kinds of 'games of communication,'" including the game of communication that marks the threshold of culture and in doing so calls into question the opposition of the human and the natural and therefore the opposition of the human and natural sciences: genetic communication. Each level thus exhibits a structure: defined by Althusser in his notes as the "distinct model of a reality" that is, according to Lévi-Strauss himself, both a system "consisting of elements such that the modification of one would entail the transformation of all other elements" and "a group of transformations."[27] It is precisely the formal character of structure in general that allows specific structures to be compared and even to help explain one another, even though they pertain to very different realities.

Herein lies the problem for Althusser, even in his early and relatively sympathetic examination of Lévi-Strauss. If the latter avoided the pitfalls of a spiritualist conception of the social totality by making the levels irreducible in their specificity and by emphasizing that structure as a model was not to be found in the region of reality under consideration as the essence hidden behind appearances but was the "theoretical construction" through which its systematic nature became intelligible, he did not entirely escape its effects. In particular, the different levels of social reality, each with its own model, could not be understood in their unity unless we can establish the model of models. "Is it possible to construct a model of all models?" Althusser asked in his seminar on Lévi-Strauss.[28] His answer, near the conclusion of his exposé: only if one, in opposition to Marx or Freud, will proceed to establish a "universal combinatory" or a universal grammar, the "order of orders" to use Lévi-Strauss's own phrase.

At this point Althusser argued it was important to distinguish what Lévi-Strauss did from what he said. In "Philosophie et sciences humaines," an essay published in the summer of 1963 (and which therefore must have been written during the seminar), Althusser contrasts the "admirable concrete analyses" of Lévi-Strauss from the "philosophy that he joins to them." In a long critical note devoted to Lévi-Strauss, Althusser begins by praising the notion of "bricolage," as it is developed in *La pensée sauvage*, as an important contribution to the understanding of certain kinds of ideologies, the most contemporary example of which is the ideology that informs Lévi-Strauss's own work. This ideology masquerading as philosophy has been "put together from pieces of Jakobson, von Neumann and cybernetics, with fragments of myths and codes" to "bring about a miraculous short-circuit between nature and culture. A certain vulgarized 'structuralism' seeks this short-circuit everywhere, making it the miracle of everyday life. A skillful manipulation of metonymy and metaphor, for example, or of paradigm and syntagm has produced, at least if the accounts are to be believed, rapid and astonishing results. Certain of these studies have already been published; others will be very soon. A great expansion of structuralist production can be predicted."[29]

Within a very few years, Althusser's position on Lévi-Strauss in particular and structuralism in general would shift in an increasingly negative direction.[30] If Lévi-Strauss's genealogy, as it was reconstructed by Althusser, made him a partial ally of the materialist cause, his work produced effects (which, more than any reading, accurately reflected its meaning, according to Althusser) in the period immediately following the seminar on structuralism that tended to undermine this cause. Althusser refers to two commentators in particular, both of whom expressed considerable enthusiasm for Lévi-Strauss's structuralism in ways that underscored the idealist elements in his work. Paul Ricoeur, as a formidable representative of French phenomenology, might have been expected to respond to *La pensée sauvage* as critically as Lefort and Lyotard had to *Les structures éleméntaires*. In fact, his review published in *Esprit* in 1963 was the declaration of a truce between what had previously been the warring tendencies of French thought: phenomenology and structuralism.[31] The ease with which this truce was declared and the obviousness of its terms confirmed Althusser's suspicions. In 1964 Lucien Sebag published a manifesto of structural Marxism, *Marxisme et structuralisme*, which contained not a single reference to Althusser and in which Sebag tended to see in the model of society offered in *Structural Anthropology* and *La pensée sauvage* as the solution to the key dilemma of Marxism: the relation between base and superstructure.[32] Althusser regarded Sebag's attempt to formulate "a 'structuralist' Marxist theory of ideologies" as making explicit what remained latent in Lévi-Strauss: the operation of an expressive causality in the very theory of social levels that Althusser had initially regarded as the site of the materialist element in Lévi-Strauss.[33]

In "Structure and Hermeneutics" Ricoeur begins by acknowledging what would appear to be the irreconcilable opposition between structuralism and hermeneutics. The former is a science whose object is regarded as existing independently of the observer, while the latter consists of a philosophical interpretation that takes as its point of departure the "hermeneutic circle," in which an object can be approached only through the mediation of the subjectivity through which it is experienced and from which it can never be successfully disentangled. Rather than oppose these "two ways of understanding" or even simply juxtapose them, Ricoeur seeks to construct a total theory of knowledge of which they will be separate but necessarily linked components. He will show that, despite its use of formal models and quantitative techniques, structuralism must rely in the last instance on the human mind as its unifying principle, as that which alone can render the entire field under consideration intelligible. For Ricoeur, the linguistic model, especially the phonological model of Trubetzkoy and Jakobson, is perfectly valid. He rejects the usual phenomenological criticisms of the model as "ahistorical" in its focus on synchronic relations at the expense of the questions of genesis and origin, arguing that the synchronic for Lévi-Strauss, far from being static or timeless, is the principle that allows diachrony or history to be understood. Instead, for Ricoeur, the problem lies in the generalizability of this model to domains other than language: the structural analogy between other social phenomena and language, considered in its phonological structure, is in effect very complex. In what sense can it be said that their "nature is related to that of language itself? . . . All that can be affirmed is that the linguistic model directs research toward articulations similar to its own, that is, toward a logic of oppositions and correlations, that is, finally to a system of differences."[34] Althusser, let us recall, argued in his seminar presentation that Lévi-Strauss's notion of society as consisting of distinct levels that were "irreducible but comparable" was a refusal of Hegelian negativity and the spiritual whole that it produces.[35] In opposition, Ricoeur, citing Lévi-Strauss himself, argues that such a strict correlation between language and culture must be founded on a third term that guarantees such a rigorous correspondence: the human mind. If Lévi-Strauss is not to fall into the absurdity of "a Kantianism without a transcendental subject," a combinatory of combinatories that would itself somehow not form part of a larger combinatory, he must seek the foundation that is the object of hermeneutic inquiry: human subjectivity, the act of understanding, "the apprehension of similitude that must precede and found any formalization."[36]

Lucien Sebag's *Marxisme et structuralisme*, written at about the same time as Ricoeur's text, took the question of the origin of language and culture (or ideology) even further, arguing, if from a different perspective, that structuralism is not only compatible with a certain reading of phenomenology (even at the extreme, what Althusser called a Marxist humanism) but in fact finds its validation only in the foundation that such a phenomenology provides. This interesting work, translated within ten years of its publication into Spanish, Italian, and German, remains little known in the English-speaking world. Sebag, who left the French Communist Party (Parti communiste français [PCF]) in 1956 in response to the Hungarian revolution and who later became a student of Lévi-Strauss, brought to structuralism a Marxism in certain important ways opposed to that of Althusser. It was a Marxism influenced by the group around Socialisme ou barbarie (whose members included both Lefort and Lyotard) and thus a Marxism with Hegelian and Husserlian inflections, whose most important reference point was Lukacs's *History and Class Consciousness*. Sebag explicitly identified Hegel as providing the initial premises of structuralism: "spirit is the total system of possible forms, the structure of structures, the system of systems."[37] In this sense, Hegel becomes the thinker of the synchronic for whom history is the selection of elements from a preexisting set of possibilities. The truth is indeed, for Marx (read by Lukacs), as well as for Hegel, the whole, but the whole understood as a formal system. Structuralism, like Marxism, will ultimately resolve the problems that it confronts only when it has achieved the knowledge of this whole, this system of systems. It is, according to Sebag, the merit of Marxism to have recognized that this is not simply a problem of knowledge but a problem of practice as well; rejecting every form of transcendence, even that of scientific knowledge, Marxism alone has posed the question of the material conditions of adequate knowledge, that is, knowledge of the totality. While certain forms of phenomenology follow Kant in posing this question in an idealist form and are thus condemned to turn endlessly in the hermeneutic circle of the subject that yearns to know the world but can only know itself, attaining knowledge only by bracketing the world as it is independent of its experience, Marxism begins by arguing that not all subjects are the same. The totality can only be apprehended from a certain place and from within a certain practice within it, that is, the proletarian class position from which alone the totality can be grasped.

Furthermore, like Althusser, Sebag found the existing Marxist conceptions of the totality inadequate. In particular he subjected the conception of the totality as founded on the base-superstructure relation to a severe critique; nearly half of *Marxisme et structuralisme* is devoted to the development of a scientific analysis of ideologies. For him, the argument that economic changes cause ideological changes (he cites Engels's discussion of the causes of the Reformation) is miscast and can only lead to an impasse.[38] Such an analysis denies the systematic, rule-governed nature of religions; in fact, it denies the existence of the synchronic dimension altogether, relying on mystical concepts like expression or reflection (Calvinism reflects capitalistic social relations) to explain the emergence of a particular variant of religious ideology.

For Sebag, the very theory of "the primacy of the economic in human history" is "badly posed and tends to disappear in the course of scientific investigation." To the traditional mode of explanation characteristic of Marxism, Sebag counterposes a method heavily influenced by structural anthropology. Accordingly, the analysis of ideologies must begin "at the level of the synchronic" to construct a model that will reveal "the principle of organization regulating a set of elements reciprocally defined. . . . It is only once the structure of this system is understood that its variations can be explained in a meaningful way. In our opinion, the principle human sciences, to different degrees, are facing the same problem that linguistics had to resolve: the possibility of understanding change presupposes a comprehension of the essence of that which changes."[39]

Each field in the human sciences must thus be subject to an "autonomization" that defines them as wholes, the combination and permutation of whose elements are governed by a specific set of rules: systems of kinship, economic relations, myths, and language. Of course, Sebag recognizes that this autonomization will inevitably be seen as a form of idealism that declares structures intelligible only by dissociating them from the activity of "real men," especially that activity without which there can be no society, no economic activity. In response, he argues that such structures or systems only come into being through human activity and have no existence apart from it. Nor is structuralism an antihumanism as he understands it. If the systems under consideration must first be separated in order to be understood as wholes whose elements are rule governed, it is not to render society a mechanical totality of indifferent parts but instead to render the systems of which the totality is composed comparable and even equivalent. It is "a priori possible" to establish between these levels or fields correspondences that are either "lexical (the content put into play)" or "syntactical (the mode of organization of this content)." Such an a priori possibility is itself founded on a common origin: the human mind, which acts as the guarantee of the unity of the whole and the equivalence of its levels.[40] Lévi-Strauss would, of course, take this one step further, moving from the human mind to the human brain and thus from culture to nature, from the social to the biological, as the ultimate unchanging cause.

Although Althusser was quite dismissive of Sebag in the few passages in which he is mentioned, Sebag's attempt to develop a "structuralist-Marxist theory of ideologies" served him as a useful index of the elements in Lévi-Strauss's work that invited criticism. Sebag made explicit that which often remained implicit in Lévi-Strauss, in particular, showing the way in which structuralism was only too ready to furnish solutions to the problems Althusser sought to identify in Marxism: the problem of base and superstructure, the nature of ideology, the concept of historical causality proper to historical materialism, and the question of how to complete the "episte-mological break" that would permit the emergence of a science of history. Because Sebag also regards these problems as central, the answers that he brings to them and the support he finds for these answers in Lévi-Strauss's work need all the more to be criticized. Accordingly, Althusser's short essay on Lévi-Strauss from 1966 (which remained unpublished during his life-time, although it circulated in mimeographed form among a fairly wide circle), in which Sebag's name is not mentioned, nevertheless focused on precisely the solution to the problem of base and superstructure and the unity of the social whole that Sebag extracted from structural anthropology and linguistics.

For Althusser, the absence of the concepts of modes of production and relations of production weighs heavily on Lévi-Strauss's texts, creating a gap that must be filled with other preexisting concepts ("ideology abhors a vacuum"). In particular, kinship structures, the avowed centerpiece of Lévi-Strauss's work through the mid-1960s, remain unfounded and indeter-minate. Althusser identifies two separate explanations of the specific form these structures take, both equally inadequate. The first is the formalist ex-planation: each kinship structure is a variant of a set of possible kinship structures, a universal combinatory. This "determination," however, must itself be explained: What determines the existence and specific form of this combinatory, the universality of which begs rather than answers the ques-tion? Here, as earlier noted in relation to Sebag, Lévi-Strauss's flight first into idealism (the structure of all kinship structures, the system of all pos-sible kinship systems, is determined by "the structure of the human mind") and then into a biologistic materialism that derives the structure of struc-tures from the "wiring" of the brain. In his contribution to Althusser's "Phi-losophy Course for Scientists" (1967–68), Alain Badiou put it this way: "Lévi-Strauss confers on cerebral complexity the honor of the structure of structures, the ultimate support of structurality itself."[41] This "explanation" of kinship structures by recourse to the two most popular sanctuaries of ignorance (to use a Spinozistic phrase favored by Althusser), which brings Lévi-Strauss's theory into the range of Cavaillès's critique of the impasses of phenomenology and logical formalism, reveals its utter inadequacy, Althus-ser argues, when confronted with the following problem:

> One of the most spectacular results of his theory is that it is *totally incapable* of accounting for the fact that kinship structures in primi-

tive societies are neither everywhere nor always the same, but manifest important variations. These variations are for him no more than
variations of a purely formal, tautological *mode of combination* which
explains nothing. When you postulate a mode of combination that
permits an infinity of *possible* forms in its combinatory matrix, the pertinent question is not that a given reality (a given observable structure
of kinship) is truly included as possible among the variations of the
combinatory (for it is tautological to argue that the real is *possible*), the
pertinent question on the contrary is this: Why is it that this reality
and no other that has become and therefore is real?[42]

Lévi-Strauss's formalism has led him to take a theory of possibility for a
theory of necessity, placing him in a long theological tradition, the very tradition, in fact, against which part one of Spinoza's *Ethics* is directed.

The second inadequate explanation of actually existing kinship structures
past and present that Althusser extracts from Lévi-Strauss's works is incompatible with the first, which, of course, does not prevent it from coexisting
undisturbed with its contrary. In opposition to the transcendental solution
to the problem of the determination of structures, Lévi-Strauss (without
ever noting this opposition) poses a second "historicist" solution, which
takes the specific form, according to Althusser, of functionalism. The functional explanation of kinship structures accounts for the different types by
referring them to the society in which they exist and regarding them as
means to the reproduction or survival of that society: kinship structures are
thus explained by the end they serve. For Althusser, this functionalism "is
still a form of subjectivism that endows 'society' with the form of existence
of a subject having intentions and objectives."[43] As such it requires a further hypothesis, that of "the unconscious," which describes the order that
individuals obey without knowing it, the reproduction of a social system
they carry out even as the case may be against their will. It is this hypothesis that more than any other appeared to Althusser to connect Lévi-Strauss
to hermeneutics. The goal of ethnography would thus be to read the true
social intentions beneath the conscious desires of individuals; it is to em-
pathically intuit the spirit of the whole, that mentality of which individual
minds are only so many partial functions. The ethnographer seeks the truth
of what is said and done in the system that alone confers meaning on individual acts. Althusser even entertains the possibility of a biological functionalism, according to which individuals would unconsciously reproduce

a certain biological (today we would say genetic) state, sacrificing their individual interests to that greater imperative of "life" or "the species" (or the adaptive gene), the system that would in turn constitute the truth of the merely human system.

Both avenues (the transcendental or the functional) lead inescapably back to idealist notions of the totality. While Althusser seemed in his seminar of 1962–63 to regard Lévi-Strauss's notion of the isomorphic nature of the different levels of society as a quasi-materialist defense of their irreducibility either to each other or to a transcendental term, by 1967 he would regard the concept of isomorphism as a means of "the negation of their difference." Althusser, judging Lévi-Strauss's work by its effects, recognizes that there have been those who, although critical of Lévi-Strauss's treatment of kinship structures and most notably his failure to situate them in relations of production, will face greater difficulty critically appraising his analysis of myths, especially as the basis for the analysis of ideologies (Sebag, of course would be the primary reference point here). Thus, not only does the concept of isomorphism or homology not "solve" the problem of which the base-superstructure model is an index, but "the isomorphism of structures is the modern form of expressive causality," which denies "the different instances of social complexity."[44] Althusser refers here not simply to the transcendental or ideal origin of the homologous levels that after all could be bracketed out but also to the effect of the concept of homology itself, which reduces the entire social field to a formal identity in which no instance is dominant over others because all are expression of the form that is immanent in them. There is no more striking instance of this than Lévi-Strauss's assumption that the economic level or instance is primarily the site of exchange (as it must be if it is to mirror the exchange of women and words) rather than a sphere of production and surplus extraction.

Interestingly, neither Althusser nor any of the young philosophers around him produced the kind of reading of Lévi-Strauss that Althusser himself recognized as the only adequate reading of philosophical and theoretical texts: not a denunciation (and "On Lévi-Strauss" for all its interest remains at the level of denunciation rather than analysis) but a reading that draws lines of demarcation that make visible the antagonism and conflict around which a given text is constituted. Instead, the task was left to a philosopher close to Althusser in certain ways, and quite distinct in others, writing at exactly the same moment (the second half of 1966). It was Jacques Derrida who demonstrated the coexistence of two opposed notions of structure in Lévi-Strauss's work, one compatible with a long metaphysical tradition, the other marking a rupture with it. The essay "Structure, Sign, and Play," published in *L'écriture et la différance* in 1967, was presented in October 1966 at the symposium the Languages of Criticism and the Sciences of Man at Johns Hopkins University.[45] Like Althusser, Derrida begins his essay by placing the concept of structure in a history, the history not simply of the social sciences but of Western philosophy itself. He finds that the current use of the term *structure* is marked simultaneously by "a rupture and a redoubling" or by difference and repetition.[46] Structuralism has posed the possibility of an infinite "structurality" even as it in fact finds itself forced to suspend this structurality. By *structurality*, Derrida refers to a new way of conceiving the relations between elements or parts of a structure, system, or whole, according to which none would be privileged or dominant a priori over any of the others and every relation of dominance and subordination would be temporary or conjunctural. None would be reducible to any of the others or to a term outside the system. This new concept of structurality, however, is in every case suspended as soon as it is posed by the actual theoretical form of structures; each structure is organized around a center or an internal principle that limits the movement of substitution and displacement and thus transcends the "play" of elements that it founds and makes possible.

Derrida argues that this very notion of decentered structurality is itself the consequence of a certain historical "decentering" that has displaced or "driven" Europe from its position of dominance in the world and in turn permitted a break with ethnocentrism and therefore a new kind of knowledge, "ethnology." Derrida is very clear that there is nothing "coincidental" about the end of European dominance and the "dislocation of the history of metaphysics." At the same time that it is the consequence of the overturning of European domination, ethnology, however, inescapably borrows from (and is therefore bound to) the tradition whose weakening made it possible. Because this borrowing is inescapable, the possibility of breaking with the tradition in which one necessarily participates, poses for Derrida, as for Althusser, the question of strategy and alliances. How does one use a tradition without being used by it? Lévi-Strauss's work serves perhaps the most salient example of the uneven and contradictory nature of the conceptual "rupture" characteristic of structuralism (it also "weighs heavily on the contemporary theoretical conjuncture").[47] Lévi-Strauss, who often reminds his readers that he began his academic career in philosophy only to find it pointless and stifling, not only imagines that he has stepped outside of philosophy with its perpetual (because insoluble) puzzles, but he explicitly seeks to root out its remnants in the social sciences. Derrida examines a passage from the *Raw and the Cooked* in which Lévi-Strauss denounces the notion of structure as totalization and hence the very notion of totality as "meaningless." Derrida finds however that two distinct critiques of the operation of totalization "coexist in a non-express manner in Lévi-Strauss's discourse."[48] The first is an empiricist critique that is entirely philosophical in the sense that it legislates jurisdictional boundaries for knowledge from a point outside of it: before an infinite reality a finite subject can neither see nor say all that is. Derrida's account of the empiricist critique of totalization is similar in many respects to Althusser's account of the notion of the model (a critique explicitly aimed at Lévi-Strauss) in *Reading Capital*: the conception of theory as a model presupposes a superabundance and transcendence of the "concrete" or "life," whose richness the theoretical model always falls short of.[49]

But there exists another, different notion of structure in Lévi-Strauss, a notion of a decentered structure, a structure whose elements are not regulated by an origin or controlled by a privileged term. The absence of a center allows an infinite play of substitutions and displacements. Perhaps most importantly, Derrida insists that such formulations are merely the "negative" face of what might be the structuralist discovery: the determination of "the non-center as something other than a loss of center."[50] There is perhaps no point at which Derrida and Althusser so closely converge as this one. The very proximity of the notions of the infinite play of substitutions and displacements and overdetermination, however, allows us to pose questions we can answer satisfactorily only at a later point: To what extent do these notions help us to think the singularity that structure as a concept both affirms and negates, and conversely to what extent, not only in their origin but in their effects, do these notions work to prevent the apprehension of singularities? The fact remains, though, that unlike Derrida, Althusser did not produce a symptomatic reading of Lévi-Strauss despite a clear sense of the anthropologist's importance and the complexity of his oeuvre, a complexity that would require from Althusser more than denunciation. Perhaps there is something at work that deserves closer scrutiny, an unanalyzed residue from the operation of structure itself or from the texts of Althusser himself.

Between Spinozists
The Function of Structure in Althusser, Macherey, and Deleuze

Up to this point, Althusser has appeared to speak from a point external to the field so imprecisely designated as "structuralism," outside the game and its rules, to use a Derridean figure, able to observe and judge precisely because he was not in play. The very concept of the theoretical conjuncture, a concept that replaces the image of the game and its rules with that of struggle, of war, a war that "leaves nowhere for a shelter," excludes in advance any place outside of or beyond the conflict: every thesis about philosophy is simultaneously a taking of a position within philosophy.[1] Indeed, if Althusser was able to think critically about structuralism, it was only because he simultaneously confronted the contradictory development of the notion of structure in his own work. To adopt a critical relation to his own texts, however, was more difficult than might be imagined; the innumerable critiques that arose in relation to his first major works made the task of self-criticism more, rather than less, difficult. The overwhelming majority of these critiques took as their starting point the very positions that Althusser set out to criticize: against Althusser and his structures were historicism (or diachrony against synchrony), man (or conscious subjects free to choose their own destinies), even the teleology of the economic base understood as the sole explanation of historical change. It was perhaps inevitable that the most salient and effective critique of his work would come not from one of his many adversaries but rather from within his circle of collaborators.

On May 10, 1965, Pierre Macherey, having just reviewed the manuscript of the soon to be published first edition of *Reading Capital*, wrote to Althusser:

I have wanted for some time to write you concerning a point that has troubled me a bit. It is the idea of the *structured whole* found on pages 41 and 127: I understand all that you have said about the nature and efficacy of structure and about the relations between structures. But it seems to me that when you speak of a set (*ensemble*) or of a whole, you thereby add a concept that is absolutely unnecessary to the demonstration and which may later become an obstacle (the idea of the real whole in opposition to that of the spiritual whole is not very clear: the idea of the whole is really the spiritualist conception of structure). Everything you say about the conjuncture is very valid: but isn't to know the conjuncture precisely to know it insofar as it is a lack (*manque*)? And the analogy you make to theatrical production (*la représentation théâtrale*), however important in itself, risks further being very ambiguous. . . . You see that I have taken the side of the "naturalists" and of the logic of the diverse. But perhaps I've failed to understand this at all.[2]

Althusser's response, dated May 13, 1965, is complex. He agrees in principle with Macherey's critique of the notion of the structured whole but feels constrained by a theoretical and historical barrier from moving beyond this notion:

I would really like you to shed further light on what you say about the structured totality. I agree with what you say about the totality as an ideological conception of structure: there is something there which needs to be defined more precisely. I have felt this for some time. But I must say, provisionally at least, that it seems difficult to go further (doubtless because I can't see very clearly in this difficulty), and I have a tendency to take refuge in certain of Marx's texts where there is a reference to an "organic whole," in the same way that I have taken shelter behind Mao's texts on "contradiction." I do not now feel able to leap over the barrier of the "organic whole" and "contradiction." To leap over this barrier means of course to replace the provisional concepts with better defined concepts. I still lack the latter. If you can help me and enlighten me, I ask you to do so immediately. It's of the greatest importance . . . to know if it is possible today to go further.[3]

In a letter dated the following day, Althusser repeats his request for Macherey to expand his "reflections on totality," to explain further his critique and the direction to which he is now inclined.

In response, Macherey (on May 14, 1965) admits that it will be possible to replace the provisional concepts of "structured whole" and "contradiction" only when "the means are there," and thus the solution to these problems will "take some time." He repeats, though, that, "each time [he has] encountered the phrase 'structured whole' in what [Althusser has] written, [he] was struck by the problems that it raises." The elements of an alternative, he argues, are to be found in Lucretius and Spinoza: "everything concerning the infinity of attributes, as well as the letter to Oldenburg from November [16]65; Deleuze's article on Lucretius is also important. . . . On contradiction: I wonder to what extent it would benefit us to use the word as little as possible (by substituting other terms for it: opposition, conflict, discordance . . .) even if we are still not capable of accounting for the difference."[4]

Macherey's arguments, however, remained "enigmatic" to Althusser (Althusser to Macherey February 19, 1966) until he had read a draft of Macherey's critical analysis of structuralism destined for publication in *Les Temps Modernes* as "L'analyse litterarire: Tombeau de structures" (Literary analysis: Tomb of structures) in a special issue devoted to the topic of structuralism in 1966. Althusser himself had initially urged Macherey to contribute to the issue "for now decisive theoretical and political reasons," proposing that the latter write "an article on the structuralism of Barthes and Foucault.[5]" Eight months later, after having read the essay, Althusser responded to Macherey's worry that the final pages of it were "confusing" by writing, "on the contrary, I found them illuminating, and much more striking, fruitful and exciting than the entire critical section. I will even say that the critical section does not take on its full meaning and direction except on the basis of your final, positive, pages. This is why I had to read you twice."[6] He praises the "peculiar power" of Macherey's text, a power of decoupling or disconnecting (*décrochage*); "reading the essay is like boarding a boat and, without realizing it, its lines are untied and one is carried along in the current of a river." At the heart of the letter, however, is Althusser's belated response to Macherey's critique of the previous May:

> But I am writing above all to tell you that I have understood what you meant when you told me that the concept of the "latent structure" appeared dubious to you. Do you remember that? You alluded to my use of this phrase in the article on theater. I now see clearly what you[7] meant, and I see what I couldn't see when I wrote that text: that it is

ambiguous, divided between a conception of structure as *interiority* (the "latent structure" or "latent dynamic" of the work) and therefore as the correlate of an *intention*, or at least of a *unity*—and another conception, very close to your own, in which structure is thought as *absent exteriority* (the concept of the *dialectique à la cantonade*).[8]

Little has been written on Macherey's forceful critique of the notion of structure in "L'analyse litterarire: Tombeau de structures," a critique carried out with instruments forged from the very compound he had suggested to Althusser: Lucretius (as read by Deleuze) and Spinoza (especially his discussion of parts and wholes in the letter to Oldenburgh from November 1665 and *Ethics* I–II). To measure the force exerted by the essay, we may note that Jean Pouillon, editor of *Les Temps Modernes*, found it necessary to criticize Macherey's essay in the introduction to the special issue on structuralism. While granting that Macherey was "right to contest the conception of the literary work as having its meaning within itself and as being able to be studied without reference to what it is not," Pouillon declares him simply wrong "to identify structuralism with an inquiry of this type."[9] The fact that Macherey's critique of the use of the term "structure" outside of a specific linguistic context could provoke this sort of reaction is itself noteworthy; among other things it shows quite clearly the extent to which an interrogation of structuralist approaches to literature and culture was doomed to provoke theoretical defense mechanisms.

To begin to analyze Macherey's critique, we might follow Althusser and think of the essay as carrying out an operation of decoupling or disconnecting (décrochage): rather than simply reject the use of structure as it exists in literary studies on the basis of a norm external to it, Macherey demonstrates that two irreducibly different and opposed meanings, whose divergence has remained invisible, correspond to the word "structure." Macherey begins by noting that structuralist criticism has assumed without question that, because literary works are "works of language," concepts developed within the domain of linguistics (especially in the fields of phonology and syntax) can be appropriated without modification and applied to literature. While Macherey is quick to point out that such borrowings are always problematic, in that concepts are not automatically transferable between fields of knowledge, his more important point is that linguistic structure and the structure of the literary text have nothing in common but the name. The latter represents an attempt by literary critics to mask a very traditional metaphysical and hermeneutic operation in the guise of a rigorous scientific method: "The notion of structure, which seems to come from linguistics where it is legitimately applied to literary objects, is in fact used by literary analysis in a very different sense. It is based on the very unscientific hypothesis that the work contains its meaning within itself (which doesn't mean that the work says it explicitly); it is what paradoxically permits it to be read in advance, even before it is written."[10]

Macherey shows that such an approach approximates the most traditional interpretive activity: the extraction of a meaning deposited within the work and concealed within its depth. The spatial metaphors are crucial here: inside/outside and surface/depth, which are both in turn related to the theme of appearance/essence. The act of knowledge takes the form of a reduction or a translation, but a reduction to what? Previous theories of literary criticism argue that the work is the realization of the expression of an authorial intention that becomes the origin, end, and thus meaning of the work. Structuralism, ostentatiously indifferent to the author, nevertheless does not mark a genuine break with the model of intention: every narrative is one possible product of a set of elements and the rules that govern the combination of these elements, a structure of structures. Thus a theory of "personal intention" is replaced by a theory of "abstract intention," while the problem of explaining the process of genesis or creation, that is, how this text rather than any other came into being at this time and place, remains unanswered and unanswerable. At the same time, the structuralist approach, insofar as it is a formalism, refuses to reduce the work to a presence external to it and seeks instead to discover the meaning hidden within it, a latent meaning that resides in the work's "secret coherence."[11]

The work only appears disordered and heterogeneous; in fact, it possesses the unity and coherence of an organism in which even the smallest and most insignificant elements have a function in the structure of the whole. It is this "imaginary organism" that structural analysis seeks to make manifest.[12] The very diversity that the work presents is no more than the realization of what the work finally is, a totality. Macherey isolates this concept as that which most haunts the structuralist enterprise: the literary work consists of parts linked together by an internal necessity that assigns to each element its place and function in the whole. The totality possesses its meaning, its principle, its spirit, and it is this that structuralist criticism seeks to recover insofar as it permeates the whole through each and every one of its elements. Even the structuralist analysis of myths (and Lévi-Strauss fares better in this essay than Barthes and Genette) does not entirely escape the spiritualism of the concept of totality, with its search for the structure of all structures ending at the human brain, a destination that makes structuralism, as we have noted, perfectly compatible with humanism: "structure is man." Totality and whole: Macherey appears to have adopted as the objects of his critique the very categories whose appearance in Althusser's contribution to *Reading Capital* moved him to write to Althusser in May 1965. Is it possible to read "L'analyse litterarire: Tombeau de structures" as a critique, in part at least, of Althusser's text?

In order to answer this question, we must recall that Macherey does not reject the concept of structure, as if it were destined forever to coincide with that of totality or organic whole, but, on the contrary, he seeks to show the way in which a certain conception of structure as it has been put into practice can be decoupled from such notions. Once we reject the notion of structure as a latent meaning realized in the hidden order of the work, that is, once we reject the notions of the interior and exterior and surface and depth of a work, we then "must ask where the structures of the literary statement (*énoncé*) are situated. If there is structure, it is not in the book, in its depths or hidden: the book belongs to it without containing it. Thus the fact that the work can be related to a structure does not imply that it is in itself, in its letter, unified."[13]

Macherey has accordingly deprived the work of its interiority—that space within, beneath the surface, where the "secret rationality" of the work, its hidden order—and thus the integration of each of its elements into the harmony where the diversity of the work must be resolved, if it is not to become an aesthetic failure. As Macherey learned from Spinoza, to reject the interior or depth, to take the work as pure surface without secrets or mysteries, is simultaneously to reject the postulate of order. No work exhibits order on its surface; hence the need to declare the surface mere appearance in a hermeneutic operation designed to reconcile apparently antagonistic and contradictory elements into the order of the whole. To accept the work as surface in which nothing can be hidden marks the first step in specifying a new concept of structure. Structure cannot be in the work but only outside of it; it is therefore not the hidden order of an only apparently disordered work but that which maintains the work as it is in its irreducible complexity: "structure 'holds it (*la tient*)' all the more in that the work is diverse, scattered, irregular. To see structure is to see irregularity."[14] Structure now becomes the principle of the work's "irregularity" and scattered-ness, the principle that not only allows us to see its irreducible diversity but makes that diversity intelligible without resorting to hermeneutic procedures. "Structure is then that which, from outside the work, dispossesses it of its false interiority" and confers significance on "its real disorder (its disarray)," which is no longer conceivable as a defect but rather as that which informs us of the necessity by which the work has become what it is.[15] But if structure "holds" (*tient*) or maintains the work in its disarray, it is nothing other than that necessity itself, the necessity that governs, organizes, and "structures" the irreducible diversity of the work, a necessity that is then no more present outside than inside the work, as if it were a presence to which the work might be related. Instead, structure is "a new type of necessity: through absence, through lack."[16] We may now understand the conclusion that Althusser drew from Macherey's essay: structure as "absent exteriority," the absent cause of a determinate disorder.

Interestingly, the penultimate sentence of the essay as it appeared in *Les Temps Modernes* (as well as in *Pour une theorie de la production littéraire*) is absent from the English translation: "Rather than that of structure, the essential concept of such an analysis would be that of *décalage*";[17] as if the work is produced by the action of a conflict that separates it from itself at the moment it comes into being. If Macherey concludes his essay with a displacement of structure from the conceptual center of literary analysis, he has nevertheless endowed it with a necessary, if subordinate, function: it rules out the inevitable reading of the essay as endorsing a view of the text as indeterminate and therefore unknowable, a threat he repeatedly acts to counter: "The work is not made by chance, according to the law of an indifferent freedom, but because it is at each of its moments and each of its levels precisely determined. That is why the disorder and chance are never pretexts for appearance of confusion, but are indices of an unwritten truth: through them the work is what it is and no other."[18] Macherey has broached the topic of singularity, "what the work is and no other," the problem of what conjoins the disparate materials of which the work is composed even in their heterogeneity to make the work what it is. It may well be in fact that "singularity," despite the occasional appearance of the word, is the unthought, and thus "invisible," concept whose absence discomposes Althusser's contribution to *Reading Capital*.

In 1966 Althusser made a note to himself "to write an article on Pierre [Macherey]," which would be "self-criticism concerning 'latent structure.'"[19] On March 10, 1966, he wrote to Franca Madonia, certainly alluding to the same project, stating that he was considering writing an article for *Les Temps Modernes* on "the Marxist conception of structure." Of all the possible projects before him, this would be the project that would prove the most difficult. He would have "to reread Lévi-Strauss, read Sartre, reread Lacan and reread Marx . . . what a job!"[20] For whatever reason, the self-critical text on structure never appeared, and the self-criticism took the far less effective form of a series of unexplained and unnoted excisions from the second edition of *Reading Capital* published in 1968, a number of them clustered in the last section of "The Object of *Capital*," particularly around the notion of structural causality.[21] While such an act in no way contested the assertions or answered the objections of the many critics of this passage, it had the effect of rendering the criticisms unintelligible to a later cohort of readers, especially those of the foreign language translations, which tended to be based on the 1968 edition.[22] At the same time, this silent operation did nothing to change the perception of Althusser as a structuralist, given the persistence of the term "structure" even in the second edition.

Of the excised material, two long passages, each about a page in length, are particularly pertinent to the question of structure as discussed in the exchange with Macherey. To read them in their original context is to note exactly where and how Althusser drew a line of demarcation within his own work, analyzing his own text like any other, making visible, if only through the void of a distance taken from certain statements, the coexistence of two concepts of structure whose antagonism, whose irreducible difference, had before remained concealed.

The first occurs in section seven of Althusser's introductory essay, "From *Capital* to Marx's Philosophy," written after all the other contributions to *Reading Capital*, including his own, "The Object of *Capital*." The chronology is important in that it is in this introductory essay that Althusser discusses the act of reading, or rather the different acts designated by that term. This meditation comes and could only have come at the conclusion of the endeavor itself, as the theorization of what had first to be practiced before it could be understood. On April 18, 1965, Althusser wrote to Franca Madonia: "I have begun my preface to the two volumes on *Capital* and find myself engaged in a new undertaking in which I've had to develop, in order to explain how we *read Capital*, an entire *theory of reading* for which there is prior support (what I have suggested in my paper on Leonardo [Cremonini] and your letter which developed it further) (then what I have done this year in my course on Rousseau). It will be a theory of the *symp-*

tomatic reading in the epistemological domain in which I will say a few new things."[23] Althusser's extended discussion of what it means to read begins with the memorable statement: "However paradoxical it may seem, I venture to suggest that our age threatens one day to appear in the history of human culture as marked by the most dramatic and difficult trial of all, the discovery of and training in the meaning of the 'simplest' acts of existence—seeing, listening, speaking, reading—the acts which relate men to their works [oeuvres] and to those works thrown in their faces, their 'absences of works' [leurs 'absences d'oeuvres']."[24] Althusser goes on to name the three men "to whom we owe these staggering knowledges [les connaissances bouleversantes]": Marx, Nietzsche, and Freud.[25] While Freud initiated the inquiry into listening, speaking, and refraining from speech (Althusser says nothing more about Nietzsche's place in this pantheon), it was Marx who allowed us to begin to think about the meaning of reading and writing. Marx's only predecessor in this domain was, of course, Spinoza, who showed us that the Bible was the model of all texts and biblical interpretation the model of every reading. Behind the "religious myth of reading" is "a theory of expression," a theory according to which the meaning of a text is expressed in all its parts, each of which in turn is read insofar as it is reduced to the meaning that pervades the whole. Spinoza and Marx nearly alone have blazed a trail that will lead us out of this wilderness and on to the path of knowledge.

Marx, Althusser argues, reads as he writes, or rather his writing constitutes a reading out loud, a reading to the reader. He reads not only to support his assertions but to situate himself in relation to the field of political economy. To look closely at Marx's reading, as Althusser does, is to discover that it "puts into practice two radically different principles of reading."[26] The first, unsatisfactory, reading is based on a theory of knowledge as vision. Adam Smith's text represents what he sees; what it omits, what it fails to say, is what he did not see, what he overlooked. Such a reading reduces the object of Smith's discourse to "the mere condition of a given." What Smith failed to see could have been seen by him but for "a weakness of vision," from which Marx did not suffer, a fact that allowed the latter to see what was present to be seen. Such a theory of reading reduces knowledge to the act of seeing an object fully present to the spectator and thus also "reduces Smith to Marx minus the myopia—it reduces to nothing the gigantic effort by which Marx tore himself from Smith's supposed myopia."[27] In this way, the theoretical text is nothing more than a representation of a pre-given reality external to it. The act of reading necessarily deprives the text of any substantiality and restores it to the truth of which it was a mere expression.

Marx's second, irreducibly different reading not only refuses any notion of knowledge as vision but in doing so grants the text a material existence. Thus, he reads the failure of Smith's text not in relation to a reality external to it, but in relation to itself, the failure on the part of the text to see what it itself does, to see what it itself contains, even, as Althusser puts it, to see what it itself sees without seeing that it sees it. Smith's text has produced more than it knows, the answer to a question that it did not and cannot pose and is thus registered in the text only as a lack or a silence, which disturbs the fullness that it appears to exhibit. What is invisible to Smith's text is then not what is not in it but precisely what is in it and defined from within, by a necessity that remains to be specified, as excluded, repressed, prohibited by a "darkness of exclusion" that is internal to the text itself, which is constituted in order not to see the objects it nevertheless exhibits. Indeed, the theoretical field that is coextensive with the texts of political economy has no external limits: "the paradox of the theoretical field is that it is an *infinite* because *definite* space, i.e., it has no limits, no external frontiers separating it from anything precisely because it is *defined* and limited within itself, carrying within itself the finitude of its own definition which, by excluding what it is not, makes itself what it is."[28] The text is marked by the operation by which it excludes what it has produced and necessarily continues to contain; it is thus divided into the visible and its invisible, that which it asserts and that which is denied and disavowed in the very assertion itself.

At this precise point in Althusser's argument, the first edition of *Reading Capital* (and the revised and restored third edition offered the following theorization of the conflictuality proper to texts according to Marx's second protocol of reading, a theorization removed from subsequent editions and therefore unknown to Althusser's English-language readers:

> Once again we must be clear that the excluded is not the pure other, a pure anything at all, or what a philosophy with quantitative pretentions [une philosophie comptable] hastens to call a "remainder" [résidu]. The theoretical foundation of the *definition* is not a "free" "choice" between two regions whose border it would inscribe in the facts, nor a simple "cutting up" of the facts that would give to all

those who cut up or cut off [trancheurs] states, lineages, carcasses or heads the thrill of being of the same blood as science and to the scientists themselves the thrill of participating in God's freedom. The great division of definition is nothing more than the product, in the limited sun of the obvious, of a solution that only emerges from the repression of what, from the problem posed in the depths of the field in which theory is born, would cast a shadow on its victory. The repressed is not just anything—but a determinate content which could pertain to the latent of an anterior structure, and which is only tipped into shadow like the balance is tipped into defeat, when the relation of forces tips the balance. What the definition of the field, infinite in its genre, but limited in its interiority, excludes from the existing problematic is thus *its* prohibited, *its repressed* which is covered by shadow only by having, before the defeat, in a precarious light been precisely covered up again by the shadow of the new.[29]

To replace this long passage in Althusser's text is to grasp the sense in which all that he writes about, that which will within a few lines be named a "symptomatic reading," particularly all the properties of theoretical texts that necessitate such a reading as the only way to arrive adequately at a thorough knowledge of a given text, applies to his own work. By removing this passage, Althusser has made visible the inner darkness of exclusion that traversed his own text, the discrepancy between what he said and what he did, a divergence that sets the work against itself. Of course, to use his own words, that which is repressed is not just an empty abstract other but an invisible and thus unanalyzed residue of a very specific nature. In this case, what appeared not only to Althusser but to the text itself as a single, unified notion of structure was, as he recognized in his letter to Macherey, the site of division between two antagonistic conceptions. It is indeed surprising to read the excised passage today given the extent to which it is incompatible with much of what Althusser says elsewhere in the text. To grant it a place in Althusser's argument necessitates a redefinition not only of structure but of the text or field that "belongs" to a structure, as well as the very act of reading itself. Althusser, according to the edition published in 1965 poses structure as latent in as well as anterior to a given text. In doing so, he endows the text with a depth beneath the surface, the two-level space that allows the manifest to conceal the latent, which must be recovered through an operation of interpretation. The conflict exhibited on the surface of the text, the divergence between the dominant meaning and that which it exists in order to exclude and repress, ceases itself to be irreducible. Instead, textual conflict becomes the function of a structure anterior to it, "the correlate of an intention," to cite Althusser's self-criticism, of which it must be a realization. Structure can be understood according to a principle of genesis (that which comes before, at the beginning) and simultaneously as the work's meaning, present within it, beneath the disorder of the surface. Structure in this way transcends the work, if only in an immanent transcendence, functioning as the presence, however spatially or temporally distant, that alone guarantees the truth of the text.

We may now appreciate the degree to which the omission of this passage modifies the sense of structure in the opening of *Reading Capital*. Deprived of the additional dimension of the latent, or of any genetic principle that might assume the function of an origin, the text solidifies into pure surface whose real, irreducible complexity was once mistaken for depth. It is, to cite Macherey, "shattered and on display."[30] Its conflicts are deprived of any possibility of being reconciled into a superior unity. Macherey's question, though, becomes all the more pertinent: why preserve the notion of structure at all if, even in Althusser's own work, it appears destined to transmit, as if by contagion, the ideology of the whole anterior to and greater than its parts?

The contradictions that traverse Althusser's use of the conceptual pairs whole/parts and structure/elements are nowhere more apparent in *Reading Capital* than at the work's finale, precisely the section of "Marx's Immense Theoretical Revolution," which attracted the most criticism and underwent the most extensive revision between the first and second editions: the discussion of "the new form of rationality" produced by Marx's discovery, structural causality. This "theoretical concept" arose as the solution to the "theoretical problems" posed by Marx's scientific practice, the determination of "economic phenomena" by "the global structure of the mode of production," or as Althusser will specify, "the determination of a regional structure by a global structure."[31] If Althusser appears to have set out on the path to structuralist formalism similar to that which he criticizes in Lévi-Strauss, he moves very quickly to rule out any movement in this direction by briefly summarizing three important consequences of the theoretical concepts described above.

First, there is an emphasis on singularity. Not only is it necessary to rethink the articulation of the economic and ideological levels of a given mode of production, but Althusser argues that the very concepts of the economic, the political, and the like "must be constructed for each mode of production."[32] From this nominalist position follows the second consequence: the incommensurability of the elements of the global structure of the mode of production, the fact that these elements are not susceptible to measurement and comparison and therefore to any formalization of an empiricist type. To begin by postulating the singularity and incommensurability of the elements in question is to recognize the need for a new concept of causality. Modes of production are no longer explained by the articulation between members of a pre-given and always identical set of elements (a concept of history distinguished by its inability to explain any transition from one system to another), because finally neither the elements nor the structure is identical. Instead, given that "economic phenomena are determined by their complexity (that is, their structure)," we must understand what "determination by a structure" means.

If Althusser has ruled out the "linear" and "transitive" causality of empiricist formalism, according to which the whole is determined by the direct causal relations between its parts, there exists another concept of the whole that may appear to offer the solution to the problems posed by Marx's discoveries. It is "the Leibnizian concept of expression," which also "dominates the whole of Hegel's thought. According to this conception, the whole is reducible to an interior essence present in each of its parts and therefore comprises a 'spiritual' whole whose essence fills each of its parts as God fills creation with His divine essence."[33] In fact, Althusser's anti-Hegelianism is itself reducible to this critique, the critique of the social whole as the manifestation of a spirit in each and every part, rendering the act of knowledge nothing more than a reduction of difference to the same, the detection of identity beneath the appearance of diversity. Such notions have wreaked havoc within Marxism itself, where social phenomena are often explained by reference to expression or representation of some primary presence, whether the economy or technology.

We now know the conceptions of causality, including a theory of the determination of the parts by the whole through expression, which are inadequate to Marx's discovery; from such perspectives his work will remain unintelligible. But what is the alternative, or at least, what is posed as an alternative by Althusser in *Reading Capital*, only to be called into question by Macherey and subject to significant alteration in the second edition by Althusser himself? For the spiritual whole, whose elements express a univocal essence, he substitutes the notion of a structured whole. It is this notion alone that will allow us "to think the determination of the elements of a whole by the structure of a whole." At this point in the text (and it would be at this point, given that Althusser has now identified the conceptions of causality that together dominate the history of philosophy and the history of social thought, allowing us to separate ourselves from them, and he must now pass on to the alternative), a series of discrepancies and ambiguities arise in stark contrast to the clarity of the exposition up to this point. The first problem, which will soon be compounded, is the notion of the elements of a whole being determined not by the whole itself but by "the structure of the whole." Althusser has until now used the terms "structure" and "whole" interchangeably, as if structure/elements was another way of expressing the whole/parts relation. We are thus unexpectedly confronted with the idea that the whole is not a structure, but rather it possesses a structure. He will then turn to Marx's discussion of *Darstellung*, "to think the determination either of an element or a structure by a structure."[34] It is far from clear what Althusser means when he introduces the idea of "the determination of a structure by a structure," unless he means the determination of a regional structure (regional can be equated to part) by a global structure (i.e., a whole or the whole), in which case he remains caught up in the part/whole dichotomy that, moreover, is posed here in a particularly incoherent way: why the redundancy of element and regional structure, which is nothing other than a kind of element?

Suddenly, two sentences later, in the same paragraph, without acknowledgment of any kind, Althusser himself abruptly changes terrain entirely. The question of how a structure acts on its elements is replaced with the question of how we understand the "presence of a structure in its effects."[35] The problem of the relation of a whole, which must exist outside of if not prior to its parts, and thus the relation between two distinct terms exterior to each other, is supplanted by a notion of structure not as a kind of whole or totality but rather as a cause that exists only in its effects. We are no longer dealing with parts and wholes but with causes and effects. Having left behind Descartes and Leibniz, Hegel and Marx, Althusser is heading to that future anterior point toward which his philosophy ever strives: Spinoza.

Immanence (more specifically the immanence of the immanent cause) itself, however, in these concluding pages (and how strange it is, and "symptomatic," to announce a new form of rationality only a few pages from the end of an extraordinarily dense exposition) develops in an uneven and contradictory way, simultaneously regressing toward a Neoplatonic expressionism and leaping forward toward a theory of structure as singularity, as the absent cause of the irreducible diversity of an entity. Immediately following the definition of structure as a cause existing in its effects, Althusser undertook by way of explanation a long examination of the notion of "Darstellung." This was the passage on which Macherey centered his critique and that Althusser omitted from the second edition of *Reading Capital*. It is in relation to this passage that Althusser's exchanges with and reading of Macherey take on their full significance:

> In German "Darstellung" signifies among other things *theatrical representation*, but the figure of theatrical representation is immediately connected to the sense of the word which signifies "presentation," "exposition" and at its deepest root "position of presence," exposed and visible presence. To capture its specific nuance, it might be instructive to oppose "Darstellung" to "Vorstellung." With Vorstellung there is a position, but one which is presence before [devant], which thus implies something that is held behind this pre-position, something which is represented but what is held in front of it, by its emissary: the Vorstellung. *In the case of Darstellung, in contrast, there is nothing behind*: the thing itself is there, "da," exposed in a position of presence.[36]

Up to this point in the omitted passage (and we have stopped about a third of the way through it), Althusser uses the distinction between *Vorstellung* and Darstellung to make visible a distinction between irreducibly different senses of presence (the presence of a structure in its effects) and even immanence (the immanence of a structure in its effects). Vorstellung, conceived in spatial rather than temporal form, is not representation but pre-presentation; it is the "emissary" of a more primary presence, whose existence behind it alone confers upon it its significance and function. Darstellung in contrast is not the pre-presentation of anything other than itself; there is nothing behind it and no need for anything behind it to confer meaning upon it; whatever is, is there in its pure positivity without excess or transcendence. At least that is what Althusser literally says, until in the very next sentence, he qualifies Darstellung in such a way as to render it indistinguishable from the Vorstellung from which he has just demarcated it. Indeed, the term "Vorstellung" does not appear again in Althusser's text, as if the distinction between terms is blurred and they once again merge into a troubled unity whose contradiction has inexplicably become invisible to Althusser. To continue:

> The entire text of a theatrical play is thus there, exposed in the presence of the representation (*Darstellung*), *but* the presence of the play in its entirety is not exhausted in the immediacy of the gestures or speech of any character: we 'know' that it is the presence of a completed whole that inhabits each moment and each character and all the relations between characters in their personal presence—but can only be grasped as the very presence of the whole, as the latent structure of the whole, in the whole, and only vaguely glimpsed in each element and each role.[37]

The use of the oppositional conjunction "but" is crucial in this sentence. It is as if Althusser draws back from his own conclusions, afraid to cast the play, which is here merely one example of a conjunction of effects forming some kind of singular entity (in this case a dramatic text) that is adrift from that which would exceed it in its immediate existence, completing its incompleteness, a whole that is more than the sum of characters and their gestures, speeches, and relations. This whole that the play itself falls short of, and does not exhaust, could not be apprehended in its immediacy; it is rather vaguely felt, a presence that even if it is accessible only through the mediation of the combined elements of the play is nevertheless that structure within, whose latent (as opposed to immediate) completeness we never see or hear but yet somehow feel. Althusser's qualification of Darstellung is surprisingly similar to what he denounces in his introductory essay to *Reading Capital* as "the religious myth of reading": the spirit that is present in this bread, this body, this face, and this man cannot be exhausted in the immediacy of the natural world in which it participates and whose beings are the signs of its ineffable presence. What Althusser has just described is quite the contrary of the existence of the structure in its effects; he has instead posited a whole or structure that not only exceeds its effects, is not exhausted in them, but leads a latent existence beneath or behind the manifest content, which the truth of could only be that hidden whole that is the task of interpretation to decipher.

A few lines later Althusser refers us to his essay "The Piccolo Teatro," first published in 1962 and later reprinted in *For Marx*. There Althusser's approach is almost Aristotelian. Parisian critics condemned Bertolazzi's *El*

Nost Milan, Althusser argues, because they failed to distinguish (and we can see here the provenance of the conception of Darstellung in all its conflictuality in *Reading Capital*) between the consciousness of the characters and the "dynamic of the play's latent structure," which cannot be reduced either to the sum of their characters or even to the relations between characters. This structure can properly be described as latent precisely because "even if it is implied by the action as a whole, by the existence and movements of all the characters, it is their deep meaning, beyond their consciousness — and thus hidden from them." Similarly, it is only potentially visible to the spectators insofar as it "has to be discerned, conquered and drawn from the shadow which initially envelops it."[38] Even in this early essay, however, Althusser's conclusion succeeded in calling into question the notion of the latent structure as completed whole, suggesting, on the contrary, that the play's greatness and power lay in its incompleteness, the radical absence of finality.

At this point in the passage from the first edition of *Reading Capital*, Althusser offers his own account of the apparent disjunction between these two meanings of Darstellung:

> *According to the level on which one is situated*, one can say either that *Darstellung* is the concept of *the presence of structure in its effects*, of the modification of effects by the efficacy of the structure present in its effects — or, on the contrary, that *Darstellung* is the concept of the efficacy of an absence. . . . I believe that understood as the concept of the efficacy of an absent cause, this concept serves admirably to designate the absence in person of the structure in the effects considered from the mundane [rasante] perspective of their existence. But it is necessary to insist on the other aspect of the phenomenon, which is that of the *presence*, of the immanence of the cause in its effects, otherwise known as *the existence of the structure* in its effects.[39]

We are at this point deep in Spinozist territory here, so deep in fact that there is no possibility of finding our way back to Althusser except by traversing this notoriously difficult terrain. Fortunately, Macherey has provided us with some directions. It is here that his suggestions concerning Deleuze on Lucretius and Spinoza's discussion of singularity become particularly useful. The problem that emerges in Althusser's text is undoubtedly centered on the notion of immanence, where, once again, a discrepancy between meanings emerges. At first Althusser externalizes the discrepancy, as a moment ago in the case of the Darstellung and Vorstellung distinction, by contrasting immanent and absent causes, although within a few lines the discrepancy is displaced to the notion of immanence itself. Thus Althusser will employ the formulae "present in its effects" and "exists in its effects" as if they are synonymous, while in fact they constitute the two opposing directions that readings of Spinoza have taken, the pantheist and the atheist. The idea of a cause present in (or to) its effects separates cause and effect even as it unifies them: that which is present in may also be present outside, and effects become emanations of the cause that may justly be declared present in them (the one that precedes, comprehends, and inheres in the diversity of its parts). Further, latency itself can be conceived as a form of immanence, even if a form of immanent transcendence. This is the sense of structure unmistakably communicated in the passages omitted from the 1968 edition, even if this sense is accompanied by another, conflicting conception of structure. By excising these passages, Althusser immeasurably increased the weight of this other conflicting sense of structural cause. According to this second conception, "the whole existence of the structure consists in its effects"; it is as Althusser puts it, "nothing outside of its effects."[40] The concept of structure understood as the principle of the unity of its elements, the whole whose causal significance lies in its assigning to its parts their place and function (as in a literary text), is so familiar, so "spontaneously" available as an aid and model for reflection that we resort to it even in our efforts to understand complex texts like those of Spinoza or Althusser. In contrast, the second conception, the notion of structure as the conjunction of singular entities in a larger singular entity that persists in its conjoined state for a specific duration of time, appears even to us, let alone to Althusser in the mid-sixties, as "unthinkable," a concept whose necessity for theorizing history in no way guarantees its historical appearance. Althusser has barred the way to notions of expressive causality, as well as to any recourse to finalism, that is, to intention, whether that of the individual or that of the system, even as the alternative has eluded him. But here we must be careful: there can be no critique of the present, except on the basis of what is already actual, already itself in some way present, the elements of an alternative.

It is here that Macherey's suggestions for seeking the elements of an alternative to the notion of the structured whole are particularly helpful. They are helpful because they do not merely indicate directions for future research, but they also refer to a common culture, a set of texts already familiar to Althusser and his circle, which, in ways that in part escape their understanding, have allowed them to take their distance from the dominant notions of causality. Moving beyond the simple evocation of the name "Spinoza," Macherey refers, as Althusser never does in his early work, to very specific texts, in particular, to Spinoza's letter to Oldenburg of November 20, 1665. In this letter, Spinoza seeks to answer a question posed to him by Oldenburg, a question directly relevant to Althusser's inquiry, which thus helps illuminate what is at stake here. Spinoza seeks to respond to Oldenburg's query on "how we know the way in which each part of Nature accords with the whole and coheres with its other parts."[41] He begins by warning Oldenburg that accord and coherence, "order," as generally understood, cannot be applied to nature but are products of the human imagination. Coherence and accordance must be redefined in such a way as not to refer to the oppositions of order and disorder, regularity and irregularity, harmony and discord. There exist only singularities of greater or lesser magnitude composing or composed of other singularities to infinity. Further, these are not "parts," at least in the normal sense of the term, of the universe, because the universe is infinite and its "parts" are determined by its infinite power to interact in an infinitely varied way.

In his *Hegel ou Spinoza* (published nearly fifteen years after *Reading Capital*), Macherey would return to the issues raised in his correspondence with Althusser to cite Deleuze on Lucretius in order to explicate the philosophical consequences of the infinity of the universe for Spinoza: "Nature as the production of the diverse can only be an infinite sum, that is, a sum that does not totalize its own elements. There is no combination capable of encompassing all the elements of nature at the same time; there is no unique world or total universe. Physics is not the determination of the One, of Being or of the Whole. Nature is not collective but distributive, to the extent that the laws of nature distribute parts which cannot be totalized."[42] To refuse to regard the universe as a whole, an organism whose parts would exist to perform a function in the whole, deprives the "whole" (now rather the infinite sum of infinitely varied and thus non-totalizable parts) of any finality that might be posited as the cause of its elements. Instead, according to Macherey, every thing that exists "is composed by the encounter of singular beings which conjuncturally join within it according to their existence, that is, which coexist in it without their joining together presupposing any privileged relation, the unity of an internal order." For the finalist conception that assigns each part a function according to the intention that the whole fulfills, "it is necessary to substitute an integrally causal explanation that takes into account only the external relations between bodies." In the case of the human body, a privileged model of the organic whole, its parts hold together until such time as, "the ambient conditions having changed, the relations between its elements are also modified: the assemblage is undone and its parts freed up for other combinations."[43]

If it is thus possible to read Spinoza's whole as a non-totalizable sum, it might appear that, insofar as structure has been identified with the whole, we are compelled to abandon it altogether. Indeed, it may even appear at the extreme that causal explanations have given way to an unintelligible randomness. Macherey, writing again in *Hegel ou Spinoza*, in a way directly relevant to the debates of the mid-sixties, asks whether Spinoza's rejection of the notion of nature as a whole "signifies that no unity can any longer be conceived in nature, which is thus dispersed to infinity in a circumstantial succession of encounters at the level of which no immanent necessity can be seen." He cautions that "to escape the illusion of a finalized order, it is not enough to substitute for it a representation of a contingent order of pure existences that would be nothing more than its mirror image."[44] Instead, the composite singularities exist as such through the necessity that allows the parts (themselves composed of parts to infinity) to conjoin and to persist in their conjunction. Spinoza calls the persistence of a specific conjunction the "conatus" of every singular being, its "actual essence," an essence entirely coincident with its actual state, which it neither precedes nor exceeds.[45] Further, the power by which a singular being persists is the same power by which it can be known, the principle of its intelligibility. Deleuze makes this point very clearly. In the first version of his essay on Lucretius, published in 1961, he rejects any notion that the "naturalism" of Lucretius is a philosophy of contingency or indeterminacy, arguing instead that it "requires a strongly structured principle of causality [un principe de causalité structuré] which can account for the production of the diverse, but account for it as compositions, diverse and non-totalizable combinations among elements in nature."[46] In the 1969 version of the essay, published as an appendix to *The Logic of Sense*, he will go so far as to call the clinamen or swerve of the atom (a concept necessary to account for the colliding of atoms that would otherwise fall through the void in parallel, straight lines) a kind of "conatus."[47] The swerve of the atom is not an accident that befalls it in its otherwise straight trajectory; it is the originary swerve that singularizes and differentiates the atom.

It appears then that Althusser's second notion of structure, read in the light of Macherey's textual references, is not only not opposed to singularity, as if structure were the reservoir of possible singular forms, but is something akin to what Spinoza calls "singular essence." If one of the insurmountable problems of structuralism was the necessity of a structure (a global structure) of all other (regional) structures in order for something like society to be conceivable, no such problem exists for Spinoza's philosophy. A singular thing can combine with another singular thing to form a third singular thing "without any change in its form" and so on to infinity.[48] Spinoza's philosophy is no more an atomism than a theory of expression or emanation. Structure, that is, the set of problems and questions linked to and by means of this term, allowed by its very heterogeneity not only the conception of structure as conjuncture, as Balibar has argued, but also conjuncture as structure, that is, the necessity that governs any conjuncture whatsoever in its very complexity but without that complexity made the "emissary" of an intention. It is this notion that allows the conjuncture to be thought of not as the negativity of indeterminacy, as the random encounter of primary elements that themselves require no further explanation than the positing of their irreducibility, but rather as determinate singularities both composed of and composing other singularities, even as they possess their own singular, actual essence.

Such notions, irrespective of the inability to articulate them fully, existed "in the practical state" (to use one of Althusser's favorite expressions) in even the "early" Althusser. "Contradiction and Overdetermination" was denounced on all sides, not as a structuralist text (which is inconceivable for anyone who has read it), or even as an example of the "theoreticism" to which Althusser would later confess, but, on the contrary, as a lapse into a "pluralism" and "hyperempiricism," according to which Marxism is nothing more than the observation of innumerable indifferent and indeterminate factors, to cite the critique of Althusser's comrade Gilbert Mury.[49] In part, Mury's critique, so discordant with the charges normally leveled by Althusser's critics, helps alert us to the presence of a certain "logic of the diverse" in what was perhaps Althusser's most important inaugural statement. In distinguishing the Marxist dialectic from the Hegelian, Althusser argues that the former differs from the latter "in its structure," drawing upon many of the arguments he would deploy against structuralism itself, demonstrating once again a disavowed affinity between Hegel and structuralism. From the Hegelian, or rather Hegelian-Marxist, perspective the "general contradiction" between the forces of production and the relations of production,

itself "essentially incarnate in the contradiction between the two antagonistic classes," explains, because it produces, all the other phenomena in a
given historical moment. This "moment" in turn is a totality in which all
phenomena are emanations of this general contradiction. Such a dialectic,
as we have seen, flounders against the problem of explaining change, transition, or revolution, resulting in the following paradox: on the one hand,
in order to explain the social totality every "instance" or element within
it must be grasped as the expression of the general essence of the whole,
each part not only expressing but functioning to maintain the equilibrium
of the whole, while on the other, the contradictions that drive history forward, to the extent they escape totalization and fail to express the meaning
of the whole, cease to be intelligible. From such a perspective, the failure to
totalize through a reduction or negation of difference would be the failure
of theory itself, the failure to ascend beyond the empirically given. A conscious rejection of the very gesture of totalization and reduction would then
constitute a hyperempiricism that clings obstinately to "things" or factors,
as they are present to observation, rejecting the very possibility of explaining them in their determinate existence.

From this position, Althusser's notion of a materialist dialectic remains
invisible and unthinkable: he argues that an event, a rupture, a break is not
produced by an inexplicable supersession of a general contradiction, which
would necessarily entail the immediate and simultaneous transformation
of all the phenomena in a given social totality into an expression of a new
general contradiction. Instead, an event is produced only by an "active"
contradiction, itself a composite of "a prodigious number of contradictions,
of which some are radically heterogeneous and which do not have the same
origin, the same meaning, nor the same level or site of application" but
which nevertheless "'merge' into a ruptural unity [unité de rupture]."[50]
These contradictions are not "the pure phenomena" of a general contradiction to which they might be reduced, as so many expressions of its essence,
but on the contrary they enter into a certain unity in which they lose neither
their "consistency" nor their own efficacity; they are neither mere expressions of this unity nor or is their function solely determined by it as in the
case of an organism. The encounter between these irreducibly diverse singularities produces another larger singularity, the historical conjuncture. If
we can continue to speak, then, of structure, it is in a sense that renders it
indistinguishable from singularity, the "ruptural unity" of irreducibly diverse elements, the encounter of which has formed a new singularity that in

no way negates the difference between the elements that will persist until a new encounter of a specific force will "undo" the composition.

The effects, however, of "Contradiction and Overdetermination" showed quite clearly that Althusser had insufficiently theorized the conjunction of the singular entities into larger, however provisional, unities: in Lucretian terms he had stressed the event over the conjunction. "On the Materialist Dialectic: On the Unevenness of Origins," published in 1963, marks an attempt not simply to reply to critics (thereby simply restating the theses of the first text and perhaps supplying better argumentation) but, more importantly, to rectify the inadequacy of the earlier essay on precisely this point. Lenin's texts on the Russian Revolution "have all the appearances of what might be called a 'pluralism' or a 'hyperempiricism,' 'the theory of factors,' etc., in their evocation of the multiple and exceptional circumstances which induced and made possible the triumph of the revolution. . . . Indeed, the meaning of these texts of Lenin's is not a simple description of a given situation, an empirical enumeration of various paradoxical or exceptional elements: on the contrary, it is an analysis of theoretical scope."[51] What is this analysis that is no mere description, but which has a distinct theoretical significance? It is that which constitutes the "irreplaceable" in Lenin: "the analysis of the structure of a *conjuncture* in the displacements and condensations of its contradictions in their paradoxical unity that is the very existence of the 'actual moment' that political action was going to transform in the strongest sense in a February and an October 1917."[52] Registering the irreducible diversity of the actual moment (translated into English as "current situation"), the objective of the earlier essay, is no longer enough. Althusser must now move on to the nature of that "paradoxical unity," that is, how singular elements combine and persist as a new, larger singular entity. Therefore, if this unity is "complex," it is also "structured": structure names the possibility of thinking the peculiar conjunction of contradictory elements as an individual in Spinoza's sense or as the actual moment in Lenin's. Far from theory reducing the antagonism and incompatibility of these elements, its objective must be to grasp the structure they form in their "disjunctive synthesis," to borrow a phrase from Deleuze. It is their very antagonism that constitutes the structure they form, even as this antagonism never produces an equilibrium of opposing stresses. Instead, the conjunction of antagonistic elements is always characterized by unevenness, by precise relations of domination and subordination, without the subordinate ever being the "pure phenomena" of or reducible to the dominant.[53] It is the persistence of singular entities, even in the larger entity they compose, that distinguishes for Althusser what he calls an "already-given complex structured whole" from a totality.[54]

Looking back a decade later for the purpose of self-criticism, Althusser would describe the concept explored in these early essays as a Spinozist one, an attempt, in the very terms of the letter to Oldenburg cited by Macherey, to theorize the notion of the infinite sum as a whole, although a "whole without closure that is nothing more than the active relations between its parts."[55] Thus, following the arguments of Giorgos Fourtounis, it is possible to distinguish antagonistic conceptions even the of notion of the whole as deployed by Althusser from the very beginning of his project: alongside the transcendental conception criticized by Macherey, there exists the sense of an immanent whole without end or ends (the whole that is "nothing more than" and therefore purely immanent in the active relations between "its" parts). Althusser undoubtedly sought to forestall any reading of overdetermination as chance or indeterminate and therefore unknowable disorder in *Reading Capital*, and in this attempt he produced, in the passages we have examined, the very transcendental unity against which he had argued so effectively in the essays of 1962–63. In doing so he overshadowed the attempt to think structure as singularity (Spinoza) and conjuncture (Lucretius), while simultaneously and indissociably thinking singularity and conjuncture as structure, an endeavor I have attempted to restore to visibility. Not only is such a theoretical project not exhausted, but it is perhaps only today, in the light of Althusser read through Spinoza read through Lucretius read through Althusser and so on, in a movement of reciprocal determination, that it is posed as such.

Interestingly, it was only through an encounter with another partisan of Lucretius and Spinoza that Althusser would finally separate himself from the metaphysical notion of structure that dogged his attempts to theorize these questions. One of the last, if not either the final or definitive settling of accounts with the notion of structure, critiques that was simultaneously a self-criticism would come as a consequence of a rather surprising encounter, one that shows that structure exerted a fascination, or perhaps appeared theoretically indispensable in a way that few could resist, including those, like Althusser himself, who might be thought most insensible to its lure. Some of Gilles Deleuze's texts, above all his studies of Lucretius and Nietzsche, as we have seen, played a role in Althusser's reflections on the problems of the whole and its parts, and structure and its elements, pushing him toward "a logic of the diverse," as Macherey put it. It is all the more ironic, then, that at the very moment Althusser was engaged in revising *Reading Capital* for the second edition, he would locate in Deleuze's overview of structuralism the very notion of structure as interiority that Macherey criticized in Althusser's own work. Ted Stolze has provided the definitive account of the theoretical exchange that took place between Althusser and Deleuze (and less directly, Macherey, to whom Althusser had sent off copy for comments) in early 1968 around the first draft (a transcription, in fact, of a talk Deleuze gave on December 6, 1967) of "À quoi reconnait-on le structuralisme," including the revisions Deleuze made in producing the published version, different in a number of respects from the draft sent to Althusser.[56] It is to this draft and Althusser's written response (of approximately 2000 words) to it that I will refer in the following discussion.

Stolze has described in detail the surprise expressed by Macherey and Althusser in reading the prefatory section of the essay in which Deleuze makes a case for the underlying unity of structuralism, the structure of structuralism, so to speak, a unity that belies the apparent diversity of domains, reference points, and objectives among those commonly thought of as structuralists. We recognize structuralists in those domains where there is language, "there is structure only where there is language, even if nonverbal language. There is, for example, structure of the unconscious only to the extent that the unconscious speaks and is language, there is structure of bodies only to the extent that bodies can be said to speak with a language, for example, of symptoms, there is no structure of things except to the extent that things are said to uphold a discourse, are said to pursue a language even if it is the silent language of signs."[57] According to this argument, a single object, language, forms reality, the knowledge of which the different domains of structuralism seek to produce. One might even envision a single structuralism the unity of which would reflect the unity of its object: one structure, one structuralism. Indeed, Deleuze's essay points in this direction. Althusser's response to this tendency was to warn Deleuze that his analysis "suffers from a sort of 'amalgam,'"[58] the positing of a unity where it does not exist, a unity moreover guaranteed by the identity of the object of knowledge across domains. This is, of course, the very position Macherey had so vigorously disputed in "L'analyse litterarire: Tombeau de structures," published two years earlier, and his response, expressed in a letter to Althusser, was less circumspect. He argues that Deleuze's conception of structure and structuralism "establishes a continuity where there is real disorder. It is necessary to show that in fact structuralist ideology is made of pieces and fragments."[59] Rejecting the idea that the work of linguists, anthropologists, literary critics, philosophers, and historians was united in the identity of the structure of language, Althusser counters that if that certain works in certain of these fields exhibit a unity, they are united only in what they refuse, in the concepts they, in a common front, reject.

Althusser's critical response, however, focused primarily not on the "eclecticism" of Deleuze's initial presentation of the field of structuralism but on the first of the five criteria by which one can, according to Deleuze, recognize the presence of structuralism: the symbolic criterion, the topological criterion, the differential or singular criterion, the serial criterion, and the criterion of the empty case. On Althusser's copy of Deleuze's draft, all but one of the marginal notes and underlines made in red pen by Althusser are concentrated in the two and a half pages of the first criterion, the symbolic (which Macherey in his letter to Althusser referred to as the theoretical base of "À quoi reconnait-on le structuralisme"). Deleuze begins his exposition with a general statement on the nature of "Western thought": it has been dominated by "an old tradition" in which our thought is concerned with the distinction, as well as the correlation, between the real and the imaginary. Indeed, philosophy itself has been characterized by "a kind of dialectical play between these two categories," declaring the primacy of one over the other (the imaginary, too, has its partisans, the exponents of the creative imagination). Even such categories as "the pure intellect" or "the pure understanding," which may at first sight appear to escape the dualism of the real and the imaginary, prove finally no more than a function of the apparent opposition. What other function does the understanding have if not to "give us the possibility of distinguishing the real in its reality or truth from the imaginary." The structuralist alone, it appears, escapes the tyranny of the dialectical game of the real and the imaginary by positing "a third order, a third reign," the symbolic. "Deeper than the real and the imaginary and irreducible to them,"[60] the symbolic is that reality with which the structuralist is concerned.

It is at this point that Deleuze's text exhibits what Althusser, judging from the marks on the page of the manuscript (Althusser drew a large arrow in the margin, and the sentence is underlined, both in red marker), regarded as a symptomatic lapse: "In other terms, it is the refusal to confuse the symbolic with the imaginary that constitutes the first dimension of the structuralist system."[61] Deleuze has conspicuously omitted that other term with which, it might be thought at least, the symbolic might be in danger of being confused: the real. The omission opens the possibility, realized before the end of this section, that the symbolic, already posited as "deeper" than the opposition whose hold it escapes, could come to function as the real itself or rather, to put it more precisely, as the real of the real. Immediately following the sentence cited above, Deleuze announces that, "I would like to take some examples from among the authors I have cited in order for this to become more concrete." His first example of the primacy of the symbolic over the opposition of the real and the imaginary is drawn from the work of none other than Althusser himself, specifically, the essay "Marxism and Humanism" included in *For Marx*: "For example, behind real men and ideologies, that is, behind the ideas and the images which men make about themselves and their nature, Louis Althusser claims to have discovered something deeper [quelque chose de plus profond] that he calls the symbolic order as the proper object of structure." A page later, at the conclusion of the section on the symbolic, Deleuze will make explicit the equivalence that is only hinted at in the passage on Althusser: the "third order beyond the real and the imaginary . . . should be called a structure." In the margins of the manuscript, next to this sentence, Althusser wrote "Third order: symbolic=structure."

Althusser begins his critique of this section by asking whether the symbolic when "removed from the Lacanian context (where its credentials are incontestably genuine) is not the site of ambiguity and a sort of wordplay. This is to suggest that it has a double meaning."[62] Given that Deleuze uses the terms "structure" and "symbolic" interchangeably, Althusser passes on to the very notion of structure itself in its most "legitimate" usage: linguistics. Even there, Althusser finds that structuralism is defined not by the real object that it studies (i.e., phonological, syntactical, or semantic structure) but by that with which it has broken: the "historicism and empiricism of classical philology." It is this break—rather than the discovery of structure, understood as the real beneath the apparent in language—that has set linguistics, even structural linguistics, on the road to scientific knowledge. This road, however, remains fraught with risk and littered with theoretical obstacles. In the case of the human sciences, "a certain number have discovered more or less blindly that they can exist as sciences only on the condition that they break with historicism, that is, the empiricist ideology of their 'object.'" In doing so, however, they tend, according to Althusser, to oscillate between two temptations: "on the one hand, they take theory as a 'model'

(L[évi]-S[trauss]: the concept of 'structure' designates a 'model'); on the other, they take this theory for a 'reality' (a specific modality of the 'real,' distinct from the real, but real insofar as it is a modality)?: for example, they say, and you have followed them on this point, that structure is the symbolic." According to Althusser, Deleuze's confusion of structure and the symbolic, the tendency to substitute one term for the other, is telling: rather than escaping the dialectical game of the real and the imaginary (which is itself one form of the opposition between essence and appearance, reality, and illusion), Deleuze has made "structure" that "unconscious reality, hidden beneath appearances." This realism in no way excludes, but on the contrary invites, a notion of structure as a "combinatory, the order of orders" formulated by Lévi-Strauss.[63]

We must not lose sight of the fact, however, that Althusser's critique of Deleuze's notion of structure, particularly of the confusion of a theoretical concept with an actually existing object, the symbolic, is simultaneously, even if "more or less blindly," a critique of his own work as read by Deleuze who is able to cite Althusser's notion of structure as an example of what Althusser calls the "realist" temptation (realism here referring as much to Plato as to empiricism). Deleuze's reading, as we have already established, was by no means peculiar to him; two years before "À quoi reconnait-on le structuralisme?," Macherey had already warned Althusser that structure appeared in certain places in *Reading Capital* as the hidden truth "behind" or "beyond" appearances. It seems then that Althusser's self-critique, the "self-critique of latent structure," whose necessity Althusser recorded in a note to himself in 1966, could only take the form of a confrontation with another person reading Althusser's work out loud, to him directly, as if only alienated in the words of the other could Althusser finally settle accounts with the contradictory development of his own work. Perhaps this, in part at least, is why his work so often seemed to escape and oppose him, allowing him to think of himself as a philosopher sans oeuvre, a philosopher whose works were not his own—not in the sense that what he wrote was borrowed from others, as he insisted in his autobiography, but in the sense that, as Balibar so aptly remarked, what he wrote was not what he wanted to write.

PART II

Subject

Marxism and Humanism

Althusser is perhaps best known for his contribution to the theory of ideology. It is therefore noteworthy that he did not devote a single text to the topic. The apparent exception, the essay "Ideology and Ideological State Apparatuses," is now known to have been, as one of the French versions puts it, "composed of fragments from an originally much longer study."[1] Further, the fact that this text is not an essay at all but an assemblage of more or less self-contained passages taken from their original context is made clear: both versions of the French text published during Althusser's lifetime are clearly marked with a series of ellipses that highlight visually the fragmentary nature of the text and further mark the precise point at which steps in Althusser's argument have been omitted. The suppression of the ellipses in the English translation of the text allowed readers to ignore the cautionary statement contained in an opening footnote and take the piece not as a collection of fragments but as a coherent and complete argument.

Interestingly, the posthumous publication of the manuscript from which "Ideology" was extracted, under the title *Sur la reproduction* in 1995 (although at least one of the extant complete drafts bears the title in Althusser's handwriting "De la superstructure"), reveals that far more was omitted from the published texts than even Althusser's original ellipses indicated: not merely sections on law, morality, and a number of other topics but parts of paragraphs and even sentences.[2] Even the replacement of Althusser's fragments in their original context, however, does not offer a comprehensive account of ideology. This famous extract (or more precisely set of extracts), then, was part of what was intended to be a book, a manual, in fact, of dialectical materialism whose projected audience was not limited to academic circles. As part of such a project, "Ideology," even when restored to its "complete" state, is clearly not the detailed exposition that one might have expected from Althusser. Further, as I will explore at length, the nature of the project, which was, like all of Althusser's works, an intervention in a very specific theoretical-political conjuncture as he understood it, imposed certain strategic and tactical imperatives on Althusser. He says some very new and in fact unprecedented things about the notion of ideology while simultaneously concealing the novelty of his postulates (obviously a manual for militants is not the place to announce theoretical discoveries).

Apart from "Ideology," the only other detailed exposition of his theory of ideology published during his lifetime is found in "Marxism and Humanism," which first appeared in 1964 as "Marxisme et humanisme" and was later included in *For Marx*. After his death, however, another text came to light (and has subsequently been published) in which Althusser again discusses ideology at some length: "Three Notes on the Theory of Discourse," a text written in the fall of 1966 as part of a theoretical discussion restricted to Althusser and a handful of former students and thus never intended for publication. Although "Marxism and Humanism" and "Ideology," separated by an interval of six years (and not just any years but 1964–70), are often cited together, as if they offer a single notion of ideology, they in fact differ from each other in fundamental ways. In fact, the 1970 text explicitly rejects certain of the key concepts and assumptions of the earlier piece, although without any admission on his part that in 1964 Althusser himself used some of the concepts he subjects to criticism in 1970. By analyzing the 1966 text, we can trace Althusser's itinerary through the three expositions of the theory of ideology from 1964 to 1966 to 1970, a period of rapid breaks and reversals in his thought, and a period in which the continuity of certain terms concealed underlying theoretical discontinuities.

Perhaps the most important and remarkable shifts in perspective, which remained for the most part unnoticed by readers and incompletely theorized by Althusser himself, tend to center on two key interdependent problems. First, there is the problem of the specific form in which ideology exists, is it interior to consciousness, exterior but present to consciousness, or not directed to consciousness at all? Another way of asking the same question: Does ideology consist of ideas, of discourse, practices, or apparatuses? Is its existence material or ideal? The second problem involves the place of the human individual as subject or agent: Is it a given, an origin (however mediated) or, in contrast, is it a myth, illusion, or reality constituted through practices and apparatuses? In grappling with these questions, Althusser in no way sought to limit himself nor was he in fact limited to the "theoretical raw materials" found within self-described Marxist texts; on the contrary, Althusser's trajectory can be seen as the outcome of a constant engagement with theoretical developments occurring around him; at certain times borrowing from them to think through his arguments, at others taking his distance from them, drawing that line of demarcation that separated what could be used productively from that which would block his way.

A careful reading of Althusser's earliest exposition of a theory of ideology yields some surprises, especially given the fact that the essay is most often read teleologically, as containing in embryo the postulates of the text published in 1970. By refraining from reading "Marxism and Humanism" as an anticipation of the final theory of ideology, we are permitted to see not only its unresolved internal contradictions but its surprising filiations. The history of "Marxism and Humanism," its immediate effects as well as its origins, is an interesting one. The context was one in which humanism (and, Althusser would insist, a certain liberalism) was widely viewed in the Communist parties, especially, but not exclusively, in Western Europe, as the philosophical antidote to the inhumanity, if not the systematic inhumanism, of the Stalinist regime. The writings of the Young Marx were translated and widely disseminated during this period, in part to provide credentials for this movement. Adam Schaff, a philosopher and sometime functionary of the Polish Communist Party, was a leading proponent of the notion of Marxist humanism.[3] Perhaps in the interest of stimulating debate and discussion, Schaff suggested to Erich Fromm (another important partisan of Marxist humanism and a champion of the early Marx, at that time living in the United States) that he include a contribution by Althusser in a collection on humanism for which Fromm was at that time soliciting contributions. Althusser responded by writing "Marxism and Humanism," a text that he would describe a few years later as "very short and too clear" and that was rewritten to be "even shorter and clearer." Significantly, Fromm rejected the essay: "He was distressed. My text was extremely interesting, he did not contest its intrinsic value, but it could not be part of the project, that is, in harmony with the others." From this experience Althusser drew the following conclusion: "the article I wrote for an American public must have touched an extremely sensitive point in, if not in the theoretical, then at least the current ideological, conjuncture."[4] The theoretical effects of "Marxism and Humanism" confirmed Althusser's judgment: the essay touched off what he called the "humanist controversy" (*le querrelle de l'humanisme*), that is, a wave of critical and often hostile responses, both public and private, primarily within the Communist move-ment. Even the Central Committee of the French Communist Party felt it necessary to intervene against Althusser's antihumanism, passing a resolu-tion in March 1966 declaring "There is a Marxist Humanism."[5] But the dis-quiet surrounding Althusser's analysis of humanism was not just restricted to the Communist milieu. Even Jacques Derrida, not usually considered a partisan of humanism, was disturbed enough by Althusser's text to ask, in a letter dated September 1, 1964, whether he hadn't gone too far and whether a certain kind of humanism was not still valuable.

The question of ideology, while not the primary focus of Althusser's crit-ics, is nevertheless central to the argument of "Marxism and Humanism." The essay, divided into five sections, begins by describing, in phrases rich with irony, the sense in which "socialist humanism is the order of the day." In the second section Althusser begins his critique: to understand the ad-vent of socialist humanism as a historical fact, as well as its present meaning and function, he warns us that it does not suffice to make use of the con-cepts "in which the event thinks itself." More seriously, this insufficiency is of a particular type: "the concept of humanism is a merely *ideological* con-cept." What does the term "ideological" at once descriptive and denuncia-tory mean in this context? Althusser offers a definition that will suffice to carry us through the stages of Marx's thought, which occupy the next two sections of the essay. Ideology is to be contrasted to science insofar as it des-ignates a "set of existing realities" without giving us, as a scientific theory necessarily does, the means to know (*connaître*) these realities. Ideology notes existences, while science "gives us their essence."[6] Thus, while the work of Marx before 1845 remains important, it does not and cannot supply us with the means to know the reality whose existence it registers. Begin-ning with the "Theses on Feuerbach," however, Marx not only broke with humanism, refusing to explain social development by recourse to a theory of human essence expressed in every human individual, but theorized his break with humanism by assigning it the status of an ideology.

At this point in Althusser's essay, the question not only remains but is posed with even greater urgency: What exactly do we mean by ideology? So far, it has been defined only negatively: ideology cannot give us knowl-edge, and it is not science. The fourth section accordingly begins with the recognition that "everything thus depends on the knowledge of the nature of humanism as ideology." Althusser's discussion of ideology, however, be-gins with a gesture of deferral: "there is no question of undertaking here" (in this too brief essay) a "comprehensive (*approfondie*) definition of ide-ology." What he will say "very schematically" will have to suffice.[7] As we follow the exposition of Althusser's definition of ideology, we will have reason to doubt that the inaugural gesture of deferral can be attributed to the constraints imposed by the circumstances of publication. It may be that the sketch of ideology remains "very schematic" because its own internal contradictions prevent it from developing further.

Let us examine in some detail the opening sentence of the definition: "It suffices to know very schematically that an ideology is a system (possessing its own logic and rigor) of representations (images, myths, ideas or con-cepts according to the case) endowed with a historical existence and role within a given society."[8] However schematic, this dense statement exhibits certain rhetorical features that ought not go unnoted. First, the parallel parenthetical statements, each offering the attributes proper to the notion of system, on the one hand, and representations, on the other. The paral-lelism is important; it emphasizes Althusser's division of the ideological in his definition into form and content, even as the order of the statement establishes the primacy of the system over the matter it makes use of. En-dowing ideology with both form and content is important: it sets Althus-ser's argument against the notion of ideology advanced by Marx and Engels in the *German Ideology*. There, ideology has no reality; it consists of mere "echoes" of real life, the phantoms and illusions whose only truth lies in the reality external to them and on which they depend. Ideology arises and dis-appears with the real history of which it is the phantasm. It is in opposition to such a notion that Althusser's use of the term "system," which he em-phasizes by declaring that it possesses "its own logic and rigor," as well as a logic and rigor proper to it (*sa logique et sa rigeur propres*), takes on consider-able importance. Ideology, if we follow the dominant reading of Marx and Engels's, is not so much known as dispelled, as a vision it is dispelled to re-veal the reality behind it. For Althusser ideology takes on an existence of its own; it is now a system, known not in relation to a reality external to it but in relation to the logic that governs it, the rules according to which its ele-ments are combined. The notion of a system of ideology governed by a logic necessarily evokes other systems, especially those studied by linguistics and anthropology. Ideology, as Althusser will soon show, shares with them the fact that it operates behind the backs of human individuals; they are not conscious of its existence, let alone of the rules that govern it (and them).

If this all initially sounds very structuralist, and Althusser's terms are calculated to evoke this sense of kinship, playing a certain structuralism against a reductive historicism, what follows it in the sentence takes a step back from structuralism. In postulating the matter of which the system makes use, Althusser might have been expected to refer to language, to statements or even signifiers. Instead, he answers the question of what ideology is made of with the highly ambiguous term "representations." Following this term in parentheses is a list of the possible forms of representation (unlike many such lists in Althusser's work, it is not open-ended and does not conclude with "etc."): images, myths, ideas or concepts, according to the case. The sequence of terms appears to suggest a kind of progress from the spontaneity and indistinctness of images produced directly by experience, to a primitive organization of these images into myths through the activity of individuals and groups but not by their design, to the products of theoretical reflection and labor, that is, ideas and concepts. Althusser will later say that the representations that supply the material support of the system of ideology are "usually images and occasionally concepts."[9] The term "images" is then obviously important here: it is among other things the root of the concept of the imaginary employed later in the essay, a fact missed by decades of commentators who saw in the use of "imaginary" an unfailing reference to Lacan.

Instead, "image" links Althusser's argument (and undoubtedly Lacan's as well, however distinct his concept of the imaginary remains from Althusser's) to a philosophical controversy in and around French phenomenology. On the one hand, the attempt by Sartre and Merleau-Ponty (and although there are important differences between the two, the differences do not prevent their uniting around this shared objective) to construct a phenomenology of the image that would rehabilitate it, restoring to the image, once thought of as a degraded or necessarily indistinct form of intellection, its rights as form of knowledge (which, when its "intentional structure" is described, can even be seen as a source of certainty), as well as its place in human emotions.[10] On the other, there is the identification by Gaston Bachelard of the images derived from "primary experience" as the "primary obstacle" to scientific knowledge (even as he would produce an aesthetic version of the phenomenology of the image, which he never managed to harmonize with his description of the history of the physical sciences).[11] While Althusser certainly shared Bachelard's antipathy to any notion that scientific knowledge could be derived, even in the last instance, from sense experience, it is important to keep in mind that Althusser's notion of a "*rup-*

ture scientifique" differed from Bachelard's in crucial respects. For Althusser, the scientific break is never a division between doxa and episteme but always a break within knowledge that only retroactively constitutes by a reordering and a recasting an earlier knowledge as "ideological" (ideology can also consist of concepts, as abstract as one might wish). Althusser then rejects both the privileging of the image as a kind of primary truth (even, at the extreme, the truth of language) and the devaluation of the image as primary illusion of the merely sensible world, which is forever set in opposition to scientific intelligibility.

Ideology thus defined is primarily a system of (inadequate) representation. But representation of what by what? Althusser does not and cannot specify either term. Let us take the question of the matter of which ideology is composed. Myth, according to Lévi-Strauss, is not a system of representation but a system of communication, a self-enclosed system each of whose elements function only in relation to other elements in the system, never representing a "reality" outside. Even more curiously, images and ideas seem inevitably to suggest mental phenomena, that is, phenomena that belong to the world of the mind (a Lebenswelt?, we will soon return to this thesis) separate from, re-presenting, what is external to it, namely material, concrete reality. In fact, Althusser has produced a compromise formation: ideology's immaterial, spiritual (in the sense of *geistige*) matter, images, and ideas (precisely the notion of ideology as consisting of ideas in the head of an individual in which he believes and on which he acts, a notion he will himself reject as idealist in the 1970 article) are nevertheless granted a certain degree of autonomy and effectivity by the fact that their function is determined less by the reality they represent than by the logic of the system of which they are elements. This compromise formation will suffice to allow Althusser to shift the discussion of ideology away from the notion of representation altogether, away from any definition of ideology as false consciousness or misrepresentation. Ideology, he tells us in the sentence following his definition, is opposed to science but not as non-knowledge or superstition as opposed to knowledge. Instead it is distinguished from science by virtue of its "function," by virtue of its effects. Ideology is characterized by the fact that "the practico-social function takes precedence over the theoretical function (or knowledge function)." Althusser has set aside the question of what ideology is—a question we can reformulate, in the terms that he himself will use, as the material existence of ideology—to pursue the question of what ideology does, of its function. He has not, however, resolved this question but deferred it to the future. His failure not only to answer this question but even to pose it will have profound effects on the remainder of his discussion of ideology. This failure will prevent him from answering the question with which the next paragraph begins: "what is the nature of this social function?"[12]

What emerges in place of an answer to the question of what ideology does, however, is itself remarkable and worthy of examination. Althusser begins by postulating the necessary existence of ideology in any society: "It is as if human societies could not survive (*subsister*) without these specific formations, these systems of representations (at various levels), that are ideologies. Human societies secrete ideology as the very element and atmosphere indispensable to their historical respiration and life. Only an ideological conception of the world could have imagined societies without ideology and accepted the utopian idea of a world in which ideology (and not just one of its historical forms) would disappear without a trace, to be replaced by science."[13] "It is as if": perhaps Althusser qualifies the argument that follows with this phrase in order to mark as provisional a statement that will certainly shock many of his readers.

Although Althusser has made the opposition of science and ideology the center of his argument, he nevertheless suggests that no one and no society (whatever the relations of production or the level of development of the productive forces) can exist outside of ideology, that is, to adhere to the definition advanced up to this point, to a system of ideas whose logic is always "immediately opaque" (to borrow a phrase from *Reading Capital*), always, as he will soon specify, unconscious. A few lines later, he will say it directly: "ideology is therefore not an aberration or a contingent excrescence of History: it is a structure essential to the historical life of societies."[14] Ideology is no longer associated exclusively with "class society," whether it is conceived in a functionalist manner as arising in order to justify the existing forms of domination and exploitation or simply as a reflection of these forms. Althusser's use of the verb "secretes" is significant here; the production of ideology is not goal directed nor is it the outcome of an intention (individual or collective). Instead, ideology is a by-product, although a necessary and inescapable by-product that accompanies and indeed envelops the activities required for the continued existence of a society. Ideology is the element or atmosphere in which a society, even a classless society, "breathes," to use Althusser's metaphor. It is no longer a question of which societies need or do not need ideology (the functionalist question) but rather a question of why and how ideology is necessary to any conceivable society.

Ideology is secreted, not invented; it is the effect of society as a totality. As such it neither originates nor resides in "consciousness," not least because the notion of consciousness itself is an ideological notion tied to a certain liberal individualism: ideology "is profoundly unconscious, even when it presents itself in a reflected (or reflective) form. Ideology is indeed a system of representations, but in the majority of cases, these representations have nothing to do with 'consciousness:' they are usually images and occasionally concepts, but it is above all as structures that they are imposed on the vast majority of men, not via their 'consciousness.'" Thus, a system of rules confers order, significance, and function on the images that usually comprise the substance of ideology. We are "conscious" of the images but ignorant of the logic that governs them and us, the structure of which Althusser speaks. At this point, he offers a highly ambivalent specification of the representations of which ideology is composed: "they are cultural objects perceived-accepted-submitted to (*perçus-acceptés-subis*) and act functionally on men by a process which escapes them."[15] Althusser literally objectifies the representations: they become "cultural objects," no longer reflections of things but things themselves, representations congealed into objective form, no longer interior but exterior to the subject that "lives" them. They are objects (dominating human beings by virtue of their function in a system that escapes our conscious apprehension), and they are "cultural," a term that perhaps denotes the structure that assigns them their function as well as their superstructural nature.

And yet, the objective existence of the representations is immediately undercut by the fact that they are simultaneously objects of a strange tripartite process (without a—grammatical—subject!) of perception-acceptance-submission. While the passive voice allows Althusser to evade the question of who or what perceives-accepts-submits to, the fact remains that this sequence reproduces the most classical liberal formula and suggests that, even as ideology is congealed in objects external to the consciousness that "perceives" them and exists in the logic of the system of objects which is not present to consciousness, Althusser has in no way abandoned the subject/object, mind/matter distinction that he elsewhere so vigorously criticizes. He has, it is true, displaced the perceiving subject (as well as the moral subject who chooses to accept and submit) from the center of ideology, which is now a system external to them that they passively reflect. The nature and functioning of the system of ideology cannot be grasped by a study of their lived experience but, on the contrary, only by definitively consigning "the lived" to the status of a necessarily inadequate reflection of a system that can only be known otherwise than by means of subjective experience. The content of consciousness is an effect but not an adequate representation of the system that will remain perpetually inaccessible to consciousness. Human individuals not only know not what they do, they know not what they think and feel, the basis on which they determine their actions. Even the ruling classes "believe" the myths that compose their society's ideology, that is, even the ruling classes, far from having the capacity to use ideologies as instruments of domination, are themselves governed unawares by the logic of the system. Thus, consciousness is decentered, devalued, nothing more than an element made use of by a system whose existence remains unknown to it. At the same time, however, it remains, even in its subordinate status, a concept necessary to the theory of ideology insofar as it mediates between individuals in their physical or vital existence and the system of objects that governs them.

If Althusser's essay stopped at this point, if it were reducible to the conception of ideology indicated above, it would have said nothing that a hundred other texts (and not all of them Marxist, it should be noted) had not already said. But coexisting with this notion of ideology, in fact, interwoven in it in its actual textual existence, is a tendency to conceptualize ideology in material terms. Recast in this way, a theory of ideology would have to move beyond positing it as existing outside and independent of consciousness; it would also be compelled at least to pose if not answer the question of how "consciousness" (or the attributes that such a term designates) or more generally the human subject is not a given, an origin, but rather is itself constituted. The contradiction reaches its apogee in a single concept, which remains throughout the essay (and beyond) susceptible to absolutely divergent interpretations, Althusser's use of the verb "to live" (*vivre*) and its past participle "lived" (*vécu*) which can become a noun (*le vécu*). Althusser qualifies his argument that the idea that ideology pertains to the realm of consciousness is invalid: the idea is not simply illusory; it alludes to an important aspect of the problem of ideology, which can be identified only if it is formulated in a different way. Althusser introduces a new concept in place of "consciousness," the concept of life: "men *live* their actions commonly related by the classical tradition to freedom and to 'consciousness' in ideology, through and by ideology; in short . . . the 'lived' relation of men to the world, including History (in political action or inaction), passes through ideology, or better, *is ideology itself*."[16]

It is not immediately clear how "life" marks a conceptual advance over "consciousness." To what does the phrase "the lived relation of men to the world" refer if not to the system of perception-acceptance-submission evoked earlier? In fact have not most readers, not only of "Marxism and Humanism" but also even of "Ideology," understood "live" in this context as a synonym for "experience"? No reader or indeed critic of Althusser was more qualified to certify the genealogy of the notion in "Marxism and Humanism" than Paul Ricoeur, who, with no little satisfaction, pronounced the phrase "lived relation" as being borrowed from "the vocabulary of Husserl and Merleau-Ponty."[17] Althusser himself, in fact, would write to psychoanalyst René Diatkine a mere two years after the composition of "Marxism and Humanism" to criticize Diatkine for using this same vocabulary, and the terms of his critique are uncannily pertinent to its effects in "Marxism and Humanism" (which he does not mention): "you make use of extremely dubious psychological philosophical concepts ('lived experience [le vécu],' 'meaning,' 'intentionality,' 'human experience,' etc.). To be sure you use them in passing and that entails no *direct* consequences in your analysis. But if one aligns the right you arrogate to utilize psychological or phenomenological concepts (phenomenology is the religious psychology of our time) without criticizing them," then the results, according to Althusser, could be dangerous. Because, as Althusser informed Diatkine, "no concept exists in solitude" but is always a member of a "conceptual community."[18] The use of such concepts, unless they were clearly differentiated from their meaning and function in their original problematic, would risk burying new questions and problems under an appearance of an already existing "theoretical community," effacing every trace of the break characteristic of every significant theoretical advance. The effect of Althusser's own use (if "only in passing") of exactly the phrase against which he warns Diatkine, that is, the phrase "le vécu," was to bind him to the extraordinarily complex and unfinished field of the Lebenswelt as developed in the late Husserl and as refined by such followers as Merleau-Ponty. To identify this source, however, by no means renders the task of understanding Althusser any easier; quite the contrary. Not only, of course, is the fourth section of Marxism and Humanism irreducible to any phenomenological argument, the source itself, that is, actually existing phenomenology up to Althusser's time, is far from pure, consistent, or univocal, even if we restrict our discussion to part three of Husserl's *Crisis of European Sciences* (and leave aside such interpreters well known to Althusser as Merleau-Ponty, Tran Duc Thao, and Ricoeur himself).

In fact, as the three philosophers just named were quick to admit, the notion of Lebenswelt has itself produced absolutely contradictory interpretations. On the one hand, the epoche (or bracketing) that precedes and allows the postulation of an absolute correlation between world and consciousness and that, by eliminating from consideration any notion of a world that exceeds the knowing subject, permits in turn the apprehension of the fact that subjectivity is the primal source (*Urquellend*) and primal state (*Urstätte*) of any objective representation of the world.[19] On the other hand, Husserl accuses Kant of presupposing without investigation a lifeworld to which the knowing subject belongs. Once we bracket the objective sciences, we are left with the world of life, the world we necessarily inhabit by virtue of our corporeal existence. This is the world of experience, both individual and universal, and is as valid and true in its own way as the sciences for which indeed it is the ground. As ground, it cannot be the object of a genetic investigation; instead, Husserl tells us, it is pre-given and pre-predicative. He has thus assigned the lifeworld a privileged position in a topography, that of foundation. At the same time, however, science, while erected on the foundation of the lifeworld, remains irreducibly distinct from it. Thus, geometry, the science of ideal shapes nowhere found in the lifeworld is at once "an infinite and yet self-enclosed world of ideal objects"[20] generated out of the practical concerns of the lifeworld (in particular, the need for ever more precise measurement) and emerged at its limits, becoming an additional world.

For a number of Marxist philosophers in the 1950s the shift in Husserl's thought at the end of his life toward the primacy of the Lebenswelt marked, in the words of Tran Duc Thao, the fact that "phenomenological idealism was surpassed by the practice of the analysis of lived experience."[21] This was nothing less than a materialist turn in Husserl's thought away from "the genesis of the world in absolute consciousness" and toward "the actual becoming of real history." Did Althusser then in "Marxism and Humanism," where Ricoeur was right to detect a certain residual phenomenological reference, follow them and simply import a whole conceptual apparatus without acknowledgment and therefore criticism to explain the phenomenon of ideology? Clearly not. First, we must recall that lived experience for Althusser is not an originary ground but a system of representations, not the absolute adequation of consciousness and world in which the world is "abolished" and we are left with the contents of consciousness, but as the system present to consciousness as its world, even as this system of representations inhibits rather than makes possible any knowledge. To conceive of this system as a radical origin, as pre-predicative, is merely to obscure the historical functioning of the system of representations that human individuals perceive-accept-submit to. In short, the postulate of an original lifeworld is a symptom of the unconscious character of ideology, the mark of the form of repression necessary to the ideological unconscious.

Another dimension of Husserl's materialist turn for Tran Duc Thao was the former's recognition that the lifeworld was not merely the world of perception or even the world of perception inseparably conjoined to the materiality of the body: as such it would remain at "a properly animal level." Instead the lifeworld was the world of human practice and production. The dependence of the sciences on the lifeworld became for Thao the sign of their genesis in the "real labor of the oppressed classes," whose practice produced as its "ideal" expression mathematics, physics, and biology.[22] For Althusser, science cannot emerge from the system of representations but only against and outside of it. There can be no continuity between the "lived experience" of ideology and science, not even the continuity guaranteed by human practice or productivity, which would then become merely another transcendental principle invoked to secure a teleological conception of history and progress. To emphasize this point, Althusser suggests that "vécu" is the equivalent of "the imaginary": ideology is the manner in which men live their relation to their conditions of existence, "which supposes at the same time a real relation and a 'lived,' 'imaginary' relation."[23] Counterposing the "lived" to the real in this way, of course, is to reject the notion of lifeworld as anything other than the world of ideology.

Thus, the recognition that the term "live" in Althusser's essay remains in part tied to the phenomenological tradition does not mean that in using this tradition he left it undisturbed or was simply used by it. In fact, we might well argue that Althusser preserves the term "consciousness" in order explicitly to deprive it of all the privileges accorded it by even the most Marxist variants of phenomenology. Consciousness is no longer at the center, no longer constitutive; instead it is an agent and an element of a system external to it, to which it submits to unawares. The truth of its social and historical existence is not in it or present to it (except in the form of the pre-given or the origin, terms that Althusser described as synonyms for "what must not be thought in order to think what we want to think")[24] but necessarily escapes it.

It remains, however, for us to explore the sense in which "lived" is irreducible to and perhaps even counterposed to its meaning and function in phenomenology, even the most materialist versions. We have already noted that the lifeworld in Husserl marked the entrance of the body on to the stage of philosophy; consciousness is always inescapably embodied. Of all Husserl's disciples and interpreters, none devoted themselves to developing this notion more than Merleau-Ponty, who went so far as to speak of the inescapable reciprocity of mind and body (periodically taking his distance from Spinoza in order not to be confused with his doctrine).[25] Even his work, however, finally offered no more than a compromise (already enacted in the later Husserl) that encased the mind in body (that is, every individual mind in every individual body—each can only experience its own thoughts directly) while preserving its privileges and independence. In an important sense, the passages in "Marxism and Humanism" that we have just examined do not contest this notion and perhaps even implicitly presuppose it. At the same time, however, in the very same essay, Althusser provides the elements necessary for a critique of every philosophy of consciousness.

There occurs one important phrase that calls the entire phenomenological edifice into question and allows us to assign the term "live" a meaning diametrically opposed to the meaning it assumes in phenomenological discourse (as well as in certain statements in Althusser's text): "men's 'consciousness,' that is, their attitude and behavior (*leur attitude et leur conduite*)."[26] First, the form of the sentence, the rhetorical trope that disguises an argument, the unmistakable Spinozism of the "sive," the Latin conjunction "or," which can also be understood in the sense of "that is," a rendering equivalent of two terms otherwise thought to be opposed: *Deus sive Natura*, God or Nature, God, that is, Nature.[27] It is an operation of translation and substitution: substitution because it allows us to replace God with nature or consciousness with behavior and translation because this substitution allows a rereading of earlier texts and doctrines that transforms their meaning. Of course, the reference to Spinoza is not merely to be found in the form of the statement but also its content. It replaces the stubborn dualism of even those theories most concerned to demonstrate the embodiedness of consciousness with Spinoza's refusal not only to separate mind and body (because even the partisans of embodiment do that) but to declare them distinct and different. Mind and body are not simply parallel, that is, reciprocal, but the same. It was precisely this idea that made Spinoza anathema to existentialists and phenomenologists alike: he denied the existence of subjectivity, its grandeur and its freedom. To appreciate the full effect of Althusser's Spinozist equation, we must pay close attention to the actual words he uses. "Attitude" in English commonly denotes a subjective disposition; in French, "attitude" tends to be associated with a bodily posture. Thus attitude and conduct, to translate Althusser's words literally, represent a substitution of body for mind, of external for internal, of acts for thoughts. To follow this set of associations is to see consciousness disappear into acts and mind into body; to replace "become consciousness of" or "experience" with "live," as in men "live" their relations to their conditions of existence, is not only to make ideology an affair of bodies rather than minds, but it is to materialize it altogether.

The translation of consciousness into attitude and behavior, of course, simultaneously necessitates the translation of all the terms used to signify attributes or actions of consciousness: imagination, perception, acceptance, submission, all those terms that set the human world apart from nature and make it an *imperium in imperio*, a kingdom within a kingdom, and thus ground humanism and the specificity of the human sciences in relation to the natural sciences. But into what are these terms translated? How are we to understand, for example, acceptance or submission except as acts of consciousness (if not of conscience)? Althusser's discussion of ideology is suspended at this precise point, and even a rigorous posing of the necessary question is deferred to another time and other texts.

Paradoxically, then, the very force of "Marxism and Humanism," the intensity of the effects it produced (the critiques and attacks it drew on Althusser), has obscured the extent to which Althusser's essay remained haunted by the humanism it sought to analyze, insofar as it desubstantialized ideology and vacillated between a notion of individual subjects as given (although no longer the center of their world) and a notion of the subject as illusion.

Althusser and Lacan
Toward a Genealogy of the Concept of Interpellation

Althusser returned to the question of ideology two years after the publication of "Marxism and Humanism" only indirectly, as if the question, up to this point of secondary importance in his research and apparently not one Althusser wanted or was prepared to address directly, proved nevertheless unavoidable. His reconsideration of ideology in 1966 grew out of a sustained engagement with psychoanalysis, an engagement that began before the composition of "Marxism and Humanism" but reached its peak only after the publication of the essay. As early as 1959, Althusser directed his students to the study of psychoanalysis, including the work of Lacan.[1] His seminar of 1963–64, which began shortly after he completed the text of "Marxism and Humanism," was entirely devoted to the topic. Fortunately, the two presentations that Althusser made to the seminar were recorded; a transcription was published posthumously as *Psychanalyse et sciences humaines: Deux conférences*.[2] It is instructive to compare the text of his lectures to the only public expression of the work done in the seminar, Althusser's "Freud and Lacan," which appeared in the Communist journal *La Nouvelle Critique* in December 1964. The latter text endorsed Lacan's "antirevisionism," without offering any real interpretation or analysis of Lacan or even, to adopt the terminology of the essay, the object of psychoanalysis as founded by Freud and defended by Lacan. Instead, Althusser rather more modestly attempted to "situate" this object in relation to the theories (or ideologies), and the objects that pertained to these theories, that laid claim to the conceptual space that could legitimately be occupied by psychoanalysis alone.[3] It is crucial to recognize the limited and overwhelmingly negative objective not only of "Freud and Lacan" but of all the texts Althusser devoted to psychoanalysis in relation both to Freud and Lacan (is it necessary to recall that Althusser, from the beginning, expressed misgivings even about the notion of the unconscious?): the importance of Freud and Lacan lay in the acts of refusal and rejection by which they "barred the way" (to use an expression from Bachelard) to the ideologies that previously occupied the space of psychoanalysis and in doing so secured and defended the space, making possible the development of knowledge. For Althusser's project specifically, Lacan above all seemed to suggest ways of refusing ideologies of consciousness and subjectivity without denying the objective existence of the phenomena to which they referred. While Marxist critiques of psychoanalysis argued that its object was reducible to a material substrate, Althusser sought to discover the means by which he could theorize the materiality of what was once thought to be the domain of subjectivity and interiority.

Given the fact that Althusser is often said to have borrowed heavily from Lacan to construct his theory (or theories) of ideology and that he did in fact read Lacan closely and repeatedly throughout the sixties, it is worth examining the written record of Althusser's reading. When Althusser's "Dr. Freud's Discovery," written in 1976, was published against his will in the mid-eighties, it occasioned considerable discussion, not least because Althusser's discussion of Lacan in "Dr. Freud" is apparently quite negative. Lacan, in Althusser's words, "attempted to do what Freud had been unable to do: *he attempted to constitute a scientific theory of the unconscious.*" This flight forward beyond what was objectively possible theoretically produced as its result "a gigantic edifice that has not stopped proliferating and for good reason which was that it could only pursue an object that was out of its reach because it did not exist." This edifice, increasingly built from the bits and pieces of formal logic and mathematics, constituted a philosophy of psychoanalysis rather than a scientific theory. Lacan might and indeed should have been content to wage "that struggle which might have occupied a man's whole life," the struggle to defend the "the Freudian Thing, the specificity of Freud's thought."[4] It was in this struggle that Lacan distinguished himself and in which is to be found his heroism. The Lacan of 1964 was not yet the Lacan of 1976; not only was the publication of the *Ecrits* still two years away, but he had just been "excommunicated" from the International Psychoanalytic Association and still faced an uncertain and insecure professional future.[5] Indeed, in the essay of 1964, Althusser refers to Lacan in terms very similar to those he used in 1976, although for contrary purposes: to show the importance of Lacan, rather than his limitations. Lacan intervened "to defend against the 'reductions' and deviations that dominate most of the theoretical interpretations of analysis today, the *irreducibility of its object*." Even this task, far less ambitious than that of constituting a scientific theory of psychoanalysis, however, depended on the "emergence of a new science: linguistics," which alone permitted psychoanalysis to escape the perils of biologistic reductionism, on the one hand, and the temptations of psychology, that science of "the soul," which was itself a derivative of philosophies of consciousness, on the other.[6]

"Freud and Lacan" while clearly drawn from the lectures Althusser gave in the seminar of 1963–64 is clearly a carefully calculated intervention in support of Lacan's struggle in particular and of the possibility of a science of the unconscious more generally. The lectures, in contrast, offer not only a more critical reading of Lacan but reflect Althusser's attempt to think through some of the problems that emerged in "Marxism and Humanism." The organization of the seminar is itself instructive as to Althusser's theoretical concerns and priorities. In addition to Althusser, who delivered the two lectures contained in *Psychanalyse et sciences humaines*, six participants made presentations: Michel Tort, who provided a general overview of Freudian and Lacanian concepts; Étienne Balibar, who spoke on the topic of psychosis; Jacques-Alain Miller on Lacan; Achille Chiesa on Merleau-Ponty and psychoanalysis; Yves Duroux on psychoanalysis and phenomenology; and Jean Mosconi on psychoanalysis and anthropology. The emphasis on phenomenology might seem puzzling (more than a third of the seminar was devoted to a critical analysis of the actual relations between the different variants of phenomenology and psychoanalysis). Althusser, however, explains that for him and indeed his generation "the philosophical encounter with psychoanalysis took place through Sartre and Merleau-Ponty."[7]

We might expect him at this point to undertake an analysis of the versions of psychoanalysis that took shape in their works. Instead, he tells us that their interpretation of psychoanalysis was an adulterated version of what should be captured in the purity of its source: Georges Politzer's 1928 text *Critique des fondements de la psychologie*.[8] Althusser offers a brief summary of "the meaning" of Politzer's text: "psychology does not exist, psychology is abstraction, psychology is the theory of the soul (*L'âme*). Why doesn't psychology exist? Because it is simultaneously a science that pretends to take the soul as its object, that is, an object that doesn't exist and a discipline that employs concepts that are nothing more than abstractions. Neither its object nor its concepts exist." For Politzer, according to Althusser, the future lay in a psychology without the soul. A concrete psychology, as Politzer called the new discipline, would be a "psychology in the first person," whose concepts would therefore be concrete, unlike the abstractions of a "psychology in the third person." We may now see the attraction of Politzer's concrete psychology for Sartre and Merleau-Ponty: by "concrete" he means experience in the first person, the concreteness of the absolute origin, the ego or cogito. In opposition, Althusser directs his students to the first chapter of Hegel's *Phenomenology* where the "I" that sees itself as the concrete starting point soon discovers that it is no more than an empty abstraction, like the "here" and "now" of sense certainty. Concrete psychology, like its offspring, existential psychoanalysis, remained dominated by the "prejudice of consciousness and never became conscious of the fact that the essence of its object was the unconscious."[9]

Simply declaring the importance of the unconscious did not suffice to differentiate psychological theories (or even those psychoanalytic theories that remained in fact prisoner of psychology) from the ideologies of the human sciences. First, there exists the temptation to biologize the unconscious, making it the seat of instincts or the site at which the psyche encounters the physiological (or today, genetic) imperatives of which it is finally the expression. This, of course, allows psychology to wrap itself in the prestige of genuinely scientific theories and essentially exploit them for decidedly nonscientific purposes. Such a temptation can take the most seductive forms; as Althusser notes, even Lacan himself could not entirely resist the lure of psychophysiological guarantees in such works as "The Mirror Stage," seeking to ground stages of development in the process of physiological maturation, even going so far as to ground an original human intersubjectivity in the necessity of neurological development.

At the same time, the theorization of the unconscious in terms of biology necessitates in turn, as Freud himself illustrated, a corresponding theory of the social milieu into which the biological individual is inserted and accordingly rendered problematic. Such theories not only reproduce the classical opposition of nature and culture but end up facing a dilemma analogous to that of Descartes's in his attempt to arrange a point of contact between the otherwise separate and parallel worlds of thought and extension. At what point does the individual, formed prior to and outside of society by biological processes themselves independent of any social determination, and the social meet? What is the point of contact, the modern version of the Cartesian pineal gland that will mediate between and unify these otherwise separate realms? This, according to Althusser, is the original impasse of any Sartrian psychology. Certain schools of psychoanalysis employ the concept of the superego to stop the gap, declaring it the outcome of a process of internalization. The pineal gland of this school is the family, which transmits to the individual the social norms. Finally, even Lévi-Strauss's discussion of the function of the shaman in savage societies marks an attempt to theorize the means by which the difficulties of the insertion of the individual into the collective are "symbolically liquidated" in such cultures.[10]

There is, however, another response to the problem of the exteriority of the individual and society. Certain psychoanalytic theories argue that this is a pseudo-problem or at best a secondary problem. After all what is the cure, if not the very process of analysis itself, if not a demonstration and a (re)enactment of that original intersubjectivity in which alone our very identities as individuals are formed? The concept of intersubjectivity, which Merleau-Ponty brandished against Sartre's "solipsism of the many" and which might thus have been regarded as a rejection of any philosophy of the cogito, was, in Althusser's eyes, "the fundamental concept of what one might call the existentialist, personalist, etc. current of our time, which is one of the major currents of the contemporary epoch and which streams forth from innumerable fountains of modern history." Intersubjectivity, used to designate what happens in the course of an analytic cure, often produces an image of mutual antagonism through the inescapability of mutual recognition that cannot but recall the Master-Slave relation proper to the constitution of self-consciousness in Hegel's *Phenomenology*. Althusser poses the question: "if the analytic situation is fundamentally identical to the situation of intersubjectivity, the original situation of subjectivity, what is the difference between psychoanalysis and the philosophy of subjectivity?" It is this reduction of psychoanalysis to philosophy that lies behind the idea of an existential psychoanalysis advanced by Sartre, Binswanger, and others who postulate "the identity of the doctor-patient relation and an originary being-for-others, an originary *Mit-sein*, an originary intersubjectivity." Althusser concludes his first lecture by declaring Lacan's "radical, conscious, and resolute refusal" to reduce psychoanalysis to either biology or philosophy (even what Althusser has called the "personalist, humanist, intersubjectivist current" of philosophy). His refusal, however, is not an individual act of will by a resolute person "but derives from the theoretical certitude on which what he says is based."[11]

In Althusser's second lecture it becomes apparent that Lacan's certitude has a name: Spinoza. In fact, Lacan fades into the latter, disappearing altogether from the lecture and thus appearing as little more than a variant of the heresy of all heresies: Spinozism. As in the first lecture, the importance of Lacan for Althusser lies in what he refuses: in this case, any reduction of psychoanalysis to psychology. Even this heroic and intransigent refusal produces, in the case of Lacan as in the case of Freud, a paradox: "we find in Freud as we find in Lacan a double preoccupation: to separate psychoanalysis from the discipline that appears closest to it (psychology) and in contrast an attempt to attach it to disciplines that in appearance are far from it (sociology, anthropology or ethnology)."[12] There exist, according to Althusser's argument, two primary paths that lead to a reduction of the specificity of psychoanalysis to psychology. The first is that against which Lacan directed his most powerful criticisms: a psychology of a "biological subject . . . defined by its needs." The term "biological" has a very specific function in this problematic: it places the subject outside of and prior to the social or the cultural and renders the subsequent passage into culture the source of all mental difficulties. In psychoanalytic terms (and Althusser here cites the example of Anna Freud's *The Ego and the Mechanisms of Defense*), the subject by means of the ego (which assumes the function once assigned to consciousness or will) must mediate both the demands of the id (that repository of bodily instincts and hence biological needs) and the contrary demand for the renunciation of any attempt to realize these needs (at least in their primary form) by the superego, which represents the imperatives of society in internalized form. In this way, according to Althusser, "the psychological subject becomes a subject who has a biological interiority, that of the 'id,' instincts, drives, tendencies etc."[13] The unconscious, defined here as a "biological interiority" is merely the reservoir, not yet known or explored, of biological urges. According to such a model, the human subject is motivated by need, and its actions (from the simplest efforts to secure the necessities of life to the formation of societies themselves, which make the satisfaction of needs more likely) are designed to fulfill the needs arising from the body. Language itself is another means, a tool even, by which the subject of needs achieves the satisfaction of those needs: the identity of the subject and needs corresponds to the identity of language with that which it signifies. Words "stand for" things, and the ability to speak is the ability of one subject to express his needs to another in order to obtain the things he needs.

For Lacan, "it doesn't happen this way." It is Lacan's "great discovery," argues Althusser, that there is no passage from nature to culture, but rather the inverse: there is no movement from a biological subject endowed with needs entering society in order best to satisfy those needs; rather, culture recruits biological beings, which it both precedes and makes possible. There is no outside of culture, because "culture always precedes itself" and is thus the "law of culture" (which Althusser declares synonymous with Lacan's symbolic order) "that determines the passage to culture itself."[14] It is at this point that Althusser takes the discussion in a surprising but extremely fruitful direction. Lacan's argument with psychology, at least the psychology of the biological subject, is a repetition of an earlier critique of similar positions articulated in an entirely different domain: namely, Rousseau's critique of Hobbes's notion of the state of nature, and therefore the whole edifice of seventeenth- and eighteenth-century political philosophy. This genealogy is important in that it not only shows the provenance of certain key concepts but, even more importantly, the political stakes of this critique:

> What is the meaning of Rousseau's critique of Hobbes? Rousseau says to Hobbes, and in a general sense, to all the philosophers of natural rights (*droit naturel*) that they have pretended to imagine a purely natural being, when in reality they have merely projected the very structures of the social state into the state of nature. They have pretended to represent as non-cultural a being that they have in fact endowed with all the cultural properties necessary to think the social state from which they have abstracted it. . . . And it is doubtless why an important revolution in Rousseau's thought in the Second Discourse consists precisely in not thinking the problem of the passage from nature to society in terms of the individual but in terms of the species.[15]

But the psychology of the biological subject represents only one of the temptations that psychoanalysis must resist if it is to continue to develop Freud's discoveries. Anna Freud, for Althusser a privileged example of the relapse into pre-Freudian ideology, "represents, if you will, the old classical psychology, that of the 'ego' as moral subject [Althusser will have more to say about this topic shortly] resting on the duality between the interiority of the subject and the exteriority of the objective world . . . the objective world of social norms, of the dominant ethical norms in a society, of the moral demands of a society."[16] The other path to a reduction to psychology, which appears to lead elsewhere, leads finally to the same place, the theory of the moral subject.

Here, the text exploited is not Freud's but Lacan's, and the exploiter, Daniel Lagache, will seek to reabsorb Lacan's thought (as expressed in the Rome discourse of 1953) "into a philosophy of existence, into a philosophy of consciousness, into a philosophy of intentionality." In opposition to a biologistic psychology for which the unconscious is "a biological 'id,' an interior unknowable from within the subject," for a psychology of consciousness, the unconscious is "the meaning (*sens*) lived but occulted, the non-sense (*non-sens*) that always threatens lived meaning in the intentionality of consciousness." To be more precise, for Althusser, this is a psychoanalysis of intersubjectivity insofar as the unconscious is for it a form of transcendence. The unconscious is the presence of a beyond within, not just an indeterminate beyond but the beyond of intersubjectivity, "the immanence of the alter ego" or the inescapable trace of the Other, to cite another version.[17] This second psychology has, of course, merely replaced one transcendental presence with another: for the biological, it has substituted intersubjectivity. In both cases, and this is where Lacan's critique of ego psychology assumes its full importance, the ego (*le moi*) is nothing more or less than consciousness, both an awareness (actual or potential) of the other present within as well as the faculty of will necessary to achieve knowledge and act rationally on the basis of that knowledge. As Lacan insisted from the mirror stage on, the ego is characterized above all by the *méconnaissances* proper to it, by the constant deception it operates. Further, for Lacan, the unconscious is not a hidden depth or veiled meaning but the very structure into which the subject is divided.

But Althusser's critique of psychology (which moves beyond Lacan at this point) cannot content itself with an enumeration of the errors and illusions of psychology, the science of the soul. In addition, we must necessarily pose the question of the historical material existence of psychology, the question of its commencement in the world of practices and institutions, not of its ideal origins as a science of the mind. For the persistence of the term "ego," for example, should not obscure the multiple and conflicting meanings associated with this term. Among, and perhaps most important, is the concept of the subject, a concept that Althusser refrains from defining, preferring instead to describe its functions: he refers at first to "the social division of labor" in which the worker is defined as a free subject, center of initiatives, who voluntarily enters into a contract with the employer. But this concept itself is no more than a version of the notion of the subject as "the subject of imputation of a certain number of actions (*conduites*), whether moral actions or political actions. It is not by chance that the subject designates one who is subjected (*assujeti*), while according to its classical function in psychology, it designates one who is active." It is this reversal, for example, that constitutes the paradox of a psychology whose origin is manifestly political: "the subject is one who submits to an order or to a master and who is at the same time thought in psychology as being the origin of his own actions. This means that the subject is the subject of imputation who is accountable to a third party for his own actions, conduct and behavior."[18]

What is the meaning of "imputation" here? First, it presupposes a state of domination, a relation of unequal forces. To the one who is "subject" to forces that determine his actions (the free worker who is moved as surely by hunger and cold as by teargas or rubber bullets), there is imputed a subjective determination: he chose to do thus; he could have chosen otherwise. He has thus, to give the scene its true dignity and pathos, "consented" to the work contract which, originating in his free will, is legitimate and therefore binding. "Binding" is an appropriate euphemism for the punishment that may lawfully be visited upon him when, if he violates the covenant into which he freely entered and therefore of which he is a subject, he is held accountable by that third party who happens also to possess the means of coercion and punishment. There is only apparently a paradox here: subjection that is legitimate is always self-subjection, a free subject subjecting itself to an authority. In societies that regard themselves as legitimately constituted (and few states do not so consider themselves), subjects are citizens to whom is imputed the will to submit to authority. Althusser here as earlier in the lectures clearly refers to Hobbes: the fact that a free individual in the state of nature has consented to the authority of the sovereign in no way lessens his subjection to that authority; on the contrary it renders that sovereignty absolute (within the limits of life: no subject can voluntarily bring about his own death, according to Hobbes).[19]

But, for Althusser, such a "manifestly political notion" presupposes another conception of the subject, namely, the subject of truth: before Hobbes, Descartes. The Descartes that interests Althusser, however, is not the Descartes of the *Meditations*, but the author of the *Treatise on the Passions of the Soul*. Here, Althusser discovers a psychology of the ego in which truth rests on the freedom of the soul to master the pathologies that afflict it and prevent it from ascertaining the truth: inattention, confusion, poor memory, the weakness of the very will to clarity. In the absence of this freedom to direct the soul in accordance with an "ideal normality" against which the pathologies of truth are defined, there can be no apprehension of the truth.[20] There thus arises alongside the subject of truth, which corresponds to this ideal normality, a "subject of error," which haunts it like a shadow, a subject whose pathologies render it too feeble to direct itself as it should to the truth. At the same time, however, as Descartes argues, the only antidote to a weakness of will is resolution "founded only on the knowledge of truth."[21] Thus, we arrive at the following paradox: one must then already know the truth in order to fortify the soul sufficiently to undertake the arduous task of knowledge production, whose object is precisely the truth. The imputation of a subject of truth, a moral subject, a political subject, that is, the imputation of an ego or consciousness that precedes and causes the production of truth or the production of the relations of domination and servitude, thus rests on an abyss; rather than provide a foundation for truth or political legitimacy, such notions render them unthinkable. Althusser poses a series of questions: Why must the truth be expressed, and why must it be expressed in Descartes in the form of the ego? Why must the truth be expressed through the constitution of a subject of truth? Why the emergence of a subject of truth as the constitution of the truth itself? These questions do not constitute an anachronistic rejection or even merely interrogation of seventeenth-century philosophy from a twentieth-century vantage point; on the contrary, the same questions were asked and answered in the seventeenth century itself, even if the refutation of Descartes (and Hobbes) was "a refutation that disappeared into history, that was literally submerged by the development of a later problematic, and which has perhaps still not resurfaced, except in a marginal and allusive form." It will surprise no one that it was Spinoza who "escaped the category of the subject of imputation projected on the subject of objectivity, insofar as he formulated a critique of the identification of subjects, a critique of the constitution of the subject (the psychological subject, the ethical subject, the philosophical subject) as having been imposed by the structure of the imaginary, that is, by a social structure that necessarily produces this subject in order to continue to exist."[22]

Spinoza took as the very object of his critique the Cartesian cogito and the notion of the ego as the center of the cogito. The question would be whether Spinoza's abandonment of the subject of objectivity as condition of possibility of any affirmation of truth does not entail a radical modification of the subject of this pathology of truth. To put it in another way, the question would be to know if the status of the subject of the passions of the soul in Descartes, which is defined as the possibility of the alternative between error and truth and is therefore conceived on the basis of the subject of objectivity, is not profoundly modified in Spinoza precisely by virtue of his suppression of this subject of objectivity. Furthermore, does *The Passions of the Soul*, instead of opening a psychology, that is, a pathology of the subject of objectivity, open for Spinoza what one might call a theory of the imaginary?[23]

Why does Althusser formulate his arguments (or perhaps hypotheses) as questions? Certainly not for rhetorical reasons alone: the propositions concerning Spinoza's theory of the imagination that follow are elliptical and undeveloped, suggesting that Althusser was thinking out loud, moving in a direction not yet entirely clear to him. It is possible, however, and indeed necessary if we are to understand Althusser's notion of ideology, to make some of the connections left suspended in the text and situate his assertions concerning Spinoza in particular texts. The connection between the subject of truth and the subject of the passions, that is, the moral subject, and the theory of the imaginary is made very explicitly and in reference to Descartes (one of the few philosophers to be named) in the *Ethics*. Spinoza twice cites Descartes's assertion that there is no soul so weak that it cannot acquire absolute mastery over the passions, what he calls an entity of the imagination. He not only does not presuppose the existence of free will but instead, in the appendix to *Ethics* I, seeks to explain how such a notion could originate. Men believe they are free because they are conscious of their volitions and desires but have neither thought nor even dreamed about the causes that have determined them to desire and will. The notion of an act of will by a subject determined by nothing other than itself, which would be the precondition of any knowledge of the truth (a will to objectivity) that must precede knowledge as its necessary condition, a notion central to Descartes's philosophy, is thus rejected by Spinoza as an illusion. Because truth is the standard both of itself and of falsity, we must already possess true ideas before we can distinguish between the true and the false. To use a phrase very dear both to Althusser and to Foucault, we must be in the true even to formulate hypotheses to be verified. Spinoza will go so far as to say that the real problem to be answered is thus not how to accede to truth but rather how do we come to have false ideas. Further, Spinoza's denunciation of the free will as nothing more than the way human beings tend to imagine themselves (and God who is a mirror not of them as they are but as they merely believe themselves to be) necessitates a rejection of the moral subject, the individual as the unconditioned origin of action and speech. But the moral subject, thus defined, is not just any entity of the imagination: it is invested with extraordinary significance and is thus laden with consequences; the moral subject is thus necessarily a pathological subject from the perspective of the norm to which it inevitably fails to conform, that is, a bad subject who is detested for simultaneously failing to be what it is not possible for him to be and for being what he necessarily is.

It is precisely this point that returns us to Althusser's discussion of the relevance of Spinoza's theory of the imaginary. If the notion of the subject whose actions are determined by nothing other than itself is an imaginary notion, does this mean that it is nothing more than a subjective illusion, that is an illusion on the side of (and internal to) the subject, a false belief that it has about itself? For Althusser, the answer is no: the imaginary is not mere illusion, because the imaginary would no longer be for Spinoza "a psychological function, that is, a function internal to the mind, but would almost be, in the Hegelian sense of the term, an element, that is, a totality in which psychological functions are inserted and on the basis of which they are constituted." Althusser thus insists that for Spinoza the imaginary exists outside of and prior to the mind of the individual. He concludes his counterposition of Spinoza and Descartes by the complete desubjectification of the imagination: "the imagination is not a faculty of the soul, it is not a faculty of a psychological subject, imagination is a world."[24] What then is the nature of this element or world of the imaginary? The reference to Hegel (an interestingly positive reference at a time in Althusser's career when few such references to Hegel and to totality could be found) might appear to point in the direction of a kind of *Weltgeist*, a totality or (to employ the terms of "Marxism and Humanism") a system of images that both precedes and exceeds individuals. But Althusser instead invokes the Spinozist distinction between the (three) kinds of knowledge in part two of the *Ethics*. There imagination is no longer merely the mental or spiritual act by which an individual pictures that which is not present to the senses, but rather the imagination is a nonmental, nonspiritual transindividual element in which images circulate by means of bodies encountering other bodies, immanent in those encounters. To the extent that such encounters are inescapable, so is the imagination.

But Althusser is more interested in what he calls the most remarkable example of the imagination in Spinoza, the example of its historical existence as described in the *Tractatus Theologico-Politicus*. Spinoza, he argues, relates the functions of psychological subjects, and in particular of the prophets, to their function in this world of the imaginary. It is not the subjects who are the origin of the world of the imaginary, but rather it is the reverse: subjects are functions of this world. For Spinoza, the message of the prophets (and he begins his discussion of prophecy by reminding us that the Hebrew word for prophet means "interpreter") is determined less by the God who was the source of that which was to be interpreted than by the material circumstances of the particular prophet. The cultivated man would perceive God's mind in a cultivated way, the rustic would inevitably have a vision of cows and oxen, whereas a soldier's vision would involve armies in battle. Here, the imaginary does not only exist external to the individual subjects, determining the content of the individual imagination, but it is itself determined (again in content, if not in form) by the material conditions that characterize its historical moment). If Althusser left his argument at this point, however, there would be little to distinguish it from the very model of base and superstructure that he criticized so convincingly during the same period. But he did go further, concluding his lecture with a statement that points the way to all that will be most fruitful in his subsequent work on ideology: "it was not by accident that Spinoza escaped the category of the subject of imputation projected onto the subject of objectivity, insofar as he formulated a critique of the identification of subjects, a critique of the constitution of the subject (the psychological subject, the ethical subject, the philosophical subject) as having been imposed by the structure of the imaginary, that is, by a social structure that necessarily produces this subject in order to exist."[25]

Element, world, social structure: Althusser has not only desubjectified the imaginary (it is no longer a mental act or state and thus is no longer contained in the individual), he has excluded any notion of the ideality of the imaginary, its externality to a material world defined as real. But even as he moves from element to social structure he defers any characterization of its specific existence. At the same time, the subject is no longer understood as an illusion or fantasy, but now as a form necessarily imposed upon the individual by a social structure that needs to impute free will, responsibility, and guilt upon the individuals that compose it. Althusser has thus posed the problem of the constitution of the subject, that is, of explaining the particular necessity that produces it. Such an explanation requires in turn an explanation of the process of production, and the means of production. At this point, terms like *world* or *social structure* no longer suffice and in fact appear as nothing more than gestures in the direction of the materiality proper to the imaginary, a materiality that could never be separated from that of ideology. Althusser's second lecture from the 1964 seminar on psychoanalysis ends without further reference to Lacan; indeed, its crescendo is the gigantomachy that pits Spinoza against Descartes in an epic battle that in no way belongs to the past. This battle is our present, if not our future, extending before us and all around us: there is no neutral territory to which we might flee given that the very idea of neutrality is one of the ruses employed in the battle itself. Althusser had not yet finished with psychoanalysis (or Lacan). It was to this field that he would return to answer the very questions that he had posed in his extraordinary seminar.

In 1966 Althusser made his own linguistic term. In a series of drafts written for the consumption of his inner circle, Althusser reformulated the problems he had encountered in the 1963–64 texts on psychoanalysis and ideology, declaring the existence of a conceptual link between the concepts of the unconscious and ideology. The "Three Notes on the Theory of Discourse" marks a decisive shift in Althusser's thought in that he attempts for the first time to specify the materiality of both ideology and the unconscious, eliminating the entire lexicon of interiority according to which an inner world would stand opposed to an outer world.[26] Such an attempt necessitated in turn a theorization of the constitution of the subject, a theorization already implicit in Althusser's notion of the subject of imputation. Althusser begins by asserting that psychoanalysis is a "regional theory" that can explain "the structure and function of its object" but which nevertheless lacks the "general theory" that would "provide objective proof of its scientificity" by relating this object differentially to other neighboring theoretical objects.[27] Althusser here repeats an argument he has already made on a number of occasions: most attempts to construct a general theory have failed insofar as they sought to reduce the unconscious to "some other theoretical object (that of biology, psychology, philosophy etc.)."[28] Freud himself never ceded to this temptation, even as he borrowed from other theories in order to think the general theory that finally eluded him. Lacan went further: his work exhibits "1) an awareness of the need to elaborate a general theory; 2) a correct [Althusser later amended "correct" to "certain"] conception of the nature of a general theory; and 3) the beginning of an elaboration of this general theory."[29] To make Lacan's achievements visible, Althusser draws a line of demarcation through Lacan's texts separating "his use of linguistics"[30] from "the (highly ambiguous) use to which he puts the thought of certain philosophers (Plato, Hegel, Heidegger). It is quite striking that the use to which Lacan puts linguistics in elaborating the concepts of psychoanalytic theory is totally exempt from the effects of misperception (méconnaissance) that haunt these examples."[31] Even Lacan's use of linguistics, however, encounters the "objective limits" that prevent him from moving forward. In particular he is faced with the temptation either to declare linguistics (in its current state of development) as the general theory of psychoanalysis, or, in opposition, to declare psychoanalysis the general theory of linguistics (and perhaps the "human sciences" more broadly).[32]

At this point, Althusser sets out to establish "the character of the unconscious."[33] The unconscious is not the latent content of the manifest, that is, the essence behind or beneath appearances. The unconscious "exists in its effects"[34] and nowhere else and its effects take the form of a discourse, the discourse of the unconscious, which, Althusser goes on to argue, is one among a number of "forms of discourse," including ideological discourse, scientific discourse, and aesthetic discourse.[35] Later in his exposition, he will face the consequences of such an argument head on: to posit the unconscious as a "discourse" is to so desubjectify it that we lose sight of that to which the discourse of the unconscious must ultimately refer, namely the drives, both libidinal and aggressive, that must "lie behind or between the lines of this discourse. . . . Something that finds expression in its words or that slips in between them."[36] Althusser's uncompromising response: the passions and their intensity are "nothing but this discourse itself" in relation to which there is no inside or outside, only the discourse and its effects. It is this discourse and nothing else that "the analyst encounters in his practice: if I affirm that unconscious discourse 'produces the libido effect,' I do so in order to show that the libido is so far from being external, anterior or transcendent to the forms of 'its' discourse that we can conceive of it as the specific effect of that discourse."[37]

The notion of discourse has thus allowed Althusser to abandon the concepts whose use by others he found so unsatisfactory, even as he couldn't quite avoid employing them himself: the notions of consciousness, interiority, lived experience, etc., the references to a subjective world in opposition to the objective. But, having embarked on an exploration of the material objective reality of discourse, he immediately encountered the question of discourse itself: what was its specific character? Here, Althusser cautions us that discourse is not identical to the object of the same name conceived of by linguistics. Discourse as he understands it exceeds the domain of linguistics and to theorize it would be to call into question some of its most important concepts. The very opposition of *langue* and *parole* (and, by extension, competence and performance) is problematized by the notion of discourse which is neither the system of elements combined according to rules (*langue*), nor the individual "use" of that system (*parole*), but the actualized state of language in which such an opposition is possible. Althusser would go so far as to argue that "language (*la langue*) does not exist: only discourses exist."[38] If discourse is not the system of elements and the rules of their combination the existence of which is always potential, greater than that which can ever be actualized, neither can it be understood as possessing the concrete existence of a practice: "the structure of a discourse is not that of a practice. Not only because a discourse produces only effects of, let us say, meaning, whereas practices produce real modifications-transformations in existing objects, and, at the limit, new real objects (economic practice, political practice, theoretical practice, etc.). This does not mean that the discourses cannot have effects on real objects, but they do so only by virtue of their insertion-articulation into the practices in question, which then make use of them as instruments in the 'labor process' of these practices."[39]

This passage highlights the contradiction that continues to haunt Althusser's effort to develop a theory of ideology: even as he separates himself from any sense of ideology as a form of consciousness, as possessing an existence internal to the mind by positing it as a system of images (Spinoza's imaginary) or a kind of discourse, he nevertheless re-creates a kind of dualism. Just as in "Marxism and Humanism," the imaginary stands outside of and opposed to the real, so in the "Three Notes" discourse appears less real than practice. It produces effects, Althusser agrees, but only effects of "meaning." Practices, in contrast, produce "real" effects. Discourse is thus situated outside of reality, its effects incapable of affecting that reality, given that these effects remain internal to the realm of discourse itself: effects of meaning, linking words or "signifiers" (a term that Althusser finally rejects as inescapably caught up in a notion of language as representation). To escape what threatens to become an unbridgeable gap between the discursive and the real, Althusser reaches for the following expedient: discourses are not condemned to hover insubstantially over a world that they cannot affect. They can and do act effectively on real objects but only by virtue of being "inserted into" or "articulated to" practices which then make use of discourses. It is perfectly obvious, for Althusser himself has provided all the means necessary to analyze his own dilemma, that he has arrived at the very problem that confronts every form of dualism, a problem made particularly visible in Descartes's fantastic "solution" to it. Substances that are as separate as mind and body, matter or spirit, or, in this case, discourse (or language) and reality (or being), substances whose very exteriority constitutes their reason for being (so, for example, that the spirit will not be contaminated by matter, or the soul by the flesh) offer no point of contact at which the one might affect the other. Hence, the need for the pineal gland. Here Althusser repeats the very dualist gesture he has denounced in others: if discourses are not in the real, how can they be "used" by practices to produce real effects?

Althusser, however, is saved by his own inconsistency. For it appears that discourses, despite what he has just said, produce at least one very real effect (that is simultaneously discursive and nondiscursive, which thus become, in Spinoza's sense, not two distinct substances but two ways of understanding a single reality), an effect in no way reducible to "meaning": "If we compare the different existing forms of discourse, that is, the forms represented by unconscious discourse, ideological discourse, aesthetic discourse and scientific discourse, we can demonstrate the existence of a common effect: every discourse produces a subjectivity effect. Every discourse has as its necessary correlate a subject which is one of the effects, if not the major effect, of its functioning."[40]

By the end of the "Three Notes" Althusser will modify his position. Not all discourses "produce" a subject position; on the contrary, that effect can be traced to ideology (or, at this point, ideological discourse) alone. Let us therefore trace Althusser's exposition of the constitution of the subject, now no longer an illusion or an error but an effect. The subject produced by ideology is now not merely the mythical origin imputed to actions and practices to render them either legitimate or illegitimate as the case may be, but possesses a structure that Althusser sets out to describe: the subject "possesses a structure of speculary centering; the subject induced is duplicated by a producing subject (the empirical subject duplicated by a transcendental subject, the man-subject by God, etc."[41] If the subject is "centered," as it must be to give its consent or voluntarily alienate its labor power, its centering is "speculary," a duplication. The idea of the speculary here is derived less from Lacan than from Ludwig Feuerbach, on whose work Althusser was at that moment preparing to write. In spring 1967 he produced a substantial but unfinished manuscript on Feuerbach, which repeats in a more developed form some of the ideas explored in the "Three Notes."

Althusser claimed to find in Feuerbach's text's the effects of a "ruse of unreason";[42] although the latter produced a theory of ideology (one that was employed without modification by the early Marx), his theory could in no way serve "as the foundation of a (Marxist) theory of ideology." Even in its inadequacy, however, in the midst of its errors and unreason, Feuerbach's theory "does provide us with a remarkable description of certain essential features of the structure of ideology."[43] For Feuerbach, God is not a fiction or myth, the product of ignorance and fear or a noble fiction created by priests and despots; God is nothing less than the alienated essence of man, an essence that (for reasons Feuerbach cannot entirely explain) can only be grasped in the form of externality, an essence proper to an other. The formulation in the "Three Notes" ("the induced subject is duplicated by a producing subject")[44] suggests that the duplication proper to ideology rests on an inequality between the terms: one represents, while the other is the represented, one produces while the other is produced. That which, for Feuerbach, is initially experienced as the object set in opposition to the experiencing subject is revealed by the gesture of unveiling, the fundamental gesture of philosophy, not to be an object at all, but the "Supreme Subject," who is not only the alienated essence of the individual subject confronting this object (and the entire world as it is experienced by the subject is nothing more than the consciousness that apprehends this world, even as it persists in regarding it as other), but an essence that transcends the individual, the species being of which he is only a partial manifestation.[45] But this only captures the fact of inequality, or its form: its content is the unrecognized "absolute subordination of the first subject to the Second Subject," a subordination that, according to Althusser, is both moral (and political) and epistemological. Moral because the first subject is "accountable to the Second Subject" and by virtue of this accountability can be said to be "subjected to the Second Subject, who is Sovereign and Judge."[46] The much vaunted freedom or agency of the subject is simultaneously constituted as responsibility before a power ready to hold the subject accountable and with the means to punish if the subject should be found guilty. The subject's freedom is thus not an abstract freedom, the freedom that one would enjoy in a void; it is instead, a freedom to obey or disobey commands that precede him and in relation to which his actions become something other than involuntary motion of the body, the commands of the Subject, producer and maker, to whom he owes his very existence, in the absence of which freedom and agency have no meaning. At that same time, the subject cannot know he is a subject unless he is recognized as such by the Subject, whose existence as Sovereign alone will guarantee that the subject truly exists as subject: "the speculary relation is asymmetrical and unequal, and . . . its true foundation is this speculary inequality."[47] Althusser has thus shown that Feuerbach's text does something other than what it says it does: in an important sense, it is not man who is at the center (and origin) of this speculary relation to whom might be reduced the entire edifice of religion, but rather God who necessarily precedes the creation to which he alone brings meaning and purpose as its guarantee and foundation. Without meaning to, Feuerbach has produced a theory of the Other whose alienated essence we are and to whom we must be returned in order finally to recover our truth. Although Althusser says remarkably little about Spinoza in the Feuerbach text (and Spinoza was a central reference point for Feuerbach), it is worth noting that Spinoza nearly alone among philosophers discusses the subject-Subject relation in a way that deprives it of any center, grasping it not as a being and its reflection, but as a reflection without an object, or a reflection whose object is always only another reflection. There can be, for him, no inversion of theology into anthropology or the reverse since neither term is primary over the other, the couple Man-God being nothing more than two sides of a single illusion, although an illusion that possesses a material existence and produces the very material effects of sadness, guilt, and pain necessary to a regime of perpetual subjection.

The "Three Notes," however, not only specifies the "structure" of the subject proper to ideology, describing the decentering necessary to the postulation of a center (and thus condemning ideology to a perpetual quest for a unity that it cannot achieve), but it seeks to describe the processes through which the subject is constituted and the forms of necessity that makes it what it is. Ideology (or here ideological discourse) "performs the function" assigned to it by the economic base of a given society: "In every social formation, the base requires the support (Träger) function as a function to be assumed, as a place to be occupied in the technical and social division of labor. . . . It is ideology which performs the function of designating the subject (in general) that is to fulfill this function."[48] The economy of a given society requires a mass of individuals who will fulfill the functions necessary to it. Ideology "recruits" the "bearers" of these functions. "Recruits" is an interesting verb here: individuals are picked from an undifferentiated mass, singled out, removed from it and endowed with a unique identity, as if such a singling out or separation of individuals were necessary to the functioning of the economy. To capture the different facets of the action thus described, Althusser introduces, for the first time in his work, the term *interpellation*: "Ideology interpellates individuals by constituting them as subjects (ideological subjects, and therefore subjects of its discourse) and by furnishing them the reasons-of-a-subject (interpellated as a subject) for assuming the functions defined by the structure as functions-of-a Träger."[49]

Interpellate is a term that itself requires some discussion. Although translated as "hail," in the sense that we hail someone from afar, calling to them, it has a very particular resonance in French that 'hail" doesn't capture. In the context of the mass mobilizations and subsequent repression of the period, one of the meanings of interpellation emerges as essential: one is "stopped" by the police and therefore singled out from a crowd or singularized in relation to a background. To be thus singled out is to be ascribed an identity, which one is then called upon to verify (today by means of one's "papers" or "I.D."). To be called upon in this way is both then to be separated from others and to be regarded as able to identify oneself, to answer questions that presuppose the agency of the individual in question: not only, "Who are you?" but also, "Where are you going?" "What are you doing here?" etc. In this sense, interpellation both separates the individual and simultaneously declares the individual the cause of his own actions which, except in the case of "accidents" or "circumstances beyond his control," he has voluntarily committed. To be thus declared responsible (morally, because causally) is to be declared free, or rather to have been free before one was interpellated, and therefore a moral and legal subject. Althusser insists again on the speculary relation of the interpellation by which individuals are singled out and endowed with the gift of freedom (or rather again the gift of having been free before being "detained"—this is the meaning of the "subject of imputation"), the status of a moral and legal subject, who unlike a slave or servant is determined by no one other than himself. An individual must be interpellated by an other to whom he must account for himself and his actions to become a subject. This specular relation is, as Althusser has explained, an unequal relation; in fact, "interpellation" as opposed to "recognition" implies an inequality of force: we obey the police officer and furnish proof of our identity (the singularity of a face or a fingerprint) who stops us not because we require his recognition to become conscious of ourselves as subjects, but because he demands it of us and his demand takes place in the context of physical constraint, real or threatened, together with violence and physical pain enacted or left in suspension. It is in fact, as Althusser noted in a handwritten addendum to the "Three Notes," "the Prefecture of Police who furnishes the individuals whom policemen interpellate the identity papers that these policemen request (demand) that one show."[50]

Althusser, however, does not go on to specify the material circumstances within which the specular relation of interpellation takes place, except insofar as we can speak of the materiality of discourse: up to this point Althusser regards interpellation as a discursive effect, even the separation of the individual from the mass is conceived as a discursive separation, a summoning in speech or writing of an individual thus imputed with the properties of a moral subject. The ambiguities that characterize Althusser's concept of discourse allow his argument to regress toward the very vocabulary of interiority and even consciousness from which he has otherwise disengaged himself. Interpellation is neither a "commandment," an act of "naked violence," nor "an injunction pure and simple," he tells us, but "an enterprise of conviction-persuasion."[51] It is ideology that "must guarantee itself to the subject."[52] To follow Althusser's argument is to conclude that the subject precedes its own interpellation; that is, its own constitution insofar as it must be persuaded to undertake the act of recognition which, in the absence of such persuasion, it would not consent to undertake. Subjection in the double sense of the term begins with self-subjection. The subject according to this strain in Althusser's thought is no longer "imputed" except in the sense that it imputes to itself in an originary act the status of subject which, if successfully "persuaded," will subject itself. Thus interpellation begins, logically if not chronologically, with the subject's recognizing himself in order then to be recognized by the other, constituting himself within himself as subject in order to be able then to recognize the recognition that the other extends to him. The stark contradiction that animates Althusser's attempt to think interpellation in the "Three Notes," the contradiction between a notion of interiority as constituted from the outside and a notion of an interiority that precedes and founds the outside is captured in his example, again, from religious discourse. "Hence the duplication [redoublement] of the subject within the structure of ideology: God, in his various forms. 'I am that I am,' the subject [note the lower case] par excellence, who guarantees to the subject that he is truly a subject, and that he is the subject whom the subject is addressing."[53] God is thus a "subject" before he is the "Subject;" an act of self-affirmation, the positing of the subject by itself (I am that I am), that is, a doubling of the subject by which it not only is affirmed but affirms itself and knows itself to be affirming itself, necessarily precedes what emerges as a second duplication of the subject into subject-Subject. Each individual subject must be as a God in order then to subject himself, by his own action, to God.

But even this strain in Althusser's text exhibits its own contradictions. For if, according to this line of argumentation, there must exist an element outside of the material mechanism of interpellation in order to supply it with the foundation of "conviction-persuasion" that it requires in order to "take" that which, within each individual, must be persuaded to subject itself in order to be subjected, the operation of interpellation does not leave this element undisturbed. Althusser goes on to argue that the very "interpellation of human individuals as subjects"—that is, the process by which an individual comes to speak of himself in the first person in order to account for himself to the Other, the Subject who is judge and Sovereign, and therefore the process by which the individual is imputed ownership of and responsibility for the speech and actions said to be his—"produces a specific effect in them, the unconscious effect."[54] If it is in ideological discourse that individuals are assigned a subject position, the very same process produces a discourse of the unconscious. Althusser stresses the simultaneity of these discourses: there can be no genesis of the unconscious in ideology or the inverse. Instead, like the simultaneity of mind and body in Spinoza, the discourse that constitutes subjects is doubled by a discourse that "ejects" the subject it produces or rather produces an always-already ejected subject, a subject whose place is always empty. Althusser will add, although we will want to question the compatibility of this addition to the body of the argument, that the production of the discourse of the unconscious is necessary in that it "enables these human individuals to assume the function of ideological subjects."[55] Soon afterward, Althusser will have to confront the fact that he has produced or appears at least to have produced a functionalist argument, warning his interlocutors that the ideas of the unconscious being essential to the functioning of the ideological and produced by it "represent nothing more than first approximations, introduced not in order to solve the problem of the constitution of the unconscious, but in order to think the determinations of its articulation with and in a particular reality."[56]

It is, of course, possible to follow Althusser's suggestions and move in the direction of theorizing an essential link between Marxism and psycho-analysis, with their respective objects ideology and the unconscious and their structures and elements (Subject, Other, Law etc.).[57] It may, however, be worth considering whether Althusser's invocation of psychoanalysis and more particularly, the unconscious, here as elsewhere, does not serve instead a more restricted but perhaps vital role: that of excluding any recourse to a conception of consciousness, no matter how subtle or mediated. The notion that inescapably accompanying the constitution of a subject is the process by which the subject is ejected undermines any stable foundation for the "conviction-persuasion" by which Althusser wants to argue ideology oper-ates. In place of this foundation is an oscillation between presence and ab-sence such that the question of "whom" ideological discourse addresses itself becomes undecidable. At this point it is no longer possible to conceive of ideology as a discourse that interpellates someone who already exists to recognize himself in the specular image and respond to the summons of the Subject. The "individual" interpellated emerges from Althusser's argument as its unthought remainder, neither biological nor psychological. If it is to be theorized, the very notion of ideological interpellation must be recast.

Althusser and Foucault
Apparatuses of Subjection

Spinoza showed that, paradoxically, no text was more difficult to read than the Bible, whose very ubiquity identified it with the rise of mass literacy in seventeenth-century Europe. In part, the difficulty of reading the Bible derived from the fact that it was so often and so universally read that certain habits of interpretation had become inseparable from the experience of reading the text itself. Even for the reader forewarned against them, the task of disencumbering oneself of the prejudices and assumptions that inevitably accompanied every reading, imposing one meaning instead of another (or, indeed, others), establishing certain connections while suppressing or ignoring others, was no easy task. But Spinoza insisted that this difficulty did not simply, or primarily, exist in the mind of the reader but in the text itself in its literal existence. Translations (which presupposed certain interpretations not only of words and phrases but of narrative events and the doctrines they were said to illustrate) and even editions of the Hebrew text itself connected the disjointed and resolved the discrepant, with the justification that the original itself was irrecoverably lost. Commentary (often designed to reconcile the apparent contradictions in the Scripture) was thus not simply superimposed upon the text but was now woven into it. To read the Bible with Spinoza was then actively to recover its original unevenness and inconsistency by interjecting the empty spaces in the full space of the text. Such an act consists both of a rejection of previous interpretations and an active intervention in the text itself to restore the absences that were not so much properties of the original text as signs of the fact that there never was an original text that was itself not already a composite. To follow Spinoza and with him, especially on this point, Althusser, one of his most perceptive readers, however, is to recognize that a reading of this type cannot originate in a mere act of will on the part of the reader, as if all that had been lacking up to this point were sufficient resolve or attention, but rather this kind of reading must itself accompany an encounter between the body of the text and other bodies in which their very conjunction determines the production of new effects.

We would do well to bear this lesson in mind when approaching Althusser's most widely read and influential text, "Ideology and Ideological State Apparatuses."[1] The editorial history of this text, as I have already noted, follows a path uncannily similar to the history of the Hebrew Bible, from an initial foregrounding of its fragmentary nature to a suppression of the ellipses, spaces, and lines by which Althusser initially called attention to the fact that parts, perhaps important parts, were excluded from the text and that it was thus not only provisional, as he liked to repeat, but both discontinuous and unfinished. In 1970 Althusser described it as consisting of "extracts" from an ongoing study," perhaps a more optimistic view of the project of which it was the sole published expression than that expressed in the version published in 1995 in which he tells us that the text "is composed of fragments from an originally much longer study."[2] The language of "extracts" and "fragments" might lead us to regard the posthumous publication of the manuscript from which the "Ideology" essay was taken as the solution to the problem of reading the text. We might imagine that by returning the essay to its original source (it was published as *Sur la reproduction* in 1995, with at least one of the extant complete drafts bearing the title "De la superstructure" in Althusser's handwriting) we could both identify what was removed or excluded from the published version and replace what was originally there. In fact, the text of "De la superstructure," far from clarifying the "Ideology" essay, only adds an additional layer of difficulties.[3]

"De la superstructure" belongs to a genre of writing that Althusser dabbled in repeatedly during the late sixties and early seventies: the manual, in particular the manual of Marxism-Leninism. A work of this type (whose audience exceeds the boundaries of academia) will not only explain "the fundamental principles of Marxist-Leninist Theory" but will do so, as Althusser wrote in his "Reply to John Lewis," "plainly and clearly, in a way that can be understood by all our comrades."[4] This was at least what Althusser wanted to write, or said that he wanted to write; it is not, however, what he wrote. Both "De la superstructure" and "Ideology" exhibit a striking combination of a crude rehearsal of a "fundamental principles" "-like mode of production, base, and superstructure and absolutely unprecedented notions like the interpellation of the subject, whose exposition in "plain" language renders them more rather than less obscure, more rather than less open to misunderstanding. Much of what Althusser excluded from the published version pertains to "fundamental principles";" much, but not all, and herein lies one of the insoluble mysteries of the text.

All of this could, and in fact to an extent did, divert the attention of critics and readers of the "Ideology" essay from that which was an irreversible break with all preceding theories of ideology, which, once noted, prevents any regression back to a notion of ideology as ideality in both senses of the term: a system made up of ideas that in turn possesses an ideal (i.e., immaterial) existence of the conviction-persuasion of the minds of individuals who then determine themselves (or more precisely, their bodies) to act in witting or unwitting obedience to this system. Althusser poses a fundamental question, the answer to which will allow us to begin to define ideology: "how is the reproduction of the relations of production secured [assurée]?"[5] Beyond the physical maintenance and reproduction of the worker, beyond reproduction of the skills necessary to a given level of development of the productive forces, the subjection of the worker itself must be reproduced. It is not enough that a worker has ingested sufficient calories and possesses sufficient knowledge to perform the activity proper to his place in the economy; this only defines him as capable of performing his allotted task. The processes that actually determine him to do so, that determine him to be a worker rather than a vagrant or criminal, must also be specified. Marx, of course, already advanced his own version of an explanation: in addition to the sphere of production, which guarantees, under normal conditions at least, the physical survival of the worker and whatever offspring he may have, there must exist a supplement to this sphere, an ideological superstructure that arises on the basis of the sphere of economic production and exists in order to rationalize it. Even as Althusser recognized that the base-superstructure model marked an absolutely decisive turning point in the conception of society, culture, literature, and art insofar as one could never again regard culture as independent and innocent of the relations of exploitation and subjection upon which it rested, it remained little more than a theoretical holding operation that allowed this essential point to be defended, even as it could go no further.

The base-superstructure model rested on a profound dualism: the materiality of the economic as opposed to the ideality of the superstructure, a realm of bodies and a realm of minds. Althusser moved beyond this model, not by rejecting it but by drawing a line of demarcation within it. For even as Marx referred to the superstructure as the place where people become conscious of the real relations that determine them, he simultaneously placed at the heart of this "ideological superstructure" a very material element: the state. There is nothing ideal or immaterial about the army, the police, the courts, or the prisons; it is impossible to conceive of them or of their role in the reproduction of the relations of production without recognizing the materiality of their interventions, which involve confinement, pain, and death as means to secure "obedience to the law." Marx, of course, recognized this fact not only in his analyses of the revolutions of 1848 and the Paris Commune but even in *Capital* itself, where the role of legal and state violence in the emergence of capitalism is described in lurid detail. If the relation of the state as part of the superstructure to the economic infrastructure is no longer one of the ideal to the material, of the expression to that which is expressed, then the ontological hierarchy between base and superstructure begins to collapse. How does this collapse challenge existing notions not simply of the state but of the plainly ideological, a phenomenon as apparently dependent on something more real than itself in its illusory existence as religion? Here, Althusser takes the decisive step, a step that separates him from all previous attempts to theorize ideology, including his own.

The reproduction of the relations of production is secured by two kinds of state apparatuses. The first is the Repressive State Apparatus (RSA), possessing all the means of coercion and violence used or merely brandished against those, workers and others, who fail to respect the laws of property (by occupations, strikes, and even slowdowns) or public order (with "riots," demonstrations, and picket lines). The second is not an apparatus in the singular but a set of apparatuses united by the fact that they secure the relations of production not by violence but, and this is as symptomatic a gesture as any Althusser analyzes in others, "by ideology." The RSA "'functions by violence,' while the Ideological State Apparatuses [ISAs] 'function by ideology.'"[6] No statement in the "Ideology" essay so cogently exhibits the contradiction that animates it from beginning to end as this. Of course, the statement that ISAs function by ideology is formally speaking an empty tautology (at least until Althusser defines ideology), but by opposing it to the violence of the RSA, he appears to endorse a political dualism of force and consent (terms that, it should be noted, are conspicuously absent from the essay and from Althusser's work in general), of a double but asymmetrical domination that exercises force and violence on the body, but force only as a last resort, the preferred mode of domination being that which persuades the mind to choose of its own irreducibly free will to subject itself to the powers that be. The servitude that is freely chosen will prove much more durable than that which is forced upon an unwilling subject in that it is lived as legitimate and lawful. Ideology here becomes indoctrination, the inculcation of beliefs (whether true or false) that will inevitably find expression in the actions of the individuals who "possess" them. There thus appears a linear sequence: ideas (the ruling ideas) are communicated to individuals who form beliefs that cause them to act. That such a sequence is fundamentally incompatible with the elements of Althusser's definition of ideology in the final section of the essay did not prevent many readers from taking the "Ideology" essay as a variant of the traditional theory of ideology. For this very reason, it is worth (re)tracing the line of demarcation that separates what is new and unprecedented in this extraordinarily complex and heterogeneous work from the images, words, and even concepts that preserve a continuity with nearly everything that has previously been said about ideology.

In fact, the most important word in the phrase "the Ideological State Apparatuses function by ideology" was all but elided from the innumerable critiques and interpretations: namely, the term, "apparatuses."[7] Outraged critics immediately took Althusser to task for grounding ideology in the state, thereby neglecting the distinction between the state and civil society, public and private, force and consent. The fact that Althusser explicitly rejected these distinctions, referring somewhat disingenuously to Gramsci, for whom these distinctions were far from unimportant, was seldom addressed. What these critics failed to recognize in Althusser's argument was the fact that making ideology not a set of ideas, beliefs, or convictions contained in the minds, the inner world of individuals who would then act upon these ideas, but instead containing it within an apparatus, fully material and external to the mind of the individual, not only rendered the idea of consent meaningless but made visible the way in which the very notion of consent is inextricably bound up with the forms of subjection characteristic of capitalist societies. Critics thus focused on "state" and "ideology," overlooking the "apparatus" in a way that preserved intact not only previous theories of ideology but all the oppositions that sustained them: matter and spirit, mind and body, force and consent. This oversight, of course, was not simply a fault on the part of his readers, a failure to direct sustained attention to what Althusser actually said, but was already inscribed within the text itself as an element that, however uneasily and at whatever cost, co-existed with what was genuinely new in the essay.

And what was genuinely new is almost exclusively contained in the section "On Ideology," in the context of which alone the definition of ideology as existing in apparatuses that function by ideology takes on meaning. The very persistence of the term "ideology," together with "the imaginary" and "the real," undeniably prevented most readers from understanding the extent to which Althusser's arguments were incompatible with all previous theories of ideology. To read this section carefully, however, is to see the way in which Althusser regarded himself, as he said of Marx and Freud, as "a fatherless child," compelled by circumstances "to be his own father" and to fabricate as best he could, with the materials at hand, the theoretical space within which something new could be thought.[8] While the formulation "the ISAs function by ideology" tends to reinforce rather than problematize existing notions of ideology when it first appears in the text, Althusser proceeds to complicate the notion of ideology to such an extent that there remains in it very little of what was traditionally associated with the term, even if, in a gesture whose meaning remains undecidable, Althusser persisted in using terms whose ambiguity allowed something new to be thought even in the guise of the old.[9] We should be very careful about assigning this gesture a strategic function like that of the double truth that Leo Strauss claimed to discern in Maimonides and Spinoza, the gesture that simultaneously reveals and conceals a truth deemed too profound for most readers. Such a reading of Althusser prevents us from grasping the combined and uneven development of the concepts underpinning the theory of ideology that emerges.

Two short paragraphs suffice to allow Althusser to draw an initial line of demarcation within the concept of ideology, making visible on the one side a theory of the genesis of ideas (whether this genesis is ideal or material is irrelevant to Althusser) and on the other a space that he opens by stating four theses. These theses, he emphasizes, while not exactly mere "improvisations," will have to be "supported and tested, that is, confirmed or rectified" by other future studies. Althusser's first thesis, in all its apparent simplicity, gave rise to absolutely divergent interpretations. "Ideology has no history" appeared to repeat the formulation, so disturbing to many readers of *For Marx*, that ideology would not disappear even when classes and exploitation disappeared but was the necessary condition of social life. Althusser, however, responded provocatively that the proponents of the theory of the eventual disappearance of ideology presupposed a version of the same thesis, albeit a "positivist" version with little in common with Althusser's. For them, as for Marx in the 1840s, ideology had no history in the sense that it was a shadowy reflection of a reality entirely external to itself, whose transformations it automatically expressed: "it is the pale, empty, inverted reflection of real history." And, although Althusser does not say it explicitly, the logic of his argument leads to the conclusion that such a theory is also a functionalist theory of ideology: societies create the ideologies they need to allow them to realize their ends. Ideologies are thus explained by their functions, apart from which they have no existence. In Althusser's essay, in contrast, the statement "ideology has no history" excludes a functionalist theory of ideology, instead raising questions about "the structure and functioning" that make ideology "a non-historical, that is, omni-historical reality in the sense that this structure and functioning are, in the same form, immutably present in what is called the whole of history." Citing the notion of Freud's statement that "the unconscious is eternal," Althusser specifies that by "eternal" or "omni-historical" he does not mean "transcendent to all (temporal) history" but rather immanent in it. The immanence of ideology is "organically linked" to the immanence of the unconscious, an immanence Althusser had begun to explore in "Three Notes on the Theory of Discourses" as the simultaneity of the constitution of subjects and the empty place that such a constitution leaves as its remainder.[10]

In fact, it is at this point, that is, at the end of the discussion of "ideology has no history," that Althusser announces that he is "approaching the central thesis on the structure and functioning of ideology," although he leaves the reader in suspense, saying nothing more about this "central thesis," which is that of the interpellation of the individual as subject. It may appear that Althusser has simply given public expression to the concept first developed some years earlier in "Three Notes," but to follow the ensuing pages of the "Ideology" essay is to find the concept radically transformed, along with the concept of ideology to which it is linked. To open the way to what he regards as the central thesis on the structure and function of ideology, two preliminary theses are required, "one negative, the other positive."[11]

Althusser states the negative thesis in two slightly different versions in rapid succession (the versions are separated by an interval of two sentences); "ideology is a 'representation' of the imaginary relation of individuals to their real conditions of existence," and "ideology represents the imaginary relation of individuals to their real conditions of existence."[12] We might dismiss the inconsistency as a mere infelicity were it not for the fact that the discrepancy appears in both the original and the published version, and we know that Althusser reviewed the published text line by line. It is not necessary to attempt to discover Althusser's intention here, or even to declare the inconsistency and effect of a certain theoretical blindness. It is instead enough to judge the discrepancy by its effects. In the first version of the thesis, "representation" (in quotation marks in the text) appears to describe not what ideology does (which would require a verb, as in the second version) but what it is, its nature: ideology is a representation (a formula that appears to repeat, although in an arguably less rigorous manner, the definition of ideology as "a system of representations" from 1964). To make the matter even more obscure, ideology is a representation of something that is already itself "imaginary," and it is therefore like Plato's "phantasm," a representation of what is already an inadequate representation of the real. Given that the notion of ideology as false consciousness or a system of false representations (as in the theory of reification) was dominant, it is no wonder that the remainder of the sentence, let alone the arguments that followed it, were rendered null and void.

The second version, at least once we note and make visible the discrepancy between the statements, opens the possibility of another way of thinking about ideology. Here, Althusser, by employing, "represents," a verb in place of the noun, focuses on what ideology does, rather than what it is. Moreover, he insists at the conclusion of the section that the latter question, what is ideology, was not discussed and had been deferred to a later point. Even the former question, that of the activity of ideology, however, must be postponed until Althusser clarifies the precise nature of "the object" that ideology "represents." The discussion that follows holds some surprises in store even for readers already familiar with the essay: Althusser takes great care to disavow the very "object" almost universally understood as that which ideology, even as he himself understands it, appears to "represent." Ideology is commonly regarded as a "worldview," which can in principle be critically examined "as an ethnologist studies the myths of a "primitive society," that is, knowing full well that they "do not correspond to reality." Even as these ideologies, like the myths of which they are perhaps a derivative, exhibit the character of an illusion, "it is agreed that they allude to reality and that it is sufficient to interpret them to discover beneath their imaginary representation of the world, the very reality of this world (ideology = illusion/allusion)." Althusser cites the example of Feuerbach who saw in religion an alienated and disavowed comprehension of the essence of man. Such notions lead to the conclusion that "in ideology men represent (or represent to themselves—*se représentent*) their real conditions of existence under an imaginary form."[13]

Several paragraphs later, Althusser makes explicit the difference between his position and the one outlined above: "it is not their real conditions of existence, their real world, that 'men' 'represent to themselves' in ideology, but above all their *relation* to the conditions of existence that is represented to them there. It is this relation that is at the center of every ideological and therefore imaginary representation of the real world. It is in this relation that is found the 'cause' of the imaginary deformation of the ideological representation of the real world." What is imaginary then is not the way the world is represented but individuals' relation to the world or to their conditions of existence. While Althusser's attempt to clarify that which distinguishes his theory of ideology from others—by directing the attention of his readers away from illusory worldviews that function, like Plato's noble fictions, to conceal individuals' relation to their conditions of existence—went unseen and unremarked by the vast majority of readers, this lapse in part is undeniably determined by the text itself. What precisely does Althusser mean by the phrase "the relations of individuals to their real conditions of existence"? What relations and what conditions? Althusser partially answers the latter question in the penultimate paragraph of the section by "speaking a Marxist language" to say that the phrase "real conditions of existence" can be translated as system of production.[14]

Something then would appear to be lost in the translation: Is Althusser's thesis on individuals' relation to their conditions of existence reducible to their place in the process of production? Is that all Althusser means by "relations"? The question with which he concludes this section of the essay suggests otherwise; here he appears to speak of relations beyond the relations of production, referring not only to social and thus "collective" relations but even relations within the life of the individual: "why is the representation given to individuals of their (individual) relation to the social relations that govern their existence and their collective and individual life necessarily imaginary?" To answer this question, however, which in fact Althusser defers until his consideration of "the central thesis on the structure and function of ideology," the thesis on the interpellation of the individual as subject, he must first answer another question, the very question with which he has struggled since the early sixties: "what is the nature of this imaginary?"[15]

To pause at this point in the essay is to confront the fact that its movement is not that of a linear, cumulative progress but a movement of dissociation where the arguments not only diverge from each other but move in opposing and incompatible directions. Nowhere in this section does Althusser acknowledge the fact that he had earlier defined ideology as made of apparatuses, and it is indeed difficult to conceptualize apparatuses as representations, let alone imaginary representations (or representations of the imaginary, a formulation that Althusser substitutes for the former, even if it is not the same thing). His warning that ideology was not a false representation of "reality" but rather of "relations" in no way prevented readers from continuing to understand ideology as a false representation even if of a different object. This reading could only be sustained, however, through a suppression of what Althusser called his "second, positive thesis," and indeed a review of the extensive commentary on the "Ideology" essay reveals how little notice was taken of this thesis. The claim that "ideology has a material existence" is the theoretical center of the essay, whose contradictions and inconsistencies are exhibited there in a particularly concentrated way.[16] It is the crucible through which any reader who seeks to understand what is singular in the essay and irreducible to all previous theories of ideology must pass: the reader will enter with notions of an imaginary representation of the real, that is, with a certain philosophical dualism intact, and leave it bereft of any notion of interiority, or anything other than bodies and forces.

Althusser begins his discussion of the material existence of ideology by reminding those who may have forgotten that ideology, despite the name, does not consist of ideas, true or false, or at least ideas possessing an "ideal" or "spiritual" existence. Instead he asks us to assume that "'ideas' or other 'representations'" (both terms now in quotation marks) have a "non-spiritual, but material existence." He then reintroduces the ISAs, reminding us that each of them is the "realization of an ideology." Now, "realization" in this sense is, for a number of reasons, not a notion we would expect to find in Althusser. It seems that we are to understand that the ideology precedes its expression in the materiality of an apparatus, as an idea precedes (and causes) an action. This would of course mean that ideology has an (ideal?) existence prior to its material incarnation, a notion that is ruled out by what

Althusser has just said, namely that ideas do not (ever) have a spiritual or ideal existence, only a material one. Without taking up any of these questions, Althusser (in the same paragraph) restates ("returns to") the thesis: "an ideology always exists in an apparatus, and its practice or practices. This existence is material."[17] The restatement, of course, changes the meaning of the original statement in certain important respects, given that "always exists in" is not the same as "is realized in." The reformulation eliminates the suggestion of the temporal and causal priority of ideology in relation to the apparatuses and thus eliminates any notion that ideology can exist external to its material form.

But while the second formulation solves certain problems associated with the first, it also poses new questions. I refer specifically to the use of the preposition "in": ideology always exists *in* an apparatus. Let us go further and combine the two formulations to achieve the full effect of the paradox: ideology always exists in the apparatus that is its realization. Thus ideology is neither the cause (in any commonly accepted sense of the term) nor the effect of the apparatuses that constitute its material form. We can now understand Althusser's comment elsewhere in the essay that when it comes to the question of ideology, "to be a Spinozist or a Marxist . . . is to be exactly the same thing."[18] As is well known, Spinoza questioned the model of every conception of the originary subject (or actor or agent of an action): God. For the relationship of God to the created world cannot be that of an actor separate from his action, which would thus be the expression of a preexisting intention. God can only be an immanent cause whose will and intentions exist solely in an actualized state: "God could not have been prior to his decrees nor can he be without them."[19] Human beings insist on imagining God as a transitive cause, whose will precedes his actions and decrees because they, argues Spinoza, imagine themselves (or their minds) to be the free causes of their actions, whereas in fact mind and body, thought and action are simultaneous and inseparable and determined by the same causes. Perhaps Althusser deliberately refrained from directly using the Spinozist language that caused such controversy when it appeared at the end of *Reading Capital*, but the concept is there: ideology is immanent in its apparatuses and their practices; it has no existence apart from these apparatuses and is entirely coincident with them. Ideas have thus disappeared into their material manifestations, becoming like causes that "exist" only in their effects (or, to add a Freudian reference that is entirely in keeping with both Spinoza and Althusser, ideas in this sense are causes that are ever only constituted *nachträglich*, retroactively, as the effect of their material effects).

It is certain that someone will object at this point, stating that ideas, even those that have disappeared into their material forms, must originate somewhere. And even if we are not methodological individualists who trace all action back to an original actor (or actors) and all thought to an originating "thing that thinks," is it not the case that consciousness or mind retains a place in this scheme if only as a relay point that facilitates the translation of "ideas" and "thought," however instantaneously, into ideological practices that, after all, depend on the corporeal obedience of individuals? Must these individuals not first (be made to) believe in order to then obey? But Althusser denounces even this notion as "an absolutely ideological 'conceptual' device (*dispositif*)" insofar as it separates ideas ("endowed with a spiritual existence") from "(material) behavior" (*comportement*) and institutes the priority of the former over the latter.[20] So, according to this conceptual device, if an individual "believes" in God, then he or she will go to church and pray. If an individual "believes" in the law, then he or she will obey it. What if an individual does not act according to the beliefs that he or she proclaims openly or "knows" secretly that he or she holds? The individual is then either a hypocrite or, more interestingly for our purposes, does not know what he or she believes. It is probable that Althusser, at this point in the text, had in mind a passage from Descartes's *Discourse on Method*: "In order to ascertain their real opinions, I ought to take cognisance of what they practiced rather than of what they said, not only because, in the corruption of our manners, there are few disposed to speak exactly as they believe, but because very many are not aware of what it is that they really believe, for as the act of mind by which a thing is believed being different from that by which we know we believe it, the one is often found without the other."[21]

Althusser subjects such statements to a symptomatic reading: despite the insistence on separating spiritual ideas from material actions, as internal intentions that are externally realized, this "ideology of ideology," faced with a discrepancy between the ideas and beliefs on the one hand and actions on the other, must, precisely to preserve this conceptual device, posit ideas other than those that the originating subject thinks it has, ideas that "correspond" to the actions the subject performs. The fact that these interpolated ideas do not preexist "their" actions, that is, the actions that correspond to them, can mean only one thing: "the ideology of ideology thus recognizes, despite its imaginary distortion, that the 'ideas' of the human subject exist in his actions." The formula is repeated: just as ideology always exists in an apparatus, so do ideas (of individual subjects) exist in (their) actions. It is at this point that Althusser crosses a certain threshold in his "restatement" of his thesis concerning the ideas and actions of individuals: "his ideas are his material actions." A few lines later, as if to blunt the force of his critique or to obscure the tracks of his theoretical detour (through Spinoza, whose name is not mentioned once in the section "ideology has a material existence," arguably the most Spinozist part of a very Spinozist essay), he tells us that while the term "ideas" has disappeared from further considerations of ideology, the notions of "belief" and "consciousness" survive.[22] This is a very revealing moment in that it shows Althusser's desire to preserve or, rather, appear to preserve an entire conceptual vocabulary, with the sole exception of the term "ideas." It is as if it would be too much altogether to eliminate the terms "belief" and, even more, "consciousness" (the importance of which for Marxist thought in all its diversity can hardly be overestimated). But do these terms and, even more importantly, the notions of interiority that they suggest actually survive in Althusser's text? Should we, as so many readers have done, take Althusser at his word?

In fact, the word "consciousness" appears only once in the remainder of the essay. Not only is it placed in quotation marks, but it is immediately qualified in the following way: the reproduction of the relations of production is assured "in the 'consciousness,' i.e., in the behavior" (*dans la conscience, c'est-à-dire, dans le comportement*) of individual subjects. Consciousness, that is, behavior: Althusser has preserved the language of interiority, the words "belief" and "consciousness," in the very same sense that Spinoza preserved the concept of God, in order more effectively to subvert it. To illustrate this point, Althusser takes an example from Pascal, condensing into a single sentence a series of arguments and postulates from the *Pensées*: "Kneel down, move your lips in prayer, and you will believe." This "wonderful formula," he writes, "will enable us to invert the order of the notional schema of ideology."[23] The order to which he refers is of course the causal order according to which thought precedes action as its cause: if an individual kneels down and prays, such an action is the consequence of that individual's belief in God and his desire to act upon his belief (for he might suffer from "a weakness of will"). Pascal's hypothetical libertine, however, poses more complicated problems. His difficulty concerns belief not action:

convinced that his destiny has been wagered, he wants to believe in God but cannot; he desires to desire God but feels only emptiness where the desire he desires to feel ought to be. Pascal's advice to the libertine is truly "scandalous": what you do is more important than what you believe. Perform the prescribed gestures and utter the prescribed words and your lack of belief will not matter. But perhaps even more scandalously, he reassures the libertine that action (at least, if it is conducted according to rituals performed within the apparatus of the Church) or practice, to use Althusser's term, will *produce* belief, thus instituting a tendential primacy of the body over the soul, of matter over spirit. To invert "the notional schema of ideology," however, is not necessarily to call it into question. For Pascal's position appears to resemble a kind of behaviorism, a theory of the conditioning of the mind through the body that makes the soul a mere reflection of the body without substance or material form.

Althusser, however, has set for himself the directly opposite objective: to demonstrate the material existence of ideas, beliefs, and consciousness. Accordingly, he immediately translates Pascal's language into "a more directly Marxist vocabulary" in order to show that "we are not dealing with an inversion at all": "where only a single subject (such and such an individual) is concerned, the existence of the ideas of his belief is material in that *his ideas are his material actions inserted into material practices governed by material rituals which are themselves defined by the material ideological apparatus from which derive the ideas of that subject*."[24] Althusser's translation is again a betrayal of the original in that every notion of a sequence and a separation between the mental and the physical, the soul and the body, spirit and matter has disappeared, and further, the ideas that "are" the actions of an individual no longer transcend physical existence insofar as they are always already "inserted" into practices, which are in turn governed by the rituals of an apparatus. The four repetitions of "material" in this passage are important. Words may remain (e.g., "belief," "consciousness"), but Althusser has effectively banished any notion of interiority, or rather he shows that the internal is always already translated in the Spinozist manner into the external "expression," which it cannot be understood to precede and outside of which it has no existence. There are only exteriorities, not only the materialities of actions and movements but also the materialities of discourse, whether written, spoken, or silent and invisible but still material, still producing effects as only the material can, not originating "inside" us whether in intentional speech acts or the unintentional but nevertheless eloquent speech that is spoken to us in the secrecy of sleep, the speech that is ours but is spoken only where we are not. Ideas, beliefs, consciousness are always immanent in the irreducible materiality of discourses, actions, practices.

In a late text on Spinoza, Althusser makes explicit the assumptions guiding these passages from the "Ideology" essay: "the soul (the *mens*, the activity of the mind) is in no way separate from the activity of the organic body; on the contrary, the soul only thinks insofar as it is affected by the impressions and movements of the body, therefore it thinks not only with the body but *in it*, consubstantially united to it prior to any separation."[25] Against the entire liberal tradition from Hobbes (who was the immediate object of Spinoza's critique) to Kant (and beyond), which posits a human interiority free and separate from the laws (and forces) that govern the physical world as if it were "a kingdom within a kingdom . . . that has absolute power over its actions and is determined by no other source than itself," Spinoza argues that whatever decreases or limits the power of the body to act simultaneously decreases the power of the mind (mens) to think.[26] Several years after the publication of the "Ideology" essay, Althusser, again referring to Spinoza, would explain the sense in which "the imaginary relation," of which ideology is a "representation," is itself "endowed with a material existence": "Spinoza's 'theory' refused every illusion about ideology and about the primary ideology of the time, religion, by identifying it as imaginary. But at the same time, this theory refused to regard ideology as simple error or mere ignorance because it bases the system of this imaginary on the relation of men to the world 'expressed' by the state of their bodies."[27] Althusser no longer conceives of ideology as a system of representations or as discourse, both of which definitions as we have seen separated ideology from something more real than itself. The materiality of ideology consists of its immanence in bodies and forces, in the indelible traces of language itself, the utterance, the word, the signifier in all the forms irreducible to anything more primary than themselves. If ideology has no history, this immanence is the form of its omni-historicity. If ideology "represents" the relations of individuals to their world, we must understand "represent" here as a transformation, a reworking and refashioning, the product of which is as real and material as that which was transformed.

As radical and fruitful as these theses may be, they render the "central thesis of the essay" ("ideology interpellates individuals as subjects") more rather than less problematic, calling attention to the fatal ambiguity of the term "interpellate" as it is employed in the essay. Althusser introduces the drama of the interpellated subject here as a drama of "recognition" (*reconnaissance*). We are "stopped" and, in acknowledging the summons, "recognize that we are recognized."[28] Even in the case of mistaken identity, when we are not the one sought by the police but nevertheless turn toward the voice that calls out to us "knowing-suspecting-believing" that it is indeed we who are sought, haunted by the sense that "our time has come." Individuals then are "always-already subjects," not only in the sense that the subject position preexists them in the apparatuses, practices, and rituals that make them subjects but also in the very different and opposed sense that they must already be subjects (conscious actors) in order to undertake the act of recognizing their recognition, which act marks their self-subjection. A certain form of subjectivity, then, necessarily precedes the double action of subjection as its original condition. This drama thus understood is, of course, nothing more or less than a version of the concept of intersubjectivity that Althusser so vigorously denounced in others; it is, moreover, heavy with overtones of a certain Hegelianism (again, significantly, a reading of the master-slave dialectic as the human condition, which Althusser himself denounced in one of his earliest publications) and even, at the extreme, elements of Sartrian inspiration. Of course, the terms "Hegelian" and "Sartrian" should not be taken as indices of some failure or fault on Althusser's part, as if any filiation with these philosophies automatically calls a theory into question. On the contrary, they are meant to suggest that Althusser's relation to both Hegel and Sartre is more complicated than has been suspected up to now and that this might prove a productive area for further research. In any case, it appears that consciousness, banished by the arguments comprising "ideology has a material existence," has returned unnoticed to the scene as the origin of the recognition that is interpellation. Has Althusser then, following the intransigent Spinozism of the previous section, lapsed back not to a theory of original intersubjectivity but of the originary place of individual consciousnesses in the drama of recognition that constitutes interpellation?

Not entirely: alongside the theory of interpellation as recognition, a theory that, as Michel Pêcheux noted with great acuity, has proved only too easily reconcilable with theories based on some variant of individual consciousness, there emerges a second, let us say materialist, version irreducible to the first, constructed according to the premises of "ideology has a material existence."[29] If, with Spinoza, Althusser holds that "mind and body . . . are one and the same individual thing," recognition cannot be an act of consciousness but must be immanent in the actions of the body.[30] The will is nothing more than a disposition of the body, Spinoza would write, while Althusser argued that if we think, "we think with and in our bodies." These statements, which might appear to invalidate the theory of ideological interpellation, in fact, furnish its foundation. The individual is endowed with a factitious if not fictious or imaginary interiority, after the fact of bodily action, a paradoxical interior that, having no place in us, is constructed around us, outside of us. We are so endowed with subjectivity, declared free subjects, originators of our acts, especially the acts of submission and consent, retroactively to demonstrate to us that we have always already consented to authority, which having received our consent enjoys the right legitimately to dominate us. Interiority and consciousness (and the internal acts that supposedly occur within these unconditioned spaces) function as the supplement of servitude, its supplemental origin, the origin of the origin, the mark of a domination that folds back upon itself to add to its superior force the guarantee of its own legitimacy. The imposition of human servitude through force and fraud is not enough; it must retroactively produce its origins (in the modern epoch at least) in the will of each and every subject, "man by man," as Hobbes would say, creating a foundation that simultaneously rises upon and buries the violence of its origins, where "conquest, enslavement, robbery, murder, in short, force play the greatest part."[31] In the liberal tradition this scheme takes the form of the "acts of will," the "intentions" that originate nowhere else but *in* ourselves (it is in this sense that each individual in his or her freedom is a "kingdom within a kingdom"), which found the political order (at least *our* political order) and are the guarantees of its legitimacy. This interiority is thus the site of origins, but origins that were never present: the consent that we have always already given and "founds" the power that rises against us, the rights that we have always already transferred to the powers that be, which, having received our authorization, cannot really be opposed to us. Althusser says it brutally: we are interpellated as subjects so that we will freely choose (or more precisely will have already freely chosen) our own subjection. But interiority is not an illusory presence to which the materiality of the body (with which we think) might be opposed, for the "interpellated" interior is itself "constituted" and therefore fully real, being not opposed to the exterior but its continuation. The interpellation of the subject is not merely a matter of recognition, except insofar as this recognition arrives fully embodied and fully armed: we are thus recognized not by another consciousness but by the apparatuses that recognize only what they themselves in one and the same gesture have created. Not only are we, as subjects who enjoy all the rights and privileges guaranteed by law in our free societies, held accountable for our choices and liable to punishment for those evil acts voluntarily undertaken, but we must be first, in order to be judged, "recruited" from the undifferentiated mass, separated, singularized, and granted an identity as a fixed, constant knowable entity, not a mere thing, to be sure, but a unique irreplaceable person. The idea that we are the cause of our actions, that our relation to our bodies is one of absolute mastery, is thus imaginary, but in no way is it immaterial or illusory: on the contrary, this imaginary relation is fully materialized not only in the ideological apparatuses but also in what Althusser has termed the RSA, the means of coercion and of inflicting pain and death on "bad subjects."

If we adopt the perspective of the second reading of ideological interpellation outlined above, what are we to make of the distinction, sketched out earlier in the essay, between the violence of the RSA and the "ideological" functioning of the ISAs? It is certain that Althusser rejects the dualism inherent in Gramsci's formulations on hegemony: the centaur, half beast, half human, inhabiting simultaneously the world of ideas and beliefs (in which consent in shaped) and the world of force and violence. Althusser himself admitted that there was no absolute distinction between the RSA and the ISAs, arguing that every apparatus is characterized by a "double functioning." Even apparently purely ideological apparatuses such as the school or the church "use suitable methods of punishment, expulsion and selection, etc., to 'discipline' not only their shepherds but also their flocks."[32] If we take seriously Althusser's statement that "we think with our bodies," then we can no longer understand the distinction between violence and ideology as a distinction between the external and the internal, between the domination exercised on bodies and the domination exercised on minds. Instead, we are forced to acknowledge the "consubstantiality" of force and persuasion, that there is no persuasion (or activity at all) of minds except insofar as it is immanent in force, which may be overwhelming or subtle, force that inflicts pain, damage, or death, or force that is quietly and unobtrusively physical, managing bodies and spaces with neither pain nor harm.

If few of Althusser's readers were able to extract from the essay the line of argumentation noted above, they perhaps sensed its presence less directly in the form of what they found threatening about it, even if they most often could not fully articulate this threat. However uneven and contradictory

Althusser's critique of consciousness, it undeniably exerted sufficient force to move readers to ask how, in the absence of a mind separate enough from the material circumstances of the society in which it existed and equipped with a will strong enough to resist the powers of persuasion, there could be something like resistance to domination. Had not Althusser with his apparatuses, practices, and rituals turned human beings into machines? In a response to critics of the piece, "Notes sur les ISAS" (Notes on the ISAS), published in 1976, Althusser himself summarized this reading: "the most frequent criticism directed at my essay of 1969–70 on the ISAS was that of 'functionalism.' My theoretical sketch was seen as an attempt to claim for Marxism an interpretation which defined organs by their immediate functions alone, thus fixing society in the ideological institutions charged with exercising the function of subjection: at the limit a non-dialectical interpretation whose fundamental logic excluded any possibility of class struggle." He then went on to complain that these critics simply "did not read with sufficient care the postscript to his essay which emphasized the 'abstract' character of my analysis, and explicitly placed my conception of the class struggle at the center."[33] It goes without saying that we can give no credence whatsoever to Althusser's explanation of the effects produced by his text, which, to judge it according to Althusser's own positions, is absurd. Not only is no text innocent of its effects, but to present class struggle, conceived as the antidote to functionalism, in a postscript and therefore outside the development of his argument is to render it superfluous, nothing more than an afterthought. It is surely significant that the question of ideology in general and the "Ideology" essay in particular figured only marginally in the *Elements of Self-Criticism* published in 1974, as if Althusser, in so many other ways a perceptive reader and critic of his own texts, remained blind to the antagonisms internal to what was perhaps his most widely read work.

The history of the text makes his blindness even more puzzling. For, if the reading of the "Ideology" essay as a functionalist work is in part a response to Althusser's rejection of the phenomena of consciousness and interiority, as I have argued, the text also produced this response because Althusser took great care to excise from the published version of the text every reference not only to class struggle, resistance to domination, but even more importantly, every passage that furnished the means to theorize revolt and resistance without recourse to a philosophy of consciousness. It is puzzling indeed today to read the suppressed chapter, "Reproduction des rapports de production et revolution" (Reproduction of the Relations of Production and Revolution," or the section on "The Ideological State Apparatuses and the Ideological By-Products [sous-produits] of Their Practices."[34] In the same way, it is difficult to reconcile Althusser's reference to the "fragility" of the ISAs in the original, a phrase that captures the materiality of ideology as he conceives it, with their machinelike character in the published essay.[35]

It is no longer a question of gauging the extent to which an ideology conceived as a system of ideas is "believed" or "accepted," but rather it is gauging the force and solidity of a material apparatus that moves bodies rather than minds or minds always immanent in bodies. This fact, the very materiality both of the apparatus that moves the body as well as the body that must be moved, points to the priority of class struggle, that, as Adam Smith himself notes in the first chapter of the *Wealth of Nations*, the very body of the worker tends to resist the rhythms necessary for efficient production. Rather than offering itself as an inert material to be shaped by the machinery of production, the conatus of the worker's body, its persisting in its "actual essence," presents an initial obstacle to be overcome through an arrangement of forces and constraints. Because the ISAs arise in response to the resistance that precedes them and makes them necessary, like so many weapons of mass subjection in the never ending war between the classes, they necessarily bear the imprint of this war, the stresses and strains of conflict from which there is no respite, and the capacity under specific circumstances to produce effects other than and opposed to those they were designed for. It is no wonder then that Althusser can describe these apparatuses as fragile, capable of producing not only subjection (which for Althusser is also always a process of individualization) but "by-products" of collectivity, the composition of forces and revolt. How such by-products come into existence, Althusser does not tell us. In any case, in the absence of this excised material, the "Ideology" essay offered a merely functionalist theory of exploitation and domination in which the devaluation of consciousness could only appear as a theoretical expedient.

From the years 1964 to 1970, Althusser moves from a system of representations to discourse to apparatuses, practices, and rituals; from the imputed subject to the subject interpellated in and by discourse to the individual interpellated as subject by the ISAs. Six extraordinary years for Althusser and for the world, with the current of mobilization and revolution lifting Althusser and carrying him along. It was only this mobilization that, through the force it exerted, made it possible to see and to feel the presence of the apparatuses and the rituals; in how many cases did the fact of disobedience alone call attention to the constraint, the existence of which, until then, was unsuspected? The fact of revolt itself, rather than any acceptance of the established order, made it possible to see how many forces combined to counter the movements for change, how difficult revolution had become, and how different the strategies required to bring it about. Perhaps it was this sense of the immensity of the task and of the absurd inadequacy of oppositional theory that led Althusser to demonstrate in such devastating detail the difficulty of bringing to an end the regime of exploitation without so much as a hint of how to conceptualize the struggle. So many of the readers who criticized Althusser for his "pessimism" never confronted his arguments: they believed with all their heart that revolution was at hand, and when they discovered that it was not, they accepted with surprising ease the society they once reviled, declaring what Althusser had described as a regime of subjection the best of all possible worlds.

For many readers this was the case, but not for all. Althusser had at least one reader who took his arguments seriously enough to identify and criticize the inconsistencies and even more importantly to take what was unprecedented in the "Ideology" essay, its materialist or Spinozist tendency, and develop it beyond the boundaries of Althusser's thought.[36] Not so many years ago it was possible (or perhaps inevitable) to read Althusser's "Ideology and Ideological State Apparatuses" and Foucault's *Discipline and Punish* not only as counterposed texts but as expressions of opposing systems of thought that might be compared and contrasted, their resemblances and differences noted, but which would remain as ineluctably separate as the men who wrote them. And despite the well-known disposition of both Althusser and Foucault to question, if not reject, the very notion of authorship as exemplary of the myth of the originary subject, it remains very difficult to separate these texts from the subsequent lives and works of their authors. While Althusser's text proclaimed its Marxism on every page, *Discipline and Punish* (in which Marx is cited approvingly on a number of occasions) was nevertheless most often read as a proleptic and hence a still obscure manifestation of what would soon become Foucault's open hostility to Marxism (or at least certain kinds of Marxism), and thus it was read as a critique and rejection of the central theses of even Althusser's highly unorthodox remarks on ideology. Despite (or perhaps because of) Althusser's subtle and enormously complex attempts to turn the notion of ideology against the ideological conception of ideology, Foucault expressed suspicion of the term "ideology" from very early in his career, and his suspicions, it must be said, were often directed at Althusser's uses of the term. It was as if Foucault followed with critical attention the successive definitions of ideology offered by Althusser and felt compelled to engage, often polemically, with them. Althusser's early definition of ideology as "the lived relation between men and their world," which was opposed by "science," was vigorously contested in the pages of *The Archeology of Knowledge*, a number of whose arguments were in turn adopted by Althusser in his self-criticism of 1974.[37] But this strange "dialogue," whose participants did not directly address or even name each other (perhaps it was unnecessary), did not stop there. Almost immediately after the publication of "Ideology and Ideological Apparatuses" in *La pensée* in 1970 the terms of Foucault's critique of ideology changed, even as he himself renewed his acquaintance with Marxism and became an active participant in the extra-parliamentary Left. The problem with the concept of ideology was no longer that it seemed to denote a realm of *doxa*, of belief and opinion in opposition to the sanctified world of scientific knowledge, but rather that ideology seemed logically confined to the realm of consciousness and ideas and therefore destined to remain idealist, diverting our attention from what is at stake in any form of subjection: the body, the body that works and whose power produces value, the body that obeys by acting or by refraining from action. In one sense, this critique of ideology cannot possibly be directed against Althusser's essay, in that its terms, its insistence on the primacy of the body, are exactly those we have just described in Althusser. But in another sense, Foucault may be understood to confront "Ideology and Ideological State Apparatuses" with its contradictions and unevennesses, developing certain of its theses (notably those concerned with the materiality of ideology) in order to show their stark incompatibility with other elements of Althusser's discussion of ideology.

In particular, *Discipline and Punish* underscores the way in which the arguments that comprise the thesis "ideology has a material existence" appear to call into question the distinction between the RSA and the ISAs as a distinction between violence and ideology (understood in turn as an opposition of force and consent). As we have seen, the "citation" from Pascal, the image of the subjected body that is determined to kneel down, move its lips in prayer, and simultaneously to "believe," suggests that while there is no question of the body being caused to act by a persuaded, indoctrinated, or deceived mind (contrary to some of Althusser's suggestions at the beginning of the essay), neither can "its" acts be understood as the effects of violence or repression (involving the army, the police, or the courts), which would, of course, not exclude a notion of a mind or consciousness that rationally calculates likely outcomes of actions and decides to choose the wiser, that is, safer course of obedience (a notion excluded by the essay's central thesis of the interpellated subject). Foucault, unencumbered by the "ideology of ideology" and having no need to turn its language against it, can argue in a directly Spinozist manner that since bodies (and the thinking that takes place in them, with them) and not consciousness or interiority are at stake in the practices of subjection, and since only bodies determine bodies, it is all the more striking that so little attention has been paid to the physical processes of subjection, processes whose divergent modalities cannot be grasped in the terms of the violence-ideology distinction: "subjection is not only obtained by the instruments of violence or ideology; it can also be direct, physical, pitting force against force, bearing on material elements, and yet without involving violence; it may be calculated, organized, technically thought out; it may be subtle, make use of neither weapons nor terror and yet remain of a physical order."[38]

Does this mean then that, as some critics have charged, humans are reduced to the level of brute beasts, not only without consciousness but without even ideas or words or thought of any kind? Here Foucault's response (which is, as Pierre Macherey has argued, more Spinozist than Nietzschean) is as well known as it is controversial: "there is no power relation without the correlative constitution of a field of knowledge, nor any knowledge that does not presuppose and constitute at the same time power relations."[39] Knowledge, which is decidedly not the same thing as "consciousness," cannot be said merely to arise, as an effect separate from its cause, from power relations (note the plural that emphasizes the conflict and antagonism that characterize power as Foucault defines it), which would then form the foundation to which it might be reduced. Knowledges (Foucault's nominalism enjoins us to speak of them in the plural) are in no way exterior to power relations, caused by them only finally to transcend them; rather, they can only be understood as immanent in the materiality of practices and apparatuses. Readers have often asked if *Discipline and Punish* is a history of ideas or a history of institutions, thereby imposing upon it the idealist dilemmas (mind or body, words or things, ideas or reality) that the work refuses from the outset. Foucault, to use Althusser's language (and in this way make it evident that, despite his refusal of the entire problematic of ideology with its paradoxes and impasses, he cannot completely escape the difficulties Althusser faced in speaking of the material existence of ideology), has written a history of the ideas that cannot be separated from the physical, material practices in which they are (always already) realized. This, rather than the functionalism and defeatism that are often ascribed to him, would appear to be what is truly scandalous about his work: his refusal to regard the histories of psychiatry, medicine, or criminology apart from their practical and institutional forms, namely, the asylum, the hospital, and the prison, the forms of the ordering and distribution of bodies in space in which these knowledges participate, the position that they, in their material incarnations, occupy in a field of conflicting social forces. If to confront the most noble ideas of human freedom with their often sordid materiality is a provocation, then nothing was more provocative than Foucault's observations on the liberal dreams of Enlightenment thinkers. Thus, what has so offended contemporary readers is not that Foucault neglected the great themes of the seventeenth and eighteenth centuries, the ideas of freedom, right, and law, but rather that he refused to regard them as disembodied ideals, existing in consciousnesses and representations. Instead, he seeks to determine their "dark side," the technologies of power, the forms of struggle and subjection that accompanied and made possible the utterances that constitute these doctrines:

> Historically, the process by which the bourgeoisie became in the course of the eighteenth century the politically dominant class was masked by the establishment of an explicit, coded and formally egalitarian juridical framework, made possible by the organization of a parliamentary, representative regime. But the development and generalization of disciplinary mechanisms constituted the other, dark side of these processes. The general juridical form that guaranteed a system of rights that were egalitarian in principle was supported by these tiny, everyday, physical mechanisms, by all those systems of micro-power that are essentially non-egalitarian and asymmetrical that we call the disciplines.[40]

From this point of view, not only is it impossible any longer to speak of an opposition between ideological apparatuses, on the one hand, whose primary function would be to produce "ideologies" understood in the old sense of ideas and beliefs, and, on the other, the repressive apparatus (always in the singular for Althusser), which would employ force or the threat of force, it is equally impossible to speak of the knowledges linked to an apparatus as being in any way external to (or innocent of) its functioning, like beautiful lies that would conceal or deny the harsh realities of the disciplinary regime. Instead, Foucault shows that the knowledges that took shape in an apparatus such as the army in the seventeenth and eighteenth centuries, knowledges that would be diffused to other seemingly counterposed apparatuses (e.g., the school), had nothing to do with what is usually meant by ideology, the "values" as Althusser suggests, of nationalism and social order. Rather, what was historically important about the army (like the police and the entire penal system) were the ideas, often nothing more than theoretical fantasies or strategic objectives (subject to the contingencies of "the perpetual battle" that characterizes the field of social forces) immanent in its multiform operations. The order that the army attempted to impose on its own ranks was, of course, not secured as much by the inculcation of values and beliefs as by the technologies of the body: the distributions according to which bodies were enclosed and simultaneously partitioned, the investments that sought, by working on bodies, by recomposing and reconfiguring them, to increase both their utility and docility, and finally the forms of supervision, from perpetual and anonymous surveillance to the examination based on a normalizing judgment.

In fact, Althusser's central thesis (ideology interpellates individuals as subjects) only takes on its full meaning in relation to what we might call Foucault's reading of the materiality of ideology, a notion rewritten as the "physical order" of the disciplines. The phrase "ideology interpellates" is, as we have noted, often read, and not without textual support, as a (tragic) drama of recognition. In this sense, the interpellation of the subject can itself be seen as a subjective process, unfolding entirely within the realm of consciousness or intersubjectivity and thus ideological in the old sense, a false idea or representation counterposed to reality. And while Althusser simultaneously supplied the elements of an objective, material theory of the constitution of the subject, it was Foucault who made this contradiction visible by arguing quite explicitly that if we can consider the individual as subject "the fictitious atom of an ideological representation of society," we must regard that fiction correlatively as "a reality fabricated by this specific technology of power . . . called discipline."[41] Further, Foucault emphasized the fact that the individual does not preexist his or her interpellation as a subject in the form of a given but only emerges as a result of strategies and practices of individualization: there is a history of the body, not only of the magnitude of its forces but even the extent to which it is integrated with or separate from other bodies.

In this way Foucault opens an entire dimension that Althusser's essay unwittingly presupposes: a history of the body, the history of the individual itself. He allows us to see the regime of individualization (or at least the descending individualization that particularizes and identifies those on whom power is exercised) as a strategy, perhaps the strategy of the disciplinary regime faced with the reality of mass movements, the reality of collective action made possible by the new enclosures of the factory, the prison, and the school: "it must also master all the forces that are formed from the very constitution of an organized multiplicity; it must neutralize the effects of counter-power that spring from them and which form a resistance to the power that wishes to dominate it: agitations, revolts, spontaneous organizations, coalitions — anything that may establish horizontal conjunctions." The same economic and political imperatives that led to the formation of masses necessitated strategies that, at the level of knowledge, tended toward reduction, segmentation, and serialization, in short, an entire "science of the individual" and, at the level of physical forces, to separation, partitioning, and cellularity. Contrary to an entire tradition that can conceive of domination only as the denial of a natural individuality through forced collectivization, Foucault argues that "instead of bending all its subjects into a single uniform mass," the disciplinary regime "separates, analyses, differentiates, carries its procedures of decomposition to the point of necessary and sufficient single units. It 'trains' the moving, confused, useless multitudes of bodies and forces into a multiplicity of individual elements — small, separate cells, organic autonomies, generic identities and continuities, combinatory segments. Discipline 'makes' individuals; it is the specific technique of a power that regards individuals both as objects and as instruments of its exercise." The fantasy immanent in the practices of discipline is to abolish "the crowd, a compact mass, a locus of multiple exchanges, individualities merging together, a collective effect" and replace it with "a collection of separated individualities."[42]

Foucault has thus described the material conditions of the possibility of interpellation, of which he proceeds to offer his own account: the individual thus abstracted from the mutual entanglements and dependencies, from the "coagulations" proper to social existence, is then endowed with a soul or, depending upon the domain of knowledge and the nature of its apparatuses, a "psyche, subjectivity, personality, [or] consciousness": "the man described for us, whom we are invited to free, is already in himself the effect of a subjection more profound than himself. A 'soul' inhabits him and brings him to existence, which is itself a factor in the mastery that power exercises over the body. The soul is the effect and instrument of a political anatomy; the soul is the prison of the body."[43]

It is at this very moment, the moment at which he most closely approaches Althusser who had written "there are no subjects except through and for subjection," that Foucault attempts to specify what separates them. In three sentences, he contrasts what is clearly the theory of ideological interpellation or at least a version of the theory with his own position, one that is both more materialist (in that it rejects the idea of subjectivity as illusion or false appearance) and more historical (the subject form varies throughout history). According to Foucault's version, Althusser sees "in the soul, the reactivated remnants [les restes réactivés] of an ideology." From this it follows that the "soul is an illusion, an ideological effect," deprived of any historical reality, nothing more than an expression of something more real than itself. In opposition, Foucault argues, we should recognize in the soul "the actual correlative of a certain technology of power over the body." To understand it, we must recognize "that it exists, that it has a reality, that it is produced permanently around, on the surface, in the interior of the body by the functioning of a power on those who are punished—and in a more general way on those who are supervised [qu'on surveille], trained and corrected."[44] Foucault's reading thus acts as a kind of mirror, reflecting Althusser's essay in a way that magnifies and makes visible by means of a slightly modified language the discrepancies between what is genuinely new and everything insufficiently differentiated from the dominant conceptions of ideology, interiorizing and then representing Althusser's theory in a way that severs it from the language of consciousness and its illusions once and for all.

But if Foucault has lifted certain of Althusser's arguments out of the inner darkness of the "Ideology" essay, he has also succeeded in making visible a new set of contradictions that significantly belong as much to his account of the subject as to Althusser's. In what is certainly one of the most illuminating commentaries on the "Ideology" essay, Judith Butler has pointed to the centrality of what Althusser himself called "a theoretical scene" and "our little theoretical theater": the allegorical figure "in which a subject is hailed, the subject turns around and then accepts the terms by which he or she is hailed."[45] The recourse to allegory, to the figural, Butler argues, is less the sign of a theoretical failure or impasse, at least in this case, than the necessary consequence of the unrepresentability of that which is not "a sequence with a before and after, in the form of a temporal succession," but that which language itself distorts into such a sequence. To describe interpellation, for Butler, is to become "trapped within the grammatical time of the subject," insofar as "it is almost impossible to ask about the genealogy of its construction without pre-supposing that construction for the asking of the question itself."[46] As if to illustrate the trap, expressed in the form of an inescapable allegorization, we may note that while Althusser writes of "interpellation policière" and of "la pratique policière de l'interpellation," phrases in which the police appear only in adjectival form, in the English translation, the adjective becomes a noun, as in "the policeman's practice of hailing," abetting the tendency to personify the work of interpellation, as if a policeman were on the scene, on stage, "representing" the impersonal existence of the law. In consequence, interpellation is often reduced, if not to recognition in the Hegelian sense (the little theater of the master and slave), to language, to a call, that is, a linguistic or speech act, rather than a summons that can be "issued" only in the context of constraint and coercion and for which the addressee is responsible and punishable. If interpellation is then more than a call from a policeman or a god, what then are the material practices of interpellation, practices that simultaneously summon and endow that which is summoned with a real existence?

It is precisely at this point that Foucault's analysis of the soul begins: read in the light of his critique of Althusser, if we can continue to speak of interpellation at all, it must be conceived less as a hailing, being hailed than the permanent production of a hold over the body, the manufacturing of a soul not only around and on the surface of the body but in it, modifying its composition. If "a soul inhabits" the individual in disciplinary societies "and brings him [le porte] to existence," it is thus "a piece in the mastery that power exercises over the body," "an effect and instrument" of that mastery. But what is the nature of this instrument that allows the body to be better administered and controlled, and how exactly does it exercise mastery of the body? To answer these questions, Foucault, like Althusser, is compelled to turn to allegory to represent the unrepresentable and to think the unthought. Here the subject is constituted (and although Foucault does not once use the term "interpellation," its range of meanings in French render it as appropriate to his analysis as to Althusser's) not by the policeman's order but by the imperturbable gaze of the prison watchtower, the center of an annular building composed of individual cells. I refer, of course, to the Panopticon, understood not as an actually existing piece of punitive—or merely disciplinary—architecture and therefore part of the means of spatial domination but rather as an "architectural figure," "a generalisable model," and finally "a diagram of a technology of power reduced to its ideal form."[47]

Allegory against allegory, figure against figure: the intersubjective relation between policeman and his subject is replaced by a relation between a watchtower, which fulfills its function only when it is "unmanned," and perhaps finally a subject's relation to himself mediated by the image or figure of the tower. Foucault's power is strangely silent: only those on whom power is exercised are "incited" to speak. As if to speak out would compromise its anonymity, power does not call out, call upon, or address; instead, it watches, supervises, and carries out surveillance, transforming the separated individualities it has partitioned into "so many small theaters," constantly visible, as well as audible, and open to inspection. It is precisely in the process of making visible, the process that assures the fabrication of docile bodies, that the soul is born and that something like subjectivity, interiority, or consciousness takes shape. This is what Foucault, in fact, will call "the major effect of the Panopticon: to induce in the inmate [le détenu] a conscious and permanent state of visibility that assures the automatic functioning of power."[48] What exactly is "a conscious state of visibility?" The visible individual becomes conscious of being visible, being watched, and he watches himself, under surveillance, exercising self-surveillance. This is very different from the action of conscience, in which an individual subjects himself to moral judgment. What Foucault has described is nothing less than the genesis of consciousness, even if this genesis, as in the case of interpellation, cannot be understood in terms of a before and after or of a sequence. The awareness of our visibility becomes "the perception of what passes in a man's own mind," Locke's definition of consciousness. Consciousness is self-surveillance, the effect and means of subjection.

Let us recall, however, that the becoming conscious of the subjected individual depends not on the knowledge that he is constantly watched but on the impossibility of such knowledge: "he is seen but he does not see." He cannot know whether the watchtower is manned or empty, and this very unknowability provokes a preemptive self-inspection. Fear is the beginning of wisdom, fear of a surveillance that may not be taking place, that may never have taken place: "a real subjection is born mechanically from a fictitious relation."[49] Fictitious: it thus appears that Foucault has reproduced Althusser's dilemmas, including an original fiction underlying material relations, and the intervention of the term "mechanical" does nothing to change the necessity of the originary illusion. The Panopticon is the figure of an anonymous Subject who creates its subjects, whose souls are born in fear and trembling.

It thus appears that the language of consciousness and its illusions is not as easy to escape as one might have thought. If Althusser and Foucault encountered a limit or barrier in their theoretical adventures, however, it was not the limit of reason itself and hence the sign of an irremediable failure. The limit that appears as a limit internal to the texts was the limit of their theoretical conjuncture. A shift in the relationship of forces had disrupted the regime of painstakingly disconnected individualities, each encased in the cage of its own subjectivity, and allowed them to break free and coagulate into mass movements that in turn disrupted and, in disrupting, made visible the rituals of subjection in factories, schools, and prisons. As the balance of power shifted so did the relations of knowledge. Each incursion of mass struggle, like a flare fired above the battlefield, revealed the obstacles, traps, and emplacements that blocked the way forward. The texts we have examined were sketches or diagrams of this battlefield, a battlefield we have not left even as we now, plunged in darkness, attempt to feel our way forward.

PART III

Origin/End

The Late Althusser
Materialism of the Encounter or Philosophy of Nothingness?

And I heard, but I did not understand, and I said, "my
Lord what is the end of these?" And he said, "go, Daniel, for the
words are closed up and sealed until the time of the end."

DANIEL 12: 8–9

More than any of Althusser's other posthumous publications, and more than a great many of the works published during his lifetime, "The Underground Current of the Materialism of the Encounter" has fascinated readers.[1] They have tended to read it in one of two ways: either as a definitive break with, and thus repudiation of, Althusser's previous work or, in contrast, as the explicit statement of what had always been the esoteric doctrine of even his most familiar texts, whose provocative and heterodox character demanded that it remain hidden, as if it were the theoretical counterpart to the confessions offered in *The Future Lasts Forever*. According to the first reading, Althusser's work is at any given moment relatively homogeneous, its contradictions residing in the discrepancies between its periods or phases. The second approach, in opposition, takes Althusser's work to be contradictory only insofar as it is the site of a double truth, an apparent meaning concealing a truth deemed too incendiary for all but a very few readers. Neither of these approaches takes the contradictions that animate Althusser's work, however, as constitutive and necessary to its very unfolding. They thus rule out in advance any symptomatic reading of Althusser's own texts, a reading capable of registering, and perhaps explaining, its specific unevenness and conflictuality. Admittedly, "The Underground Current" poses serious challenges to anyone who seeks to read philosophical works according to the protocol initiated by Althusser himself. To read it carefully is to confront the fact that the published version consists of two sections, a short autobiographical preface and what the editor François Matheron describes as "*le cœur*" or core of the work, some 37 pages of what appears to be an uninterrupted discourse, both excerpted by Matheron from a 142-page typed manuscript. Althusser's protocol of reading assumed that philosophical texts presented the dissimulation of coherence and consistency, not simply in order to supply to the reader with what is normally expected of philosophy but also, and more importantly, as a defense against the force of their own conflicts, a sort of obsessional and therefore imaginary mastery of an irreconcilable antagonism. As an "a posteriori construction," to cite the words of the editor, it differs not only from texts such as "Contradiction and Overdetermination" but even from the version of "Ideology and the Ideological State Apparatuses" published in 1970, which consisted, according to Althusser himself, of "fragments of a much longer study."[2] The latter text, although a composite, was carefully edited by Althusser and, however we may evaluate it today, exhibits a rigor and precision that are absent from "The Underground Current" with its numerous errors of fact and attribution.

What then would justify treating this now celebrated text, written, according to Matheron, by an Althusser who was no longer Althusser, as a text at all and taking its discrepancies as symptoms (and therefore endowed with theoretical significance) rather than mere accidents of its composition and publication? To begin to answer this unavoidable question, we might consult Althusser's own description of a work that he himself initially calls "strange": "As always, I have said everything in a single breath [d'un trait] trusting in some sort to the movement of a form of writing that is, as it were, 'spoken' rather than 'written'; and trusting also that readers of goodwill will meet it with something like a movement of the same kind. I have swept passed [enjambant] the difficulties flagged along the way, repeated established truths when necessary, and hastened towards its end in expectation of the sequel."[3] The text, then, spoken in one breath, or written in one stroke, the "condensation," as he says a few lines earlier, of all he is capable of saying at that moment, hastens toward its end but also toward an end to which there will be no sequel. As such, despite the insistence of so many readers on its novelty in relation to Althusser's earlier work, as if it marked an epistemological break internal to his own theory, "The Underground Current" possesses the characteristics of a last testament or confession, spoken all at once, as if he were making manifest what was heretofore latent in his published oeuvre or, perhaps more accurately, bringing what had been hidden into the open for all to see, the philosophical analogue of his auto-biography.

I propose to take seriously the description of the text as a movement toward an end and to take as a starting point the problem of chronology (both as it is practiced and as it is theorized in the text): the sense that it is organized around an observable historical development of the idea of a "materialism of the encounter" from its origins in Epicurus and Lucretius (with, it is true, a linking of this philosophy to that of Heidegger in order to demonstrate its contemporaneity or, rather, to demonstrate the non-contemporaneity of Heidegger whose work, as he himself insisted, marked a rejection of modernity and a return to the questions that occupied the Greeks), to Machiavelli, to the seventeenth century of Hobbes and Spinoza, to Rousseau, and finally to Marx. This history as presented by Althusser is all but exempt of the dramas of other such histories: it is not a time of breaks, interruptions, and reversals but a cumulative, remarkably continuous, linear time in which all that follows Epicurus and Lucretius seems little more than a progressive revelation of their doctrines as they are applied to increasingly complex historical and political problems. Of these, the most important problem is that of the origins of capitalism (and its corollary, which, as we shall see, haunts the entire narrative from start to finish, the end of capitalism).

At one point alone does the chronological organization of the argument become itself an object of scrutiny: in the conclusion of Althusser's discussion of Spinoza, who is termed the heir to Machiavelli, he declares Hobbes to be a transitional moment between Spinoza and Rousseau. He follows this reordering of the history of philosophy with the statement that "chronology hardly matters in the business, because each of these bodies of thought is developed for itself, despite the intermediary role played by Mersenne because what is in question is above all the resonances of a tradition buried and then revived, resonances which must be registered."[4] The implication here is twofold: first, because each of these works is a manifestation of a buried tradition, it is not so much the development of a theory that is at issue but the gradual excavation of what has so far remained underground; subsequently, the historical or even accidental order of revelation is not therefore identical to the logical order of which the tradition is composed. In fact, Althusser's insistence that "each of these bodies of thought developed for itself," tends to dissociate them and render relations of influence or antagonism unthinkable. But Althusser's critique of chronology remains extrinsic to the work as a whole; it is in fact, as we have noted, at odds with the organizing principle of "The Underground Current": the only exception to chronology is the inversion of Spinoza and Hobbes who were in fact contemporaries.

Why assign this lapse any importance at all? Is it not simply a lapse in rigour, a moment of confusion in an otherwise lucid text, a moment underscored by the reference to Mersenne (who died in 1648 — when Spinoza was sixteen) as an intermediary between Hobbes and Spinoza (which among other things suggests an association of Spinoza with Descartes for whom he is substituted in this passage)? Despite the fact that Hobbes is obviously (too obviously in fact) closer to Rousseau's doctrine than Spinoza, Althusser's chronological reversal allows him to avoid acknowledging the extent to which Spinoza's philosophy, and not just his theologico-political philosophy, represents a severe critique of Hobbes. This allows him to perform, the last thing we might have expected from Althusser, a Hobbesian reading of Spinoza, according to which, in a certain sense, Spinoza may be read as the anticipation of Hobbes, as laying a metaphysical groundwork for Hobbes's political philosophy.

As if to underscore the problematization of chronology in this text, Althusser begins his discussion of Spinoza by situating his philosophy in a period "less than a century after Machiavelli's death" (Machiavelli died in 1527). Almost immediately, Althusser advances the thesis, which he admits will appear "paradoxical" (although, we should note, without explaining why), that "for Spinoza, the object of philosophy is the void." Matheron inserts a note at this point in the text, informing the perhaps skeptical reader that in the very same year, 1982, Pierre Macherey "was defending much the same paradoxical thesis" at a conference in Urbino.[5] Before we can determine the extent to which Macherey's argument coincides with or even resembles Althusser's, we must first examine Althusser's account of the void in Spinoza.

To grasp the existence, otherwise disavowed, of the void in Spinoza's *Ethics*, we must note, Althusser contends, "how Spinoza begins," that is, with God, although a God who is "only nature" or "nothing other than nature." In other words, outside of nature there is nothing, *rien*, that is, *le vide*, the void. Althusser, however, is not content merely to establish the infinity of God but proceeds to posit the existence, outside of nature, of the void and to do so requires more than mere wordplay. To demonstrate the existence of the void as a concept in *Ethics* I, he takes up the theory of the attributes. The attributes, he tells us, can be read as a version of Epicurus's rain: they "fall in the empty space of their determination like raindrops that can undergo encounters only in this exceptional parallelism *without encounter or union* (of body and soul . . .) known as man, in this assignable but minute parallelism of thought and the body, which is still only parallelism, since here, as in all things, the order and connection of ideas are the same as the order and connection of things. In sum, a parallelism without encounter, yet a parallelism that is already, in itself, encounter thanks to the very structure of the relationship between the different elements of each attribute."[6]

Those familiar with Althusser, and more particularly with his commentary on Spinoza, will no doubt wonder at his use of *Ethics* II, proposition 7, to support the theory of "parallelism," a term that occurs nowhere else in Althusser's treatment of Spinoza for the very reason that it runs counter to virtually the entire of Althusser's oeuvre. In fact, it was none other than Macherey who, in his commentary on *Ethics* II, proposition 7, reminds us that "the parallelist reading of proposition 7 of *de Mente* reinscribes Spinozist doctrine in a dualist perspective, explaining all of nature on the basis of the relation between extended substance and thinking substance," a position that Spinoza has "precisely invalidated."[7] Rather than allowing the attributes to remain extrinsic to each other even as they develop in correspondence, Spinoza explains in the scholium to the proposition that "thinking substance and extended substance are one and the same substance."[8] It was precisely in this spirit that Althusser himself would write in 1970 that ideas had a material existence and the consciousness was nothing other than action. Here, in "The Underground Current," he has not only separated mind and body but has inserted between them the infinite space of the void, through which they are destined to fall in parallel for eternity.

It is possible at this point simply to dismiss Althusser's willful distortion of Spinoza's text as a more or less clumsy attempt to cast it as a slightly disguised version of Lucretius, as if the history of "aleatory materialism" were nothing more than a series of variations on a single theme. To do so, however, would be, in my view, a serious error; it would prevent us from understanding a concept the importance of which is not peculiar to Althusser: the concept of *le vide*, the void. This concept appears throughout the work of Althusser in diverse contexts and serves diverse and contradictory functions; in a sense it appears as if this entire, irreducibly complex history is staged all at once in one grand finale in "The Underground Current."[9] The passage on Spinoza's theory of the attributes, described in an editorial note as nearly covered over by corrections and only barely legible, may thus be understood as a symptom, the effect of an unrecognized conflict at the heart of the text between two incompatible notions of the void.

At no point in the text is the conflictual character of the void more apparent than the following passage from the discussion of Machiavelli. Here, the discussion of Machiavelli's theory of the non-accomplishment of Italy, the "atomized country, every atom of which was descending in free fall without encountering its neighbour," moves to an exposition of the philosophy that underlies this theory. It is a philosophy that furnishes the principles that allow Althusser not so much to transform his own philosophy as to translate it into its true form, the form proper to it. Thus, "philosophy has no object" is a "way of saying that philosophy's 'object' par excellence is nothingness, nothing or the void [le néant, le rien ou le vide]."[10] When Althusser argued at an earlier point (notably in the *cours de philosophie pour scientifiques* delivered in 1967) that philosophy had no object, he was careful to specify that by this he meant that it had no object external to it. Strictly speaking, philosophy was its own object or the element in which its own objects, philosophical objects, existed. These were the object not of a representation but of an intervention; in a striking phrase, Althusser advanced the idea that philosophy produced effects outside of itself only by intervening within itself. In its practical existence, philosophy must constantly pose to itself the question of its orientation, of the place it occupies and that which the conjuncture demands it accomplish; it must constantly ask, what is to be done? Such practical questions, however, warns Althusser, can easily "re-awaken the old religious question of destiny," which is "the mirror image of a theory of the radical 'origin' of things.'" Philosophy, to be sure, must take its distance from such notions, which in a sense surround and lay siege to it, but the void of a distance taken is not even a void, and the taking of a distance by drawing a line of demarcation did not even leave an empty space in its wake. In fact, Althusser concluded his course by drawing a line between himself and Rousseau and precisely warning against the theoretical effects of a certain concept of the void: "One does not occupy a position in philosophy in the sense that Rousseau's noble savage occupies in the *Discourse on the Origin of Inequality* an *empty* corner of the forest [un coin de forêt vide]."[11]

In "The Underground Current," the act of demarcation, of taking a distance, is substantiated: the void is not practiced but possessed or represented in the form of *le néant*, or le vide. Althusser endows philosophy, indeed, the history of philosophy with an object external to it: the nothing-ness that is the origin (or rather originary non-origin, a theoretical compro-mise that in no way escapes the implications of the concept of origins) and destiny of all things. If philosophy creates a void, it does so not to occupy a space but to unveil the heretofore concealed void that not only precedes but accompanies, like a shadow, all that exists as its secret and its truth. This ontological conception of the void, as we must call it, becomes for Althus-ser the defining characteristic, the specific difference of that "profound tra-dition" that led from Epicurus to Marx. The originary void is thus at its center, although a center denied, repressed, and forgotten by the dominant tradition, which, far from neglecting these thinkers, assimilated them into itself in order to better mute their radicalism. This tradition, Althusser tells us, gave up "thinking the origin as reason or end in order to think it as noth-ingness."[12] The question for us, as we read "The Underground Current," is whether this now openly avowed "theory of the radical 'origin' of things," to cite Althusser's own words, will "reawaken the old religious question of destiny."[13]

If Machiavelli sought to evacuate every form of providentialism and tele-ology from his political thought, Althusser argues, it was to reveal that the apparently teeming world of fifteenth-century Italy was in fact a void, "every atom of which was descending in free fall without encountering its neighbor," and therefore without the possibility of the "*carambolage*," that is, pile up or crystallization out of which nations, like species or worlds, could be created. In the most important sense, the sense that mattered to Machiavelli, Italy was a non-world of the non-accomplishment of the fact, the empty table awaiting the throw of the dice. If, for Machiavelli, Italy was the non-encounter among the lasting encounters of political atoms known as France and Spain, Hobbes will take the theory forward in a radical ges-ture that appears to abolish history, but in fact it furnished its conditions of possibility. His state of nature was less the projection onto an origin of a social, historical result, that of primitive accumulation itself, the forced dis-solution of rural communities and the emergence of a multitude of "master-less men," than a figuration of the void, the originary disorder in which individuals, "the atoms of society," sought to "persevere in their being" like so many "atoms descending in free fall parallel to each other."[14] Such a condition was not simply the origin of any society no matter how lasting, it remained in abeyance but never definitively abolished as the ever present possibility that haunted every society. It was this threat that justified and necessitated the Leviathan state.

Rousseau, in the second *Discourse*, will further refine Hobbes's theses, pointing out that Hobbes's state of nature is already a social state, even if the sole social relation is one of hostility and enmity. It is therefore a pseudo-origin, not the genuine social void that must precede any society but a counterfeit designed to justify tyranny. Rousseau, Althusser argues, returns, past the compromises that mar earlier conceptions of the state of nature, associated not only with Hobbes but even more with Locke, to "the radical Origin of everything," that is, the state of pure nature, the "truly radical absence of society that constitutes the essence of any possible society." What constitutes the "radical absence of society?" Precisely the lack of any social relation, "whether positive or negative." The "fantastic image of the primeval forest" will serve to make palpable and conceivable the infinite void of individuals without encounters. This world without event or encounter cannot itself produce society. The conjunction of individuals can only be "imposed" from without, by external causes that divide this infinity into contained spaces. That these atoms possess characteristics that allow them to conjoin, especially the pity that lies latent in them, awaiting only such an encounter to awaken, does not change the fact that this original condition constitutes the constant threat of the abyss, into which society "can fall back at any moment."[15]

It is only in Althusser's discussion of Marx, to which, as he says, all his "historical remarks are just a prelude," that the stakes of a materialism of the encounter or, more precisely, the relation of a philosophy of the void to a materialism of the encounter become apparent: "to say that in the beginning was nothingness or disorder is to take up a position prior to any assembling and ordering."[16] While there existed in Marx a theory of the dialectical progression of modes of production and, therefore, a theory of history as order, there coexisted with this first theory a second, irreducibly different theory of modes of production as aleatory encounters: "the whole that results from the taking hold of the 'encounter' does not precede the 'taking-hold' of its elements, but follows it; for this reason it might not have 'taken hold' and a fortiori, 'the encounter might not have taken place.'"[17] Capitalism might never have come into existence.

Of course, it might at this point be objected, and Althusser is well aware of this possible objection, that the fact of the possible non-accomplishment of capitalism has given way to its actual accomplishment and not simply as a brief encounter but as one that has lasted. In fact, it has lasted longer than the time so many of its theoreticians allotted it, "inducing stable relationships and a necessity the study of which yields 'laws'—tendential laws, of course."[18] The encounter that produces capitalism cannot be said a priori to be any less durable than that which produces nations or even biological species. It was Althusser himself who often recalled Spinoza's analysis of the durability of the Hebrew people—an aleatory a phenomenon as one could find in human history—which in certain ways was, in the typical Spinozist manner, nothing more than a metonym for the far more provocative and perhaps intolerable question of the rise to dominance and durability of Christianity itself (once the question of its truth is set aside), a question that Spinoza never directly posed and in fact could not pose, even in his correspondence (another sign of his solitude), in spite of its theologico-political urgency. In discussing this question, Althusser will have recourse to a term that would otherwise seem strangely out of place in this text: "structure."[19] He argues that every lasting encounter has a structure, and once the encounter takes place, there comes into being a "primacy of the structure over its elements." Citing Lucretius and alluding less directly to Spinoza, Althusser must admit that not every atom, element, or singular thing is capable not merely of "colliding" with any other but of becoming interlocked (he uses the verb "*accrocher*") with it to form a being, a singular thing. Thus, although this order with its coherence and its laws has arisen from disorder, it is no less an order. In fact, it might well be said that this is what haunts Althusser's text: the fear of the aleatory encounter that once established will persist not for eternity but, again to cite Spinoza, indefinitely; a fear of that which, in Althusser's words, *dure longtemps*, lasts a long time, that which fails to end on time, as expected and predicted. It is as a defense against even a theoretical possibility of this type that Althusser must postulate an origin, an original abyss from which all comes and to which all must return, the "radical instability" that haunts the most interlocked structures. They too are only provisional: just as they might not have taken place, they "may no longer take place."[20]

Interestingly, it is here, around an entire series of problems and references, that Althusser's theoretical trajectory more closely approaches Derrida's than at any other time in the history of their relationship. He reported in a letter in 1984 having recently reread Derrida after having earlier read him "in another context." Derrida has led him back to Heidegger (whom he has read "with the help of Derrida"), while Althusser has read Derrida in order to determine "in what respect, and how he has criticized Heidegger even while basing himself on him." And although Althusser will rather quickly report having "finished" with Heidegger ("who in the end annoyed me because of the streak of 'country priest' in him"), we would be mistaken to too quickly dismiss the brief encounter between Althusser, Derrida, and Heidegger.[21] François Matheron has dated the first draft of "The Underground Current" between July and September 1982; in October 1982, Derrida delivered an address at Johns Hopkins titled "My Chances/Mes chances: A Rendezvous with some Epicurean Stereophonies."[22] The latter text, otherwise devoted to an analysis of the notion of chance in psychoanalysis, contains a brief and extremely dense reading of Heidegger (primarily section thirty-eight of *Being and Time*) from the perspective of Epicurus and Lucretius.

It is in this context that Derrida poses a question concerning the history and function of the concept of chance that illuminates a heretofore unnoticed theme in Althusser's text, responding to it so precisely, to its words, motifs, and assumptions that Derrida might as well have been directly commenting on "The Underground Current": "when chance or luck are under consideration, why do the words and concepts impose the particular signification, sense, and direction of a downward movement, regardless of whether we are dealing with a throw or a fall? Why does this sense enjoy a privileged relation to the non-sense or insignificance which we find frequently associated with chance? What would such a movement of descent have to do with luck or chance?"[23] Derrida's questions call attention to Althusser's privileging of the rain as the image of atoms and of the fall (*la chute*) or falling (*tomber*) as their primary form of movement, a fact that becomes all the more noteworthy given the archival evidence that he read both Epicurus and Lucretius very closely and in the original languages. While the most frequent verb used by Epicurus to describe the motion of atoms and bodies is κινέω (to move) and by Lucretius *moveo* (to move), Althusser almost exclusively describes atoms as falling. And rain has no privileged place even in Lucretius, who indeed uses the expression "atoms raining in the void"; in *De Rerum Natura* the metaphors of rushing rivers, stormy seas, and blasts of wind are far more common. At the extreme Lucretius will even, in a phrase he repeats a number of times, refer to atoms "per inane vagantur," or "wandering through the void."[24]

Althusser so privileges the notion of the fall as to translate the first line of Wittgenstein's *Tractatus Logico-Philosophicus*, "Die Welt is alles, was der

Fall ist," (translated in the English edition of the work as "The world is all that is the case") as "The world is everything that 'falls,'" although modifying the translation as his sentence progresses to "everything that comes about [advient], everything that is the case—by *case*, let us understand *casus*: at once occurrence and chance, that which comes about in the mode of the unforeseeable, and yet of being."[25] The noun "der Fall" (the case) becomes a verb "tomber," conjugated in the phrase *tout ce qui "tombe."* It is clear Althusser regards the verb "to fall" as the most forceful way to render the case or the event, to separate such notions from any finalism, that is, origin or end. Is Althusser correct in his assumption or, conversely, is "fall" linked to an entire theological and philosophical history of which Althusser takes no account and therefore determines his text in ways that escape his knowledge and control?

The question of the fall leads Derrida from Epicurus and Lucretius to Heidegger in what he himself will call "an admittedly violent condensation," which produces an apparently only "fortuitous connection."[26] He refers specifically to "the analytic of Dasein" as discussed in section thirty-eight of *Being and Time*, "Falling and Thrownness" ("Das Verfallen und die Geworfenheit"), which contains the Heideggerian motifs mobilized by Althusser: "in Heidegger . . . 'things are thrown' in an inaugural 'destining,'" while his philosophy "'opens up' a prospect that restores a kind of transcendental contingency of the world, into which we are 'thrown.'"[27] It is here that Heidegger theorizes being in the world, the "*da*" or "there" of *Dasein* as a fallenness, and the belonging of being to the world is conceived as "das Verfallen des Daseins" or the falling of Dasein. The "violent condensation" of Epicurus and Heidegger proposed by Althusser and Derrida permits us to read "das Verfallen" as movement without origin, the movement by which being becomes what it is. But, as Derrida points out in a remark that may be as relevant to Althusser as to Heidegger, Heidegger himself admits only to deny and disavow the other meaning from which the term "fall" cannot be entirely disassociated: the "negative evaluation [der negative Bewertung]," the sense of a "fall" from a purer and higher "primal state [als "fall" einem reineren und höheren "Urstand"]," that is, not simply or even primarily the Christian notion of the Fall but perhaps also notions of a historically determined and therefore finite alienation (as opposed to the alienation—or inauthenticity—of being fallen into the world), of a "deplorable" state of which "more advanced stages of human culture generations might be able to rid themselves."[28] And while Heidegger takes great pains to differentiate the fall as he uses it from such theological and political notions, Derrida argues that "one is all the more struck with certain analogies with such a discourse."[29] Derrida undoubtedly refers here to the linking of Verfallenheit to inauthenticity; we might, however, apply his very brief remarks to Heidegger's (and Althusser's) discussion of thrownness (Geworfenheit).

While Geworfenheit is a way of thinking the original dispersion of being (again for Althusser as well as for Heidegger), thrownness is not precisely synonymous with dispersion and retains a theological and anthropological cast absent from such terms as "projection," "propulsion," "movement," and so on. Similarly, for Althusser, following Heidegger's commentary in the *Letter on Humanism*, the German expression "*es gibt*" ("there is," the equivalent of "*il y a*") is no longer allowed simply to function as a postulation but is returned to its origins in the verb "*geben*," to give: the "there is" becomes "it gives" and the "it" (*es*) in the expression, Heidegger insists, is being itself. "There is" becomes "Being gives." In "The Underground Current," Althusser takes a certain distance from Heidegger's formulations, even as he deploys them: the idea that "the world is a gift" gives way to the idea of *donner* as the dealing of cards; what is, is the "*donne primitive*," the original deal, before which there is nothing and thus marks the "primacy of absence over presence (Derrida)," the "horizon which recedes endlessly before the walker." Later in the text, Althusser will return to "es gibt" to render it equivalent to "there is nothing."[30] Destiny itself, (*der Geschick*, derived from the verb "*schicken*," to send) would seem to have ceased as a concept to refer to the end and instead come to signify an inaugural or originary sending, even, as Nancy and Derrida have suggested, an originary abandonment.

The world is thus falling: it has been given (away), dealt (out), sent, abandoned, all actions that the thesis of the primacy of absence over presence renders irreducible, actions before which there is nothing or no one. All of this tends to solidify and make permanent the issue and indeed the urgency of origin. "Before the world," a phrase that is repeated throughout in "The Underground Curren," there is "the non-world," before "the accomplishment of the fact, its non-accomplishment"; it is precisely in the nothing that precedes what is that philosophy dwells, the eternal void in relation to which being is mere rain, fleeting condensations of matter destined quickly to dissolve. Being is not fallen but that instantaneous falling into dissolution, into the "nothingness and disorder" (a perfect translation of the Hebrew of the second sentence of Genesis: before creation, the world was nothingness and disorder) out of which it came. It is nothingness itself that declines into being, sending that which exists to its destruction. This is precisely the doctrine Hegel, in the *Phenomenology*, ascribed to skepticism: everything is *Nichtigkeit* or nothingness. Hyppolite in his commentary suggests that this is not the epistemological skepticism of Greek and Roman antiquity but rather that of the book accused by the Rabbinical commentators of Epicurean heresy, Ecclesiastes: all is vanity הבל)) or nothingness.[31] The skeptical consciousness "declares the absolute vanishing [das Absolute Verschwinden]" and the nothingness (Nichtigkeit) of all things: "Before the silver cord is snapped asunder and the golden bowl is shattered, and the pitcher is broken at the fountain, and the wheel falls shattered into the pit, and the dust returns to the earth as it was . . . nothingness of nothingnesses, says Koheleth, all is nothingness."[32] For Althusser, however, the principle of nothingness as destiny serves not to condemn or devalue the human world in its evanescence (as is the case with Hegel's account of skepticism); it instead furnishes a principle of hope, of anticipation.

The entire principle of an originary and final nothingness is summed up in a proposition that deserves some scrutiny: "History here is the permanent revocation of the accomplished fact by another undecipherable fact to be accomplished, without our knowing in advance whether, or when, or how the event that revokes it will come about." It is worth recalling at this point that Althusser's discussion of Spinoza ends with a reference to the prophet Daniel: here it is Althusser's own hand that inscribes the indecipherable announcement of the destruction to come, of the undoing of the accomplished fact and "the dice thrown again on the empty table."[33] We should not be deceived by Althusser's insistence on original nothingness. The meaning of the void is here, not at the moment of the encounter that "takes hold" and produces a world but the moment of its inevitable destruction, not the past but the future, although a future not given to us to know, but a future to await. Is it too much to say that Althusser, writing in the 1980s, a time of defeat and despair, has thus rewritten the conclusion of Benjamin's "Theses on the Philosophy of History," producing a theory of messianicity without a messiah?[34]

But Daniel, as Althusser liked to say, following Spinoza, often did not know the meaning of his own prophecies. Is there not a meaning of the void as it is developed in this text that eludes Althusser? Indeed, if the void in "The Underground Current" were reducible to an ontology, we would be compelled to repeat to him his own words of twenty years earlier, when he described in a lecture to his students Foucault's *Folie et déraison* as finally unable to break with a theory of the origin as the condition of possibility of history's intelligibility. And the specific form of the origin that haunted Foucault's first great work would survive to haunt Althusser himself. That which the Althusser of 1963 could describe as a "transcendental abyss" allowed Foucault to argue that "the great work [grande œuvre] of history is indelibly accompanied by an absence of work, which renews itself at each instant, but which runs unaltered in its inevitable emptiness all throughout history: and even before history, since it is already there in the primitive decision, and after it as well since it will triumph in history's last words."[35] "The Underground Current" thus exhibits a strange unthought mimicry of the very "transcendentalism" Althusser once subjected to critical scrutiny, tracking it in all its ruses through the thickets of Foucault's first major text.

To discern the existence of another notion of the void, not only irreducible to the first but actively antagonistic to it, we will return to Althusser's summary of "the philosophy of the void": it is not only "a philosophy which *says* that the void preexists the atoms that fall in it, but a philosophy which makes a philosophical void in order to endow itself with existence." Althusser presents the two aspects of philosophy as if they were complementary, as if a philosophy that represents an ontological fact, that of the void that preexists all things, would serve as the foundation of the philosophy that makes a void, as if the latter's activity were to represent in discourse the former. If, however, we follow the itinerary of the statement "philosophy makes a void," not only through this text but through Althusser's work as a whole, we are forced to confront the fact that the work of "evacuating all philosophical problems" cannot leave even the void itself, especially insofar as it serves as "the radical origin of all things," untouched and unaffected.[36]

In another symptomatic moment in the text, a moment perhaps not entirely separable from the discussion of Spinoza cited earlier, Althusser attributes the position that "to say that in the beginning was nothingness or disorder is to take up a position prior to any assembling and ordering, and to give up thinking the origin as Reason or End in order to think it as nothingness," to a triumvirate of philosophers: Nietzsche, Deleuze, and Derrida. Of the three, of course, Deleuze stands out and not only as a fellow Spinozist as Althusser once addressed him in their correspondence. For it was he, in an essay well known to Althusser, who would offer a reading of Lucretius (which could legitimately be called a Spinozist reading) that passionately contested the notion that *De Rerum Natura* founded its concept of nature on an originary nothingness. According to Deleuze, Lucretius, following Epicurus, rejected all previous philosophy on the grounds that it was unable to think "nature as the production of the diverse," seeking instead to reduce diversity to identity and to overcome difference in the name of being or the one. It is in relation to this tendency alone that Lucretius's notion of the void may be understood: the problem with earlier philosophies is not that they lacked a conception of the void, a lack that he would attempt to fill, it was, rather, that "because they did not want to consider the void, the void encompassed everything. Their being, their One, and their whole are artificial and unnatural, always corruptible, fleeting." Rather than confront irreducible diversity and singularity, "they would rather say, 'being is nothing.'"[37] At this point it is difficult not to see "The Underground Current," at least in part, as a continuation of a philosophical tradition that, far from rejecting the void, makes of it, in however disavowed a form, the ground and truth of existence. We might even go further to see that Althusser makes explicit the all-encompassing void that earlier philosophies sought to conceal, saying out loud what they could only silently think. Is not the void for Althusser the principle that overcomes the difference between the brief and the lasting encounter, the principle in relation to which all things are resolved into the identity of pure nothingness, the origin and destiny of all things?

Indeed, Deleuze suggests that Lucretius's concept of the void functions precisely to counter the figure of an original nothingness that haunts philosophy, to empty or evacuate it, as it were, in order to allow philosophy to think the singular and the diverse. In a bold step he will declare Lucretius's clinamen not so much a swerve of the atom through the void as "a kind of conatus," the persistence of a singular thing not in spite of but by means of encounters and conjunctions. By thus invoking Spinoza, Deleuze points to a philosophy from which the void has already been evacuated, a philosophy whose aim is to think the infinite productivity of singularities, that is, to put it in Althusser's terms, a philosophy of the encounter without the void.

But would not the idea of a philosophy that makes a void in order to free the infinite production of the diverse and the singular from the transcendental unity imposed by the originary void mark, in its very dissociation from a reality to which it would appear to stand opposed, another form of transcendence, even a dualism of thought and extension, idea and thing, mind and body? It is at this point that Althusser's text is most in conflict with itself: the idea that philosophy does not find the void but makes it compels us to reverse many of the propositions Althusser advances. From this perspective, the void is not the condition of the encounter; rather, the encounter is the condition of the void, although understood as a verb, an activity rather than a substance, even if that substance is a negation of substance. In this sense, we can say of the void, as Spinoza does of God, that it does not exist prior to or outside of the encounters, conjunctions, and disjunctions in which it is immanent. The void that philosophy makes would not be a constatation of the real, as if it were external to that which it represents, but rather one of its effects, a means by which it frees itself of origins and ends in order to become the infinite diversity it is, the indissociable simultaneity of thought and action that Althusser once tried to capture in the phrase "theoretical practice."[38]

Why is this other concept of the void, a concept perpetually inscribed in and on Althusser's texts, at their center or their margins, sometimes visible, often invisible, so submerged or written over in Althusser's last text? Setting aside psychological explanations, we find the beginnings of a response twenty years earlier in another text, "Contradiction and Overdetermination," whose object was the aleatory, the encounter, the singular. It was as if in that moment, a moment characterized by a balance of forces so apparently favorable to an undoing of the present, one could afford to contemplate not the dissolution to come or the void to which all would return but precisely the opposite: the "véritable blocage," the "inhibition historique" that prevented a social formation or even a mode of production from ending "on time," that is, the time allotted to it by the theoreticians of historical evolution.[39] How could societies that had ripened into maturity persist for so long? How could their "decomposition" take the form of a system that could endure for decades or even centuries? Encounters of extraordinary number and variety might, it is true, bring about the destruction of a social order, but more commonly, far more commonly, such forces might serve to freeze it in place, to render it impervious and neutralize the antagonistic forces that arise in its very effort to persist in its own being.

To situate the ontological conception of the void in the context of Althusser's corpus as a whole is then to be able to assign it its symptomatic value and force. Another text, perhaps the only other text, in which the concepts of le vide and le néant play a central role is "The Piccolo Teatro: Bertolazzi and Brecht," published the same year as "Contradiction and Overdetermination," which shares many of the concerns mentioned a moment ago. What is striking about these terms in this early text is that they are the concepts that allow Althusser to think another time than that of the encounter that strikes like lightening in the void. They are the concepts of an "empty time [d'un temps vide]," "a time empty of events and collisions," a time "long and slow to live," a time in which a structure formed by an encounter long since forgotten remains silent and immobile. It is "a time in which nothing happens," nothing that is, that can be called an event, "a time without hope or future, a time in which the past itself is frozen in repetition." It is a "time in which gestures have neither result nor effect," not because the effects are doomed immediately to pass away but because there are no effects. It is a time of "unbearable vacuity [d'une vacuité insoutenable]." When will the event that in an instant shatters this world of empty repetition occur? Only "when everyone has departed," for its time is irreducibly foreign to the time of nothingness. This play, like those of Brecht, subjects the "illusions of consciousness" to the experience of an intolerable temporality: "thus, in Galileo the history that is slower than the consciousness impatient for truth, the history which is also disconcerting for a consciousness never able to 'grasp' it durably in the time of its short life."[40] "The Underground Current," then, is the chronicle of "a waiting that knows itself in vain."[41] It is a waiting in vain for a future that does not arrive late or on time, for a consciousness that confuses its time with the time of history and its end with the end of a mode of production, unwilling and perhaps unable to grasp the fact that from the perspective of a genuine materialism of the encounter, just as nothing guarantees the arrival of the best, so nothing absolutely prohibits the endurance of the worst.

The End of Destiny
Althusser before Althusser

ג׳ באין בימה הרעת אלו הן משח מציאה ועקרב

Three things come unforeseeably: the Messiah, a found object and a scorpion.
BABYLONIAN TALMUD, Tractate Sanhedrin 97a

If "The Underground Current of the Materialism of the Encounter," Althusser's "last" work, itself a found object whose discovery and publication was purely a matter of chance, unexpectedly produced a certain eschatology, if not a kind of messianism, that disrupted its connection to itself and to the materialism of the encounter that preceded and accompanied it, so another text, another object lost and forgotten, lurking unexpectedly like the scorpion with which the Talmudic verse somewhat surprisingly concludes, returns against this eschatology. In fact, it is Althusser's "first" text, the first full-length essay intended for publication: "The International of Decent Feelings," written in December 1946.[1] By following and concluding a discussion of Althusser's last work with a reading of his first text, I do not intend so much to reverse chronology as to examine the ways in which Althusser calls into question the notion of time as χϱονος, leading from origin to end or first to last. To speak here of Althusser's itinerary is to set aside notions of a point of departure and a destination. He himself insisted on the destinationless nature of philosophical work: the individual who jumps aboard a train "without knowing where he comes from (origin) or where he is going (goal)."[2] Nor should we assume that we, unlike Althusser himself, know from our historical vantage point where he is going, as if his thought finally reached its ultimate destination. The movement of Althusser's thought does not in the least resemble progress or development; it is rather a movement without an identifiable beginning or end, consisting of reversals, detours, and diversions. The greatness of Althusser, what Macherey called his "fearlessness," consisted in his refusal to confer upon his philosophical discoveries (for there are philosophical discoveries) an artificial, premature coherence, and his willingness to risk the discontinuity and even provisional incoherence of a way of thinking that never allows itself to rest.[3] His greatest texts were the products, perhaps even the by-products, of this restlessness. I refer here above all not to his most frequently cited texts but to those like "Contradiction and Overdetermination" or "Lenin and Philosophy," which provoked and continue to provoke incomprehension and anxiety in his many critics.

In the opening of *Reading Capital*, which has lost none of its lucidity or importance, Althusser describes Marx's reading of classical economics not as an identification of what is missing in the texts of Smith and Ricardo but rather what is there present and visible but overlooked: the answers to questions that have never been posed and, in a certain sense, must precede the posing of the questions, their questions, as their condition of possibility. In this way Althusser's first work may be read as the answer or an answer to the questions "The Underground Current" poses without any sense that it is doing so, as if the latter were written in the interrogative, rather than the declarative, mood. Thus, we have reason to think carefully about the celebrity of the later text and the obscurity of the earlier, for it may well be the case that a text that poses questions in the guise of their own answers is more accessible or at least more reassuring than a text that offers answers to questions that have yet to be asked. It is precisely this encounter between the first and the last or the answer and its question that confers upon "The International of Decent Feelings" its meaning and importance. Althusser has provided all the means necessary for a critique of the eschatology of his final work.

"The International of Decent Feelings" admittedly poses a number of difficulties for those accustomed to the Althusser of the sixties and seventies, not to speak of the theoretician of aleatory materialism. It is a text by all accounts written by "Althusser before Althusser,"[4] a still young man who a mere eighteen months earlier had been starving in a German prisoner of war camp, an intellectual engagé, impassioned by Marxism and by class struggle, but still a Christian, an observant Catholic to be precise (there is no religion without ritual, as he would later say), capable of employing the phrase "The Last Judgment," without irony. Its reference points and theoretical adversaries are not those of later years, Marxist humanism and structuralism, but the postwar writings of such figures as Camus, Malraux, Gabriel Marcel, and Arthur Koestler to whom Althusser refers rarely if at all after 1960. It was thus undeniably produced in a theoretical and political conjuncture very different from that he attempted to theorize in the mid-sixties.

The fact that it takes the form of what Althusser would later call an intervention demonstrates his own maxim that practice precedes theory as its precondition and that a method must be practiced before it can be stated or theorized. As an intervention, it is an essay that he himself would call, in a letter to his father, "virulent" (a term that might most accurately be translated as "venomous," that is, not simply angry or rancorous but actively poisonous, capable of destroying, in this case, a body of argument from within, perhaps by triggering a deadly autoimmune reaction).[5] His judgment of the essay was later confirmed: submitted to the Catholic journal *Cahiers de notre jeunesse*, it was almost immediately rejected precisely because of this very "virulence." The text itself, which lay undiscovered until after Althusser's death, did not escape the effects of the poison: part of the last page was torn out and had disappeared. Thus, published only posthumously, the text has been sent on its way, subject to the fortuitous encounters that will pass for its destination.

The first and the last: this "venomous" text stands in stark contrast to "The Underground Current." Althusser before Althusser and Althusser after Althusser. The "late" Althusser is all but bereft of religious or theological references, except those designed to illustrate the surface under which the materialist current flows (the very image of a buried truth of which Althusser taught us to be suspicious of insofar as it recapitulated the notion of surface and depth, of essential and inessential, affirming the idea that truth could be extracted from the dross that surrounds it).[6] The early text, in contrast, is explicitly religious, addressed to Christians in a Christian idiom, making liberal use of scriptural references and allusions to move his readers and in fact formulating nothing less than a Christian critique of the eschatologies (both secular and religious—if such a distinction can be made in the period in which Althusser wrote) that suddenly appeared so pertinent in the aftermath of the greatest slaughter in human history. What he does in this early text is undeniable: as a Christian, he not only does not reject theological discourse in the name of "reason," let alone "materialism" or "naturalism," but remains within it to draw a line of demarcation internal to it in order to make visible a distinction or difference, as if the conflict that concerns him were not between theology and an external rationality, a ratio or logos outside of and opposed to it, but the conflict internal to theology itself in which an otherness (the nature of which remains to be determined) is already inscribed. But what difference, what otherness? Could it be that a distinction between materialism and idealism (to use the terms of *Lenin and Philosophy*) rather than coinciding with the division between theology and philosophy traverses both fields, setting each against itself and calling their distinction into question?

It is perhaps helpful to recall Macherey's comment on the relation of a materialist practice of philosophy to the traditional dilemmas and oppositions that philosophy recognizes as its own: "the real process of the history of philosophy cannot be confused with the conflict of ideas that appears on its surface, the debates and traditional dilemmas in which it recognizes its true problems: freedom or necessity, truth or error, individual or society. . . . Let us take an example: the well-known opposition of reason or experience. Is this conflict an objective contradiction which reveals the material processes of the history of philosophy? Do the fundamental tendencies in philosophy, materialism and idealism, appear there in person?"[7] We might interject here that today the opposition between philosophy and theology, or philosophy and religion, is perhaps even more constitutive than those cited by Macherey, in that philosophy has historically defined itself and continues to define itself in opposition to theology and religion. Macherey's response to his examples and ours is important: "in effect, materialism cannot recognize itself in any of these pairs," because:

> there is no separate history of idealism (or materialism) in which the antagonistic position would intervene from the exterior, as if it were utterly foreign to it: on the contrary, it is necessary to say that materialism is objectively engaged, in person or not, in the history of idealism, according to the material conditions that determine the real relation of forces between these tendencies. . . . In a certain way and under certain conditions, it might be said: there is materialism in idealism, just as there is materialism in idealism. Which means nothing other than that idealism and materialism do not have two independent and distinct histories, but belong to one and the same history.[8]

From such a perspective, it is perfectly possible that an intervention within theology could produce a more forceful critique of messianism and eschatology than an explicitly irreligious text, which, as it were, might be more vulnerable to that which it regards as irreducibly foreign to it, encountering the concept of the end unawares, and thus in however secularized a manner all the more its captive.

Althusser wrote "The International of Decent Feelings" as a critique of the messianisms, both secular and religious, that arrived to give meaning and significance to the conjuncture that immediately followed the apparent cessation of hostilities in 1945 throughout the world. Instead of a general sense of relief, a sense that the world's inhabitants might return to their prewar lives and occupations, there emerged a generalized sense of dread: "two years after the most atrocious of wars, on this earth covered with peace and ruins, in the mists of the winter that is drawing nigh . . . men are beginning to see that the war waged with arms has not brought the war for souls to an end, that the peace is as murderous as the war, and still more terrible; for now in peacetime murder no longer has the clamour of arms for an excuse."[9] The occasion of this observation was André Malraux's lecture "L'homme et la culture," delivered at the Sorbonne on November 4, 1946, in which he announced, according to Althusser's rendition: "At the end of the last century, Nietzsche proclaimed the death of God. Now it is for us to ask ourselves whether, today, man is not dead."[10] The death of man to which Malraux referred was not the death of a concept but a real death, the extinction of the human species suddenly made possible by the advent of the atomic bomb. The war, hastened to its end precisely by the techniques of mass destruction, has made extinction imminent and death the absolute master whose judgment has only been temporarily deferred.[11] Against this ever present possibility, a universal alliance must be concluded; its proponents include such diverse and otherwise opposed figures as the "secular progressives," Malraux and Camus, together with Christian intellectuals such as Gabriel Marcel and, for lack of a better term, "antitotalitarians" such as Arthur Koestler. Leaving minor (and not so minor) differences aside, they are united in calling for the formation of a new international, "the international of decent feelings [L'internationale des bons sentiments]," a mocking phrase that captures what Althusser regarded as a fundamental lack of seriousness beneath the pompous phrases and declarations of alarm issuing from this "Holy Alliance against Destiny."[12]

According to Althusser, it is Camus, whose *Neither Victims nor Executioners* (*Ni victimes ni bourreaux*) had appeared in installments in the newspaper *Combat* during November 1946, who emerges as the theoretician of the secular version of the new international. For the Camus of 1946 (a Camus very different from the author of *The Myth of Sisyphus* [1942], which Althusser cites against the eschatological orientation of *Neither Victims nor Executioners*) the defeat of one totalitarianism has simply displaced the struggle to the victors: the United States and the Soviet Union. Both, according to Camus, are utopianisms struggling to realize their ideals through the most efficient means necessary, violence, now made incomparably more effective by new technologies (new forms of genocidal violence, from industrialized death camps to the atomic bomb). Not that he rules out good intentions on the part of Communists or Liberals who seek equality or freedom: it is precisely the combination of all the good intentions "that has produced the present infernal world."[13] There is no question of choosing between them; the crimes of both sides are too well known. In fact, their opposition is more apparent than real, nothing more than the effect and realization of their more primary unity. Together, they constitute another international, an international of death, to which all who seek to live and to insure the survival of humanity itself must declare their opposition. They have given the universal its positivity, the positivity of the means of annihilation of the human species, making death an absolute master in a way that Hegel could never have imagined. Death against life, men against humanity (to cite Marcel's variant): such are the terms in which the historical present has been allegorized. The twentieth century, Camus argues, "is the century of fear."[14]

Althusser notes that such a worldview willingly borrows the language of Marxism. Thus, it is not so much the case that the proletariat as maker of history has disappeared or become irrelevant. It has instead become universal: humanity in its entirety, as totality, has become the new proletariat, shaped into a collectivity not by the means and relations of production but precisely by the means and relations of destruction that, as the experience of the war shows, make use of their bodies to realize the goal of global annihilation. The struggle between worker and employer, between exploited and exploiter, once regarded as essential, can now be understood has having been an anticipation of that by which it has been superseded and whose arrival it merely prefigured: the proletarianization of humanity as such. It is the "proletariat of the human condition," and according to Camus, "the condition of modern man is fear."[15]

Thus, the effect of such a proletarianization, which operates less through material conditions than through the threat of what is to come, "the imminence of a common destiny," which is that of humanity's destruction, is the constitution of a "proletariat of fear." It is fear that unites the otherwise disparate and opposing parts of humanity into a universal community: "Fear haunts the rich man and the poor, the free man and the prisoner, it holds the soul of every man in its grip, whatever his legal or social status, from the moment he looks his destiny in the face and sees that *his destiny awaits him*." Althusser cites Matthew 5:45, from the Sermon on the Mount, typically condensing two lines into one. God "makes the sun shine on the good and the evil alike and the rain fall on both the just and the unjust (Althusser: 'it rains on the good and the evil alike')."[16] In Matthew 5:44, these images justify the argument that it is not enough to love one's neighbor or even the stranger as oneself; one must love one's enemies: "bless them that curse you, do good to them that hate you and pray for them that speak against and persecute you." For the partisans of the new international such observations are particularly pertinent: who, among the participants in humanity's worst war is worthy of judging his fellow man? How is it possible, asks Marcel, "that the same men who fought and suffered so that their country could be delivered from the Gestapo, instituted or tolerated methods not fundamentally different from those they suffered from. . . . The lies of Vichy paved the way to the lies of the Resistance."[17] For Marcel, to have resisted Nazi violence was to have exposed oneself to a "contagion" to which, once it reaches a certain threshold, no one is immune. Both the Nazi occupiers and those who physically resisted them were driven to a partisan hatred that tends to the obliteration of "the fundamental freedoms." The Germans had their death camps, yes, but the Allies are responsible for Dresden and Hiroshima. The Germans tortured civilians but so did the partisans who opposed them: "We are all murderers! Cries Camus."[18] According to Marcel, if no side is without sin, if all have participated in murder, so have all sides working in unwitting harmony produced "techniques or technologies of debasement [les techniques d'avilissement']." Somewhat surprisingly, following a period of unparalleled innovation in the practices of torture and mass extermination, the debasement to which Marcel refers is not that of one's physical being, but rather of the mind, not malnutrition or excessive labor but the techniques of mass communication that facilitate the universalization of propaganda. The community thereby created is not a properly human community but a solidarity of "sub-humans [sous-hommes]" fit only to participate in their own extermination.[19]

Althusser, after providing a brief sketch of the nonpartisan partisanship of the international of decent feelings, suggests "there is perhaps something to be gained from trying to discover what it conceals." The generalized condemnation of humanity for its proponents (both Christian and atheist) opens the sole possible form of a human community: only when each recognizes the evil he has done can he learn to forgive and accept others. All have killed (whether guarding or liberating a concentration camp, whether trying to enslave a people or to resist enslavement; indeed, did not the very inmates of the camps exact terrible vengeance on their former captors when given the chance, perhaps using the same instruments and technologies of pain and death?) and are thus not only "made indistinguishable" but positively "reconciled by crime." The relentless assertion of universal guilt paradoxically allows all men to be "absolved by crime" in a "secular absolution," which will allow the all of humanity "to clear their consciences at bargain rates."[20] Thus, the reinvention of a secular equivalent of original sin ("no murder is legitimate," Camus argues) allows these thinkers not only to oppose all partisanship but to advance the argument that a distinction between the violence of the occupier and the occupied, between inmate and guard, between master and slave only allows the perpetuation of violence and insures its universalization.[21] Althusser, however, does not stop his analysis there. The concept of original sin necessitates redemption; our (collective) past fault turns us toward the future, and we remain suspended between hope and fear.

It is significant that Camus who denounces both capitalism and communism as messianisms, in that both seek to destroy the world that exists in order to realize the world to come and do not hesitate to used armed force to hasten its coming, is himself captivated by the notion of an imminent end. He insists that his objective is "to define the conditions of a modest political thought, that is, one freed from any messianism and unencumbered by any nostalgia for an earthly paradise." A sober and modest consideration of the history that the world has just lived through may allow an indefinite postponement of the "apocalyptic history that awaits us."[22] Messianism, according to which the end justifies the means, is an eschatology masquerading as a teleology: the struggle to realize the desired goals only produces the end of humanity. Thus, Camus denounces messianism from the point of view of the apocalypse that it will bring about, that is, from the point of view of the end of humanity as such, an end whose proximity requires urgent action.

Marcel's interpretation of the postwar situation is remarkably similar:

> An extremely general fact seems to me to dominate the contemporary situation. Men have entered what we must call an eschatological age. I do not necessarily mean by this that what we call in an extremely equivocal phrase, the end of the world is chronologically near; it would seem presumptuous and even puerile to make any kind of prophetic statement on this matter. But what is important is that man as species cannot fail to appear today as endowed with the capacity to put an end to his earthly existence. It is no longer a question of a distant and vague possibility raised by some excitable astronomer from his observatory—but of an approaching, immediate possibility whose foundation is in man himself and not in the sudden eruption of a celestial body in the aftermath of some cosmic collision.[23]

Marcel, as Althusser notes, while appearing to distance himself from any prophetic discourse, does not refrain from interpreting the present from the perspective of original sin and the Last Judgment: the universalization of guilt, both because it leaves no remnant without sin and because it thereby displaces any possibility of salvation (in however secular a sense) to a future absolutely beyond being, allows us to infer that the next and final war, final because it will bring about the destruction of humanity, "will in fact be a bilateral crime. But the paradoxical notion of a bilateral crime calls for closer examination. It appears to be indistinguishable from that of sin itself."[24] The apocalypse to come, which will leave not even a just remnant of humanity, will thus be the absolute coincidence of sin and its own punishment: humanity's murder of itself as punishment for that murder. What is crucial here is that the political and social differences and forms of inequality that separate human beings and set not individuals but collectivities against each other are nullified. Their very opposition, the forms of the struggles in which they meet and, above all, the technologies driven by and in turn determining these struggles, is simply the nature of the unwitting and involuntary cooperation in the accomplishment of sin whose very realization is its own punishment.

Significantly, of all the works devoted to the theme of apocalypse (and of the fraternity that its imminence effectuates) produced by living authors, Althusser singles out Malraux's epic of the Spanish Civil War, *L'espoir* (translated into English as *Man's Hope*), published in 1937: "This apocalyptic fraternity is a pure creation of language. Looking back we can make out anticipations of it in certain formulations of *Man's Hope*, perhaps the most somber [Althusser had originally written "despairing"] book of our times: is it still possible to speak of a 'fraternity beyond death'? Fear is not a fatherland [patrie], nor is courage (we have learned this from the fascists, who now attempt to exonerate themselves by talking about their courage); more, the human condition is not a human fatherland."[25] Althusser here refers to a passage in *L'espoir* in which two former enemies, an anarchist named Puig and a Catholic military officer named Ximénès, pitted against each other in the Asturias revolt of 1934, are both now (1936) united behind the Republic, overcoming their previous antagonism by recognizing that "for Ximénès as for Puig courage was also a fatherland."[26] The Popular Front as understood by Malraux is already a human front, and those opposed to it (Spanish Fascists—often reduced for effect to their expeditionary force, the "Moors"—together with their German and Italian allies, who all together constitute an inhuman front for total destruction) are nothing more than the embodiment of a will to annihilation, the regime that they intend to put in place nothing more than the systematic destruction of humanity by itself. As Althusser points out, however, the reconciliation of former enemies in the cause of courage can and will almost certainly be extended in another conjuncture to (former or even present) Fascists themselves, as is the case in 1946. Courage, like fear or hope, is not an orientation to the present but to the future, to that which is to come, that which does not (yet) exist, but whose imminence can and should unite all, the just and the unjust, friend and enemy alike.

Further, Malraux's critique of the left wing of the Popular Front (those parties to the left of the Soviet-affiliated Communist Party) as a "fraternity of the Apocalypse" anticipates his later rejection of all forms of socialism and communism. The anarchists as he portrays them are ardent "apocalyp-ticians": one of them, Garcia, declares that the Fascist insurrection "was beaten. And beaten by the Apocalypse." Magnin, sympathetic to the Communist Party, denounces the slogan of "Land to the Peasants" (advanced by the Anarchists and the Partido Obrero de Unificación Marxista) as providing "objective aid to Franco," and he argues that Franco will be beaten by an "organization," not by an "apocalypse": "the danger is that every man bears within himself the desire for an apocalypse. And that in the struggle, this desire leads in a very short time to certain defeat. For a very simple reason: by its very nature, the Apocalypse has no future."[27] In fact, Malraux without knowing it, has already sketched out his postwar position:

neither the Left nor the Right, that is, neither the apocalypse of the revolution nor that of the counterrevolution. The Communist Party of Spain in 1936 appeared to Malraux as the defender of civilization against the objectively united forces (Fascist, Anarchist, and Trotskyist) of lawlessness and destruction. Less than a decade later in France, De Gaulle would play that role against a Communist Party, from Malraux's perspective, threatening its own apocalypse. Humanity must unite against that which in any given historical situation seeks to abolish the future.

It becomes clear at this point that the international of decent feelings was engaged in a theological-political project whose central concepts were perfectly amphibious, capable of living and reproducing in both religious and secular realms. One such concept, arguably central to the entire movement, was never pronounced by name, at least within the French context. It is the concept that Schmitt, writing at the same time as Althusser and in response to the same events, in *Nomos of the Earth*, would appropriate from early and medieval Christianity: the concept of the katechon, first articulated in 2 Thessalonians 2:1–6:

> Now we request, brothers, concerning the appearance (τῆς παρο–υσίας) of the Lord Jesus Christ and our coming together in him, that you not be shaken or disturbed either by a spirit, by words or by a letter saying that the Day of the Lord has arrived. Let no one deceive you, for that day will not come unless apostasy comes first and the man of lawlessness is revealed (καί ἀποκαλυφθή ὁ ἄνθρωπος τῆς ἀνομίας), the son of destruction, who opposes and places himself above every god or object of worship, in order to take a seat in God's temple and display himself as if he were God. Do you not remember that I spoke of this when I was here before? And you know what restrains (κατέχον) him now, that he will be revealed (ἀποκαλυφθῆναι) in his time (καιρῷ).[28]

Schmitt read this very difficult passage, subject historically to many different and opposing interpretations, as providing a "bridge" between an eschatological expectation whose sense of imminence could only lead to a suspension of all worldly activity, the vanity of which rendered it contemptible and thus, as Schmitt argues, to a kind of "paralysis," and the acceptance of the deferral of Christ's Parousia and, with it, of the need for order and culture, for a *nomos*.[29]

In this Epistle, Paul inaugurates the distinction between true and false apocalypses, the first brought about by Christ himself, while the second is the work of the "anomos (ανομος)," the lawless one. As Schmitt notes in his reference to "Adso's letter to Queen Gerberga" (ca. 950), part of the millenarian speculation that preceded the year 1000, the apocalypse associated with the lawless one, now explicitly the Antichrist, is no less destructive for being false.[30] In fact, Adso warns that there are many Antichrists, not simply the (primary) Jewish one who will be born in Babylonia, and each has many servants, earthly rulers who destroy the innocent and persecute the faithful. In the face of such evil, it becomes not simply legitimate to "restrain" (the verb κατεχώ, to restrain or hold back) the lawless one, the one who destroys law and culture, but necessary. The problem of the katechon's identity is crucial: Who holds back the lawless one? A recent commentator has identified nine possibilities ranging from God himself to Paul.[31] Schmitt's argument, however, derives from the most prominent and politically oriented of the interpretations: the katechon of Scripture was the Roman Empire. It was Tertullian who developed this theme in his *Apologetics*. Why would Christians pray for those who persecute them, namely the Roman emperors? According to Tertullian: "We know that the great force [vim maximam] which threatens the whole world, the end of the age itself with its menace of horrendous suffering, is delayed [retardari] by the respite which the Roman empire provides for us. We do not want to experience this and when we pray for its postponement [differri], we are supporting the continuance of Rome."[32]

The international of decent feelings, while sharing the forms of Schmitt's analysis of world history as the struggle of the katechon against the horrendous suffering and perhaps even annihilation that the lawless one will inflict upon the world, has supplied a very different content. The governments of the earth (or at least the most powerful among them) have since the war become the agents of mass destruction, of an annihilation, an end to the world (as Marcel noted) quite distinct from that of the Last Judgment. The struggles between these worldly powers, the technological developments that are both causes and effects of these struggles, all conspire together in one great destructive force. The citizens of the world united by the very imminence of the cataclysm must awaken to this threat, to acknowledge that the age is indeed the age of fear, a justified fear that all must confront and take on the role of the katechon themselves. The survival of the human race demands a conspiracy of the good to restrain the conspiracy of the bad.

For Althusser, this fear, which he calls "apocalyptic panic," is an orientation, a kind of captivation by an object that does not yet exist, a panic not constituted by but constitutive of its object: "apprehension [meant here as "dread"] is a collective expectation ('attente'), an *advent* in which human beings are united in spirit but not in truth and are all the more disoriented in that *they already dwell in the same void.*"[33] In this void, the empty place of what does not exist, a collectivity is shaped by the shared experiences of hope and fear: What may I hope for and what must I fear? There is a name for this void: destiny. To analyze the function of the concept of destiny and its relation to the concepts of advent and apocalypse, and thus to re-connect the notions that Derrida would have us separate, namely those of teleology and eschatology, Althusser turns to Hegel's early text, *Der Geist des Christentums und sein Schicksal*, or *The Spirit of Christianity and its Fate*.[34] This is a work with which Althusser was well acquainted by the end of 1946. Not only does he discuss it at some length in his thesis "On Content in the Thought of G. W. F. Hegel," but his close friend Jacques Martin was at work on a French translation, which was published in 1948.[35] Althusser "cites" Hegel (in fact, a single phrase from Hegel) twice, at the beginning and at the end of the essay: only at the end is the line attributed to Hegel. In the opening paragraph Althusser describes the experience of Malraux's presentation of his theses on the imminent of the death of humanity at the Sorbonne in November 1946 as watching "a man treat his destiny as an enemy." Near the conclusion of the essay, Althusser repeats the phrase, adding, however, a crucial element: "Destiny, said Hegel, is the conscious-ness of oneself as enemy." The becoming conscious of this consciousness, its self-awareness, allows Althusser to advance the following paradox: "we await ('nous attendons') . . . the end of destiny."[36]

Hegel's account of the emergence of Christianity from Judaism is strik-ingly relevant to the conjuncture in which the "The International of Decent Feelings" was written. Judaism, possessed of a positivity rather than a spirit, can be understood by means of a single anecdote: when Pompey entered the temple in Jerusalem hoping to discover in its heart the secrets "that ani-mated this exceptional people," the being that stirred such veneration in the Jews, he found only "an empty space."[37] From this image Hegel deduces the fact that the sacred for the Jews is absolutely other and thus beyond being, mediated by a set of normative prescriptions to which complete obedience is impossible. The law becomes the principle of condemnation, which reveals to the Jews that they can never become reconciled to that which is holy, a figure Hegel called "the unhappy consciousness" in the *Phe-*

nomenology. Thus irrevocably separated from the sacred, they can only lead an "animal existence," waiting for the Messiah who has not come and who will never come for them. When Jesus appeared in their midst, they rejected him and further would not rest until he and with him any hope of an embodiment of the divine were destroyed.

Hegel is very interested in the relation of law to action. For the Jews, whose world is organized around law, the necessity of punishing those who transgress the law is clear, but the punishment, designed to modify a living thing, becomes purely contingent: nothing determines its administration by other living things. Moreover, the criminal, even one who understands and condemns himself for violating the law, remains no less a criminal for having been punished. The distinction between law and life, between law and punishment, is overcome only when law becomes life and punishment is understood as destiny. Destiny is the way in which the law is brought down to earth, the form of the reconciliation of the universal and the particular. It is the means by which an individual grasps that in committing a crime it is he who is his own victim: the life that he destroys is above all his own; his crime is no longer a rebellion against law or master but rather a splitting of himself in which he is represented as his own enemy. Destiny "is consciousness of oneself, but as enemy."[38] The fear of destiny, of a void of annihilation that awaits, is finally a fear of oneself. Hegel has thus brought destiny down to earth and the future to the present. The question is no longer that of a future, the mere thought of which induces "apocalyptic panic," but of a present that can grasp itself only in the form of a future to be feared.

If the apocalypse to come is, as Hegel's analysis allows Althusser to suggest, not a matter of the future at all but rather of the present, a human present divided against itself as its own enemy, we must identify not only what is concealed in this moment but also what this moment conceals from itself. As noted earlier, the identification of destiny as a "hostile power" ("eine feindfelige Macht") not only makes possible but necessitates (if humanity is to survive) a universal alliance.[39] Social antagonisms, and friend and enemy distinctions, must be set aside: the only master, ruler, or enemy is the universal death that awaits and whose cold rule can be averted only by an equally universal, equally total response. Only humanity united as a single agent can become the katechon capable of holding back the apocalypse. The struggle of humanity against its hostile destiny is the only legitimate struggle in that humanity's very survival (the precondition of every other struggle) is at stake: "what good is it for an activist in a modern workers' party to know that he is threatened by the bourgeoisie, if he does not realize that he is threatened by death as a human being (*homme*), before being threatened by servitude as a worker." Further, the recognition of impending catastrophe renders any other struggle than that of humanity as a whole against its collective death not simply mistaken or illogical but divisive and therefore dangerous. The only proletariat that exists is now the proletariat of the human condition (that is, universal humanity): "let men learn, if there is still time, that the proletariat of the class struggle can only divide them and that they are already united unawares in the proletariat of fear or the bomb, of terror and death, in the proletariat of the human condition."[40]

For Althusser, it is precisely this drive to universalization, the panic-stricken declaration of a community of terror, which in fact resembles a state of exception declared by the katechon, the Holy Alliance against the apocalypse whose pronouncements are therefore binding to every individual as human being, that threatens to give rise to war. He attributes to the philosopher Alain the observation that "wars are born of the fear of war as sins are born of the fear of sin."[41] For the international of decent feelings, those who divide humanity with their self-interested claims and demands threaten the unity that is required to forestall the apocalypse; as such, they are not simply blind or ignorant. The fear of those who do not fear, the struggle against those who continue to struggle against anything other than destiny, becomes, as Foucault put it, a "vital" question in both senses of the term. The life of the species is at stake in the struggle against the enemies of the universal and of the human community. War against those who make annihilation inevitable is itself unavoidable.

Althusser cuts through this knot of propositions with a single statement: the proletariat of fear, of the apocalypse, in short, "the proletariat of the human condition is a proletariat of the morrow (*du lendemain*)." Destiny, however, as Hegel argued, is not a matter of the future but of the "partitioning" (*Trennung*) of the present. For Althusser, what "distinguishes the laboring proletariat from the proletariat of fear" is precisely the fact that "the worker is not a proletarian by virtue of what-will-happen-to-him-tomorrow, but by virtue of what happens every minute of the day (*mais par ce qui lui advient à chaque instant du jour*). As Camus said so well, not long ago, 'There is no tomorrow' (*Il n'y a pas de lendemain*)."[42] By citing Camus against himself, Althusser underscores the existence of a theoretical break internal to his work, the precise form of which is a regression into precisely the eschatology whose conceptual foundations he once criticized "so well." Althusser has extracted a line from *The Myth of Sisyphus* in which Camus grounds human freedom: "L'absurde m'éclaire sur ce point: il n'y a pas de lendemain. Voici desormais la raison de ma liberté [The absurd illuminates this point: there is no tomorrow. Henceforth this is the reason for my freedom]."[43] The proletariat or, as Althusser specifies, the laboring proletariat, abolishes destiny as destiny and restores the "future" to its proper place as part of the present, no longer a danger to come but a fully realized violence of the present that sets it against itself in a struggle. The object of dread is not out there in a beyond, whether near or distant, but here among us in the horror from which precisely the Holy Alliance wishes us to look away. Derrida, in his own reflection of the concept of apocalypse, reminds us, citing André Chouraki, that the term "apocalypse" as it is used in Scripture never signifies "catastrophe," a meaning that the term would take on only later. Instead, ἀποκάλυψις, apocalypse, is the Greek translation of the Hebrew verb, גלה, which means "to uncover."[44] In this sense, the apocalypse is the lifting of the veil over the present, the veil that conceals the present from itself: "The veil is upon their heart, nevertheless the veil shall be taken away."[45] In Althusser's text, the apocalypse is the uncovering of the catastrophe that is here and now and that has always been here, always been present, no longer conceivable as imminent, as the catastrophe to come, but immanent in the world, catastrophe disguised as that which will hold it back: empire as katechon, the exterminating angels of the counterrevolution. But the apocalypse takes other forms than the spectacular violence of crusades, conquests, and death camps; it appears with far greater stealth than nuclear holocaust. In 1946 in a world of still smoldering ruins, it is easy, too easy, to forget or to dismiss as irrelevant the slow, insidious, nearly invisible death that steals millions away beneath the eyes of the international of decent feelings, who are otherwise occupied searching for the signs of the destruction to come:

> The proletariat is that which has no future, not even the future of fear: poverty, in the proletariat is not the fear of poverty, its is an actual presence that never disappears, it is on the walls, on the table, in the sheets, in the air the worker breathes and the water he drinks, in the

money that he makes and that is made from his poverty, in the very gestures that conjure fear; proletarians are in poverty the way one is in the night, the way certain sick people are in the suffering, which is so closely bound up with them that it becomes part of their nature.[46]

The plague, that would figure as an allegory of the human condition for Camus, is already here for Althusser, the poverty and hunger so bound up with the proletarian condition as to be unrecognizable and invisible: a plague neither dormant nor potential but raging unnoticed throughout the cities of the world.

But at this point we are presented with a contradiction: How can Althusser reconcile the proposition "there is no tomorrow," with his Christianity, whose entire meaning is bound up with the notion of a world to come? For Althusser the Christian, the concepts of destiny, end, and apocalypse, that is, of telos and eschaton, concepts that vacillate between theological and secular registers and whose presence is perhaps most determinant when it is not suspected, are so intertwined that no one of them can be employed without at least implying the others. In the face of this, he declares the eschatological orientation of the current discussion "sacrilegious," and in particular he denounces it as "false prophecy." Those who sincerely "take the atomic bomb for the will of God" and "the tortures of the concentration camps for the Last Judgment," as if human beings are the agents of God's providence in even their most murderous acts, as well as those who merely believe that the end of the world, or rather the end of humanity, is at hand without the slightest reference to a supernatural or transcendental meaning of this destiny or end, are equally the fulfillment of the scriptural prophecy: "for there shall arise false Christs and false prophets, and shall show great signs and wonders, insomuch that, if it were possible, they should deceive the very elect." As Althusser puts it, "this false end of the world is teeming with false prophets who announce false Christs and treat an event as the Advent. . . . The paradox is plain: the end that is close for every Christian is not the end of the false prophets of history."[47] Althusser then does not and cannot as a Christian relinquish the concept of an end, indeed of an end that is "close."

The problem then becomes how does he, does one, distinguish between the true and the false end, between the event, no matter how universal and total the destruction that characterizes it (Matthew 24:2, "there shall not be left here one stone upon another, that shall not be thrown down") and the Advent? To speak of the Advent, the day that will come like a thief in the night, at all is to "usurp God's place," for "of that day and hour knoweth no man, no, not the angels of heaven, but my Father only."[48] The end that is spoken of, that is known and therefore expected, whose arrival is calculated, cannot be the true end. To adopt the position of truth is to speak out against those who speak of the apocalypse, to assert the impossibility of a discourse of the apocalypse that would be anything other than a betrayal of its meaning and being by attempting to represent in speech that which is unrepresentable and thereby engaging in an idolatry not of stone or wood but of words.[49] The apocalypse that is spoken of, that can be represented, is then destiny in Hegel's sense, the separation and opposition of the present to itself, a contradiction projected on to a temporal dimension and lived as a teleological unfolding.

How then are we to understand Althusser's retention of an "end that is close [proche] for every Christian" against the end declared by false prophets? In what sense is it close, if not in the temporal and historical dimension: the end that is coming soon? In fact, everything in the essay works to exclude any such notion. The future, in a very real sense (perhaps understood as the reproduction and recurrence of the present), belongs to "that which has no future," that which is immured in the present and determined by its social existence to ignore what is always to come in favor of what has already arrived: the proletariat. In this sense, the end, not telos but eschaton, not fulfillment but limit, can be understood not as a relation between present and future but a relation of the present to itself, a recalling of the present to itself, not in completion or fulfillment but in a recognition that "completion," like perfection, is nothing more than a comparison of the present to something other than itself. In the strict sense, the end to which Althusser remains committed is thus the end of the end, the end of the future, the end of waiting as a mode of being and acting; it is the revelation that "tomorrow will be a today," a pure present without a beyond but that is never the same. The apocalypse that reveals the end of destiny frees us not only from fear but from hope, as Beckett, yet another voice woven into the conjuncture, writing at exactly the same moment as Althusser, expressed it: "For what possible end to these wastes where true light never was, nor any upright thing, nor any true foundation, but only these leaning things forever lapsing and crumbling away beneath a sky without memory of morning or hope of night."[50]

A present without memory or hope: Would it not be a prison? As Althusser puts it: "Prisoners can escape because theirs is an objective condition, because the bars are real; real bars can be broken (*"se brisent:"* are breaking, being broken): *à nous la liberté*!" It is in fact the future that is a prison, being inescapable because its nonexistent: "The man who is afraid is a prisoner without a prison and without bars: he is his own prisoner and threats stand guard in his soul. This is an adventure from which there is no escape, because there is no fleeing a prison without bars: fear is captivity without the possibility of flight."[51] The proletariat is immured in the present, but a present forever colliding with itself and therefore a shattered present, a ruin, a heap of fragments from which they are already salvaging the materials to compose their liberation. And while the others are looking away, waiting for that which never comes, the scorpion, uncovered, scuttles over stony rubbish.

Afterword

As if a first thought, grasped (*saisie*) in having been read, persisted in
us through other unforeseen thoughts, as if phrases, reunited in our
memory, combined into new groups, producers of new meanings, as if
from one chapter to another, like the landscapes of that great walker, new
perspectives opened before us: all the more gripping (*saisissantes*) for
not having been perceived earlier. . . . There, the word has slipped out:
gripping (*saisissante*). Machiavelli grasps (*se saisit*) us, but if by chance we
want to grasp (*saisir*) him, he escapes us: ungraspable (*insaisissable*).

LOUIS ALTHUSSER, *Machiavelli and Us*

I have often thought that this description of what it is to read Machiavelli simultaneously captures the experience of reading Althusser himself,
the philosopher who shocked a generation of readers by asking a question
that had all the hallmarks of sheer sophistry, as if it were designed to divert
thought into infinite regression: What is it to read?[1] In fact, we can go further and say that every one of Althusser's most arresting (or gripping) accounts of the conflictuality specific to political thinkers and philosophers,
Marx and Lenin, of course, but also Montesquieu and above all Machiavelli and Rousseau, remind us inescapably of the conflictuality of Althusser's own work. To admit this is to acknowledge that the very activity of reflecting on the antagonisms proper to the work of others must produce its
own antagonisms and that, in a very important sense, more profound than
any intention, every one of his commentaries also represents an attempt
to grasp the uneven and contradictory development of his own work. This
is not to say that he simply projected upon others' texts the image of his
own disorder, but rather that his awareness of the necessarily contradictory
character of his own work taught him to be attuned to the dissonances in
even the most harmonic of texts, to hear the silences in their loquacity and
the asides they whispered over the head of the reader. And these experiences in turn enjoined him to return once again to his own project in order
more precisely to grasp its constant detours and divergences. As he liked to

say, philosophical practice could only ever be understood retrospectively, *après-coup*, and, in his case at least, only through intermediaries by means of whom, and at a remove, he could learn something about his work he could not otherwise discern.

It is thus possible to read Althusser's unfinished but powerful late text on Machiavelli as a commentary on the Italian philosopher that is also and no less powerfully an attempt to come to terms with and even perhaps make sense of his philosophical corpus, a body of writing that violently reflects upon philosophy's disavowed violence, a violence that has everything to do with the violence outside and all around it. To move things, to shake things up, to shift the balance of power internal to philosophy, to open the possibility of thinking otherwise required a language of force and provocation. We might recall the concluding paragraph of Althusser's essay on Bertolazzi and Brecht in which he describes himself as being "assailed," by the question of whether the essay itself, far from originating in him or with him, is not rather the play *El Nost Milan* itself "pursuing in me its incomplete meaning, searching in me, despite myself, now that all the actors and sets have been cleared away, for the advent of its silent discourse."[2] In the same way, Althusser was driven to risk phrases that pushed well beyond the requirements of the argument, phrases whose very beauty seemed to depend upon an opacity that wore away only with time to reveal their meaning to unwary readers.

There is perhaps no better way to capture the tumult of his oeuvre, its risks, its tragedies, it exultations, the way in which Althusser frantically pursues a meaning that seems constantly to elude him, even if this meaning is nothing other than the pursuit itself, than in the concluding words of his description of Rousseau's *décalages*, the gaps or discrepancies that prevent Rousseau's philosophical project from cohering. These décalages, according to Althusser, determined its simultaneous regression and flight forward, producing a theoretical order that lives and moves by means of its "failures," a philosophy that will not and cannot rest, chasing its contradictions before it until the encounter that leaves it no way out but a fictional triumph—or in Althusser's case, until it seems to disappear over the horizon of the present.[3] It was this that made Althusser's thought so gripping, as if it held us and holds us in its grasp, and, at the same time, when we attempt to grasp it, so elusive. If he remains ungraspable, it is because there is something new, a beginning, a rupture there, not a new doctrine, a new theory of history or society, but simply a new way of inhabiting philosophy, that is, the philosophical conjuncture, that makes visible the lines of force that constitute it, opening the possibility of change. Althusser, too, it appears, has slipped away: he has disappeared into his intervention, a line of demarcation that is not even a line, the emptiness of a distance taken, a cause that exists only in its effects, the shattering of obstacles that opens new perspectives.

Notes

INTRODUCTION

Why Read Althusser Today?

Epigraph: Althusser, "Is It Simple to be a Marxist in Philosophy?," 168.

1 A brief sample would include Avenas et al., *Contre Althusser*; Fougeyrollas, *Contre Lévi-Strauss, Lacan et Althusser*; Giannotti, *Contra Althusser*; Mandel, *Contra Althusser*; and O'Neill, *For Marx against Althusser*.

2 Benton, *The Rise and Fall of Structural Marxism*.

3 Lilla, "Marx and Murder"; Hitchens, "Transgressing the Boundaries"; and Judt, *Reappraisals*.

4 Althusser, "Reply to John Lewis," 60.

5 Rancière, *La leçon d'Althusser*; and Thompson, *The Poverty of Theory*.

6 Rancière, *La leçon d'Althusser*, 9. Reading *La leçon d'Althusser*, as the lines cited above show, we very easily imagine a pedagogical primal scene in which Althusser the expert, already in possession of a doctrine that he only reveals gradually to those pupils deemed worthy by virtue of their obedience and passivity, is the very figure of the master. He is the French version of pompous pedant that the Red Guards would drive from the classrooms of China with a dunce cap on his head. We too easily forget that Rancière had not simply been a passive auditor taught his lessons by Althusser, but he was in fact a participant in the 1964–65 seminar that produced *Reading Capital* and the author of a contribution to the original edition, an examination of the concept of critique in Marx. Along with a number of Althusser's students (including Robert Linhart, Jacques-Alain Miller, and Jean-Claude Milner), Rancière left the student organization of the French Communist Party (Parti communiste français [PCF]), the Union des Étudiants Communistes in 1966 to form the Union des Jeunesses Communistes (Marxiste-Léniniste) (UJC [ML]). Shortly after 1968, the UJC (ML) dissolved itself, and he pursued the theoretical and political critique of the PCF's revisionism, participating in the foundation of La Gauche Prolétarienne, a Maoist organization that was both antiauthoritarian (drawing from certain aspects, real or imagined, of the Cultural Revolution) and antirevisionist (regarding Soviet Marxism as a revision of the basic notions of Marx, Engels, and Lenin in the interests of a restoration of capitalism).

7 Thompson, *Poverty*, 202, 174.

8 Althusser, *Writings on Psychoanalysis*, 116.

9 See Althusser, "The Philosophical Conjuncture and Marxist Theoretical Research."

10 Althusser, "Is It Simple to Be a Marxist in Philosophy?," 171.

11 Althusser, "Elements in Self-Criticism," 143 (translation modified).

12 Althusser, "Lenin and Philosophy," 63.

13 Derrida, *Of Grammatology*, 24.

14 The short-lived British journal *Theoretical Practice* represented an attempt to constitute an Althusserian social theory. The self-critical texts by Althusser and Balibar propelled the editorial group into a genuine crisis of faith, leading the most notable among them to wash their hands of Marxism altogether. Other works, as well, treated Althusser as if he were a sociologist, economist, or political scientist rather than a philosopher and consequently arrived at judgments that were partially or totally negative. See also Benton, *The Rise and Fall of Structural Marxism*.

15 It is worth remarking that those closest to Althusser for a very long period, especially Étienne Balibar and Pierre Macherey, never ceased to reflect on their contemporaries, whether Lacan, Foucault, Derrida, or, significantly, Althusser himself. In fact, I would say that theirs constitute some of the richest meditations on Althusser produced in recent times. See for example, Balibar, "Eschatology versus Teleology"; and Macherey, "Althusser et le jeune Marx."

16 Some of the most interesting work on Althusser in the last decade has focused on the later writings; I refer in particular to the work of François Matheron, Vittorio Morfino, Filippo Del Lucchese, Augusto Illuminati, Maria Turchetto, Emilio de Ipola, Giorgos Fourtounis, Jason Read, Yoshiko Ichida, and Mikka Lahtinen, among others. For more on Althusser's philosophy of the encounter, see Goshgarian, introduction to *Philosophy of the Encounter*; and de Ipola, *El infinito adios*.

17 Rancière, *La leçon d'Althusser*, 9.

18 Badiou, "Althusser: Subjectivity Without a Subject."

19 Althusser, "Ideology and the Ideological State Apparatuses," 112.

CHAPTER 1
The Theoretical Conjuncture
Structure, Structurality, Structuralism

1 Benton, *The Rise and Fall of Structural Marxism*. See also, Smith, *Reading Althusser*.

2 Althusser, "Elements of Self-Criticism," 132.

3 Althusser, "On Lévi-Strauss," 19–29.

4 Sebag, *Marxisme et structuralisme*.

5   Althusser, "Sur la genèse," Fonds Althusser, Institut mémoires de l'édition contemporaine, ALT2.A11–02.01.

6   Althusser, "Remark on the Category," 94–99.

7   In regard to Althusser being inspired by Epicurus and Lucretius, see "Notes sur Lucrèce," ALT2.58–02.16; "Dossier sur Épicure et l'épicurisme," ALT2.58–04.01, Fonds Althusser, Institut mémoires de l'édition contemporaine.

8   See Althusser, *Philosophy and the Spontaneous Philosophy of the Scientists and Other Essays*; Hobbes, *Léviathan*, I:13.

9   Althusser, "On Marx and Freud," 115.

10 Balibar, "Structural Causality," 112.

11 Fortunately, this work has already begun: Balibar's "Structuralism" provides a precise account of the philosophical conjuncture known as structuralism, as does Maniglier's recent collection *Le moment philosophique des années 1960 en France*. See also, Milner, *Le periple structural*. I should add that, while hardly new, Jameson's *The Prison-House of Language* has emerged from the mass of analyses and critiques of structuralism as one of the most perceptive and rigorous.

12 Perhaps the most useful and detailed overview of the structuralist moment is undoubtedly Dosse, *History of Structuralism*.

13 Gandillac, Goldmann, and Piaget, *Entretiens sur les notions de genèse et structure*; Bastide, *Sens et usages du terme structure dans les sciences humaines et sociales*.

14 I refer particularly to Pos, "Perspectives du structuralisme."

15 Troubetzkoy, *Principles of Phonology*.

16 Jakobson, *Lectures on Sound and Meaning*.

17 Michel Foucault, *La Naissance de la Clinique* (Paris: Presses Universitaires de France, 1963), xv.

18 Deleuze, "À quoi reconnait-on le structuralisme?"

CHAPTER 2
Toward a Prehistory of Structuralism
From Montesquieu to Dilthey

1   ALT2.A40–02.01-ALT2.A40–02.03.

2   Dosse, *Structuralism*, 1: 316.

3   Althusser, *Lettres à Franca (1961–1973)*, 211.

4   Ibid., 382.

5   Ibid., 412–3.

6   Ibid., 364.

7   Fonds Althusser ALT2.A40–02.01.

8   Althusser, *Lettres à Franca (1961–1973)*, 228.

9   Fonds Althusser ALT2.A40–02.01.

10 Althusser, "Montesquieu," 21, 34.

11 See Lévi-Strauss, *Structural Anthropology*; Althusser, "Montesquieu," 36, 38.

12 Althusser, "Montesquieu," 15, 48.

13 Ibid., 46, 48, 47.

14 Hegel, *Philosophy of Mind*, 49.

15 Hegel, *The Philosophy of Right*, 5.

16 Althusser, "On the Materialist Dialectic," 214–21.

17 Althusser, "Montesquieu," 103.

18 Althusser, "Contradiction and Overdetermination," 103.

19 Deleuze, *Difference and Repetition*, 50.

20 Among the exceptions: Hyppolite, *Studies on Marx and Hegel*; Lebrun, *La patience du concept*; Bourgeois, "Althusser et Hegel," 87–104.

21 Althusser, "On Content in the Thought of G. W. F. Hegel," 36–184.

22 Matheron, introduction to *The Spectre of Hegel*, 5–6.

23 Althusser, "On Marx's Relation to Hegel," 161–86.

24 Althusser, "On Content in the Thought of G. W. F. Hegel," 171.

25 Althusser, "On Marx's Relation to Hegel," 121.

26 Althusser et al., *Reading Capital*, 94–95.

27 Ibid., 94.

28 Ibid., 97, 96.

29 See Goldmann, *The Hidden God*.

30 Gandillac, Goldmann, and Piaget, *Entretiens sur les notions de genèse et de structure*. The proceedings of the other major conference devoted to structuralism in 1959 were published as Bastide, *Sense et usage du terme "structure" dans les sciences sociales*. For a detailed account of both conferences, see Dosse, *Structuralism*, 1:173–76.

31 Derrida, "Genesis and Structure and Phenomenology," 159, 160.

32 Ibid., 160.

33 Dilthey, *Introduction to the Human Sciences*.

34 See McCormick and Elliston, "The Dilthey-Husserl Correspondence," 203–9.

35 Derrida, "Genesis and Structure and Phenomenology," 168.

36 Stanislaus Breton quoted in Gandillac, Goldmann, and Piaget, *Entretiens sur les notions de genèse et de structure*, 262.

CHAPTER 3
Settling Accounts with Phenomenology
Husserl and His Critics

1 Husserl, "Philosophy as Rigorous Science," 71–147. For an account of the Husserl-Dilthey debate, see Spiegelberg, *The Phenomenological Movement*.

2 Husserl, "Philosophy as Rigorous Science," 77.

3 Ibid., 125, 146.

4 See Althusser, "Sur l'objectivité de l'histoire," 17–31.
5 Lyotard similarly sees Aron's theory as a restatement of Dilthey's in *Phenomenology*, 106.
6 Althusser, "Sur l'objectivité de l'histoire," 18, 19, 21.
7 Ibid., 6, 7–8, 23, 29, 30.
8 Cavaillès, "On Logic and the Theory of Science," 353–409.
9 Some exceptions: Sinaceur, *Jean Cavaillès*; and Lawler, *Derrida and Husserl*, 56–65. Lawler's study remains the best overview of French phenomenology.
10 Cavaillès, "On Logic and the Theory of Science," 358, 359–60.
11 Ibid., 379, 386.
12 Ibid., 401.
13 See Derrida, *Edmund Husserl's* Origin of Geometry.
14 Cavaillès, "On Logic and the Theory of Science," 409.
15 Ibid.; see Canguilhem, "The Death of Man or the Exhaustion of the Cogito," 74–94.
16 Macherey, "Georges Canguilhem's Philosophy of Science," 161–87.
17 Ibid., 179.
18 This is no longer the case. Among the most interesting of the recent studies of Canguilhem are Macherey's own *La force des norms*; Le Blanc's *Canguilhem et les normes*, and *La vie humaine*. See also Lecourt, *Marxism and Epistemology*.
19 Althusser, foreword to "Georges Canguilhem's Philosophy of Science: Epistemology and History of Science," 161, 163.
20 Ibid., 162–63, 164, 165.
21 Macherey, "Georges Canguilhem's Philosophy of Science," 171–72.
22 Canguilhem, *La formation du concept de réflexe aux XVII et XVIII siècles*, 6.
23 See the commentary of Lecourt, *Pour une critique de l'épistemologie*, 78.
24 Althusser et al., *Reading Capital*, 62.
25 Ibid., 63.
26 Thao, *Phenomenology and Dialectical Materialism*, 7. For the underappreciated nature of Thao's work, see Herrick, "A Book Which Is No Longer Discussed Today," 113–31.
27 Thao, *Phenomenology and Dialectical Materialism*, xxi.
28 Derrida, *Edmund Husserl's* Origin of Geometry.
29 Thao, *Phenomenology and Dialectical Materialism*, xxiii.
30 Lyotard, *Phenomenology*, 42.
31 Thao, *Phenomenology and Dialectical Materialism*, xxvi, xxvii.
32 Husserl, "The Origin of Geometry," 355.
33 Althusser, "The Humanist Controversy," 221–305.
34 Ibid., 240.
35 Lyotard, *Phenomenology*, 43.
36 Ibid., 45.

37 Althusser, "On Feuerbach," 126, 132.

38 Foucault, introduction to *The Normal and the Pathological*, 8.

39 Ibid., 8, 9.

CHAPTER 4
Lévi-Strauss
Ancestors and Descendants, Causes and Effects

 1 For recent work on Lévi-Strauss, see Duranti, "Husserl, Intersubjectivity, and Anthropology"; Rosman and Rubel, "Structure and Exchange"; Zafiropolous, *Lacan and Lévi-Strauss*; Maniglier, "L'humanisme interminable"; Franchi, "Les jeux anaclastiques de Lévi-Strauss," 125–41.

 2 Althusser, "Lévi-Strauss à la recherché de ses ancêtres putatifs," Fonds Althusser, ALT2.A40–02–03.

 3 Lefort, "L'échange et la lutte des homes," 1400–1417; Lévi-Strauss, *The Savage Mind*.

 4 Jakobson, *Main Trends in the Science of Language*, 13.

 5 Husserl, *Logical Investigations*, 2:524.

 6 Ibid.

 7 Ibid., 2:526.

 8 *Études phonologiques dédiées à la mémoire de M. le Prince Trubetskoy*; Pos, "Perspectives du structuralisme."

 9 Lyotard, *Phenomenology*, 9.

10 Pos, "Perspectives," 73.

11 Ibid., 75, 74.

12 Ibid., 74–75.

13 Ibid., 75.

14 Lyotard, *Phenomenology*, 82.

15 Wallon, *Les origines du caractère chez l'enfant*. For an account of Wallon's influence, see Ogilvie, *Lacan, la formation du concept de sujet*; and Roudinesco, *Jacques Lacan & Co.*, 66–71.

16 Merleau-Ponty, *Phenomenology of Perception*, 448.

17 Lefort, "L'échange," 1407.

18 Lévi-Strauss, *Structural Anthropology*, 297.

19 Ibid., 297–98; see Morgenstern and von Neumann, *The Theory of Games and Economic Behavior*.

20 Ibid., 33, 10, 77.

21 Raymond, *De la combinatoire à la probabilité*, 51.

22 Althusser, "On Feuerbach," 134.

23 Althusser, *Lettres à Franca (1961–1973)*, 230.

24 Fonds Althusser ALT2.A40–02–03.

25 Ibid.

26 Althusser, *For Marx*, 113.

27 Lévi-Strauss, *Structural Anthropology*, 279.

28 Fonds Althusser ALT2.A40–02–03.

29 Althusser, "Philosophie et sciences humaines," 9, 12.

30 In fact Althusser planned to, but ultimately did not, write introductions to Godelier's *Rationalité et irrationalité en economie* and Terray's *Le marxisme devant les sociétés primitives*.

31 Ricoeur, "Structure and Hermeneutics," 27–61.

32 Sebag, *Marxisme et structuralisme*.

33 Althusser, "On Feuerbach," 132.

34 Ricoeur, "Structure and Hermeneutics," 30, 38.

35 ALT2.A40–02–03.

36 Ricoeur, "Structure and Hermeneutics," 52, 57.

37 Sebag, *Marxisme et structuralisme*, 36.

38 Ibid., 89.

39 Ibid.

40 Ibid., 125, 126.

41 Badiou, *The Concept of the Model*, 17.

42 Althusser, "On Lévi-Strauss," 26.

43 Ibid., 25.

44 Althusser, "On Feuerbach," 133, 133–34.

45 Derrida, "Structure, Sign, and Play in the Discourse of the Human Sciences," 278–94. The conference proceedings were published as Macksey and Donato, *The Languages of Criticism and the Sciences of Man*.

46 Derrida, "Structure, Sign, and Play in the Discourse of the Human Sciences," 278.

47 Ibid., 282. Alan Bass translates "la conjuncture théorique contemporaine," as "contemporary theoretical situation," thereby obscuring the reference to Althusser.

48 Ibid., 289.

49 Althusser et al., *Reading Capital*, 117.

50 Derrida, "Structure, Sign, and Play in the Discourse of the Human Sciences," 292.

CHAPTER 5
Between Spinozists
The Function of Structure in Althusser, Macherey, and Deleuze

1 Althusser, "Elements in Self-Criticism," 166.

2 Fonds Althusser ALT2.A6–05.02.

3 Ibid.

4 Ibid.

5 Ibid.

6 Ibid.

7 Ibid.

8 Ibid.

9 Pouillon, introduction to special issue, *Les Temps Modernes* 246 (1966): 790.

10 Macherey, *A Theory of Literary Production*, 141.

11 Ibid., 142.

12 Ibid., 152.

13 Ibid., 151.

14 This phrase is found only in the original French version of Macherey's *A Theory of Literary Production*, published as "L'analyse litterarire: Tombeau de structures," 925.

15 Macherey, *A Theory of Literary Production*, 155.

16 Macherey, "L'analyse litterarire: Tombeau de structures," 918.

17 Ibid.

18 Macherey, *A Theory of Literary Production*, 51.

19 ALT2.A11–02–04

20 Althusser, *Lettres à Franca (1961–1973)*, 663.

21 All references are to the translation of the third edition of *Lire le Capital*, Althusser et al., *Reading Capital*, and the third edition itself, *Lire le Capital* (Paris: Presses Universitaires de France, 1996), which includes, with Althusser's emended text of 1968, the excised or modified passages from the 1965 edition.

22 One of the very few to break the silence surrounding Althusser's emendations was Sprinker, *Imaginary Relations*.

23 Althusser, *Lettres à Franca (1961–1973)*, 611.

24 Althusser et al., *Reading Capital*, 15–16; *Lire le Capital*, 6.

25 Althusser et al., *Reading Capital*, 16; *Lire le Capital*, 6.

26 Althusser et al., *Reading Capital*, 18.

27 Ibid., 19.

28 Ibid., 27.

29 Althusser et al., *Lire le Capital*, 636.

30 Macherey, *A Theory of Literary Production*, 96.

31 Althusser et al., *Reading Capital*, 182.

32 Ibid., 183.

33 Ibid., 186–87.

34 Ibid., 187, 188.

35 Ibid., 188.

36 Althusser et al., *Lire le Capital*, 464.

37 Althusser et al., *Lire le Capital*, 465 (emphasis added).

38 Althusser, *For Marx*, 145, 146.

39 Althusser et al., *Lire le Capital*, 464.

40 Althusser et al., *Reading Capital*, 189.

41 Spinoza, *Complete Works*, 848–51.

42 Deleuze, "Lucretius and the Simulacrum," 267; quoted in Macherey, *Hegel ou Spinoza*, 195.

43 Macherey, *Hegel ou Spinoza*, 216, 217.

44 Ibid., 221.

45 Spinoza, *Complete Works, Ethics* III, proposition 6–7.

46 Deleuze, "Lucretius and the Simulacrum," 303–20; "Lucrèce et le naturalisme," Etudes philosophiques, series 16, no 1. (Jan.-March 1961), 19–29: 21.

47 Deleuze, *The Logic of Sense*, 305.

48 Spinoza, *Complete Works, Ethics* II, proposition 13, 1. 7, scholium.

49 Mury, "Matérialisme et hyperempiricisme."

50 Althusser, *For Marx*, 177.

51 Ibid.

52 Ibid., 179.

53 Ibid.

54 Ibid., 201–2.

55 Althusser, "Essays in Self-Criticism," 141.

56 See Stolze, "Deleuze and Althusser"; ALT2.A8–03.02.

57 ALT2.A8–03.02

58 Ibid.

59 Ibid.

60 Ibid.

61 Ibid.

62 Ibid.

63 Ibid.

CHAPTER 6
Marxism and Humanism

1 Althusser, *Positions (1964–1975)*, 80.

2 See Althusser, *Sur la reproduction*.

3 See Schaff, *A Philosophy of Man*.

4 Althusser, "The Humanist Controversy," 224.

5 See Althusser, "Letter to the Central Committee of the PCF 18 March 1966"; see also, as well as Lewis's editorial introduction, Goshgarian, introduction to *The Humanist Controversy*.

6 Althusser, "The Humanist Controversy," 221, 223.

7 Ibid., 231.

8 Ibid.

9 Ibid., 233.

10 See Sartre, *The Imaginary*; Merleau-Ponty, *Phenomenology of Perception*.

11 See Bachelard, *L'activité rationaliste de la physique contemporaine*. See also the commentary of Lecourt, *Bachelard*.

12 Althusser, "The Humanist Controversy," 231.

13 Ibid., 232.

14 Ibid.

15 Ibid., 233.

16 Ibid.

17 Ricoeur, *Lectures on Ideology and Utopia*, 135.

18 Althusser, "Letters to D.: 1966," 43.

19 Husserl, "Philosophy as Rigorous Science," 103.

20 Husserl, "The Crisis of the European Sciences," 26.

21 Thao, *Phenomenology and Dialectical Materialism*, 7.

22 Ibid., 7, 13. Althusser, "The Humanist Controversy," 233.

23 Althusser, "Humanism," 233.

24 Althusser, *Reading Capital*, 63.

25 Merleau-Ponty, *Phenomenology of Perception*, 463.

26 Althusser, "The Humanist Controversy," 235.

27 Spinoza, *Complete Works, Ethics* IV, preface.

CHAPTER 7
Althusser and Lacan
Toward a Genealogy of the Concept of Interpellation

1 See Gillot, *Althusser et la psychanalyse*.

2 Althusser, *Psychanalyse et sciences humaines*.

3 Althusser, "Freud and Lacan," 7–32.

4 Althusser, "Dr. Freud's Discovery," 91, 90.

5 See Roudinesco, *Jacques Lacan & Co.*, 531–32.

6 Althusser, "Freud and Lacan," 20, 24.

7 Althusser, *Psychanalyse et sciences humaines*, 32.

8 See Politzer, *Critique des fondements de la psychologie*.

9 Althusser, *Psychanalyse et sciences humaines*, 32, 37, 41.

10 Ibid., 56.

11 Ibid., 59, 65, 66, 69.

12 Ibid., 77.

13 Ibid., 98.

14 Ibid., 90, 92.

15 Ibid., 92–93.

16 Ibid., 102.

17 Ibid., 102, 104, 105.

18 Ibid., 107.

19 Balibar discusses the history of the concept of the subject in "Citizen Subject,"
   33–57. See also Balibar and de Libera, "Le sujet," 1234–53.

20 Althusser, *Psychanalyse et sciences humaines*, 112.

21 Descartes, *The Passions of the Soul* I, 49.

22 Althusser, *Psychanalyse et sciences humaines*, 115, 120.

23 Ibid., 113–14.

24 Ibid., 114.

25 Althusser, *Psychanalyse*, 120.

26. Louis Althusser, "Three Notes on the Theory of Discourses," *The Humanist Controversy and Other Writings*, trans. G. M. Goshgarian (London: Verso,
   2003), 33–84.

27. Ibid., 38.

28. Ibid., 67.

29. Ibid., 70.

30. Ibid., 43.

31. Ibid., 45.

32. Ibid.

33. Ibid., 47.

34. Ibid., 45.

35. Ibid., 48.

36. Ibid., 70–71.

37. Ibid., 72.

38. Ibid., 82n.

39. Ibid., 79.

40. Ibid., 48.

41. Ibid., 49–50.

42. Althusser, "Feuerbach," 127.

43. Ibid.

44. Althusser, "Three Notes," 50.

45. Althusser, "Feuerbach," 127.

46. Ibid., 130.

47. Ibid.

48. Althusser, "Three Notes," 50.

49. Ibid., 51–52.

50. Ibid., 83n.

51. Ibid., 52.

52. Ibid.

53. Ibid.

54. Ibid., 53.

55. Ibid., 56.

56. Ibid., 57.

CHAPTER 8
Althusser and Foucault
Apparatuses of Subjection

1 See Althusser, "Ideology and Ideological State Apparatuses."
2 See Althusser, "Idéologie et appareils idéologique d'État (Notes pour une recherché)."
3 See Althusser, *Sur la reproduction*.
4 Althusser, "Reply to John Lewis," 39.
5 Althusser, "Ideology and Ideological State Apparatuses," 148.
6 Ibid., 145.
7 The outstanding exception was none other than Jacques Rancière, who argued that "the fundamental theoretical lesson that the mass movement of May 1968 made clear to everyone and that Althusser's left critique had begun to systematize was this: the ideological domination of the bourgeoisie was not that of a social imaginary where individuals would spontaneously reflect their relations to their conditions of existence. It is a system of material powers reproduced by the apparatuses. . . . This problematic of the ideological apparatuses represented a political rupture as much with the opposition of science and ideology as with the conception of class struggle in theory" (*La leçon d'Althusser*, 140–41).
8 Althusser, "Freud and Lacan," 15–16.
9 Althusser, "Ideology and Ideological State Apparatuses," 145.
10 Ibid., 158, 159, 160, 161; see also Althusser, "Three Notes on the Theory of Discourses."
11 Althusser, "Ideology and Ideological State Apparatuses," 162.
12 Ibid.
13 Ibid., 162, 163.
14 Ibid., 164.
15 Ibid., 165.
16 Ibid.
17 Ibid., 165, 166.
18 Ibid., 175.
19 Spinoza, *Complete Works*, *Ethics* I, proposition 33.
20 Althusser, "Ideology and Ideological State Apparatuses," 167.
21 Descartes, *Discourse on Method* III, 23.
22 Althusser, "Ideology and Ideological State Apparatuses," 169.
23 Ibid., 168.
24 Ibid., 169.
25 Althusser, "The Only Materialist Tradition," 17.
26 Spinoza, *Ethics* IV, preface; *Ethics* II, proposition 7, scholium.

27 Althusser, "The Only Materialist Tradition," 11.

28 Althusser, "Ideology and Ideological State Apparatuses," 172.

29 See Pêcheux, "The French Political Winter," 211–20.

30 Spinoza, *Ethics* II, proposition 7.

31 Hobbes, *De Cive* IV, 1; Marx, *Capital*, 1:874.

32 Althusser, "Ideology and Ideological State Apparatuses," 145.

33 Althusser, "Notes sur les ISAS," 253.

34 Althusser, *Sur la reproduction*, 179–95 and 113–17, respectively.

35 Ibid., 119.

36 One of the few besides Foucault to understand what was truly new in Althusser's essay was none other than Rancière himself for whom the "problematic of ideological apparatuses" constituted a "rupture" with the opposition of science and ideology: "The fundamental theoretical lesson that the mass movement of May 1968 had made clear to everyone and that Althusser's Left critique [critique de gauche] had begun to systematize was this: the ideological domination of the bourgeoisie was not that of a social imaginary in which individuals spontaneously reflected their relations to their conditions of existence. It is a system of relations of material powers reproduced by the apparatuses." (*La leçon d'Althusser*, 140). He could not, however, extend Althusser's theses concerning the material existence of ideology in apparatuses to the constitution of subjects, denouncing the idea of the interpellated subject as a notion of a deceived subject whose deception could only be dispelled by Marxist science. The discrepancy between his extremely perceptive reading of the passages on the material existence of ideology and his incomprehension in the face of the notion of interpellation is absolutely symptomatic of the contradictions that haunt his denunciation of Althusser.

37 See Foucault, *The Archaeology of Knowledge*, 184–86. For Althusser's notes on the *Archaeology of Knowledge*, see ALT2.A58–02.08.

38 Foucault, *Discipline and Punish*, 26.

39 See Macherey, "Towards a Natural History of Norms," 179; Foucault, *Discipline and Punish*, 27.

40 Foucault, *Discipline and Punish*, 222.

41 Ibid., 194.

42 Ibid., 221, 191, 170, 201.

43 Ibid., 29, 30.

44 Ibid., 29.

45 Butler, "'Conscience Doth Make Subjects of Us All,'" 106. See also Fischbach, "Les sujets marchent tout seul . . . Althusser et l'interprellation," 113–45; and Macherey, "Judith Butler and the Althusserian Theory of Subjection."

46 Butler, "'Conscience Doth Make Subjects of Us All,'" 117.

47 Foucault, *Discipline and Punish*, 200, 205.

48 Ibid., 200, 201.

49 Ibid., 200, 202.

CHAPTER 9

The Late Althusser

Materialism of the Encounter or Philosophy of Nothingness?

1 See Althusser, "The Underground Current of the Materialism of the Encounter."

2 Althusser, "The Underground Current of the Materialism of the Encounter," 163–64; Althusser, *Positions (1964–1975)*, 80. On the later Althusser, see Bourdin, "The Uncertain Materialism of Louis Althusser"; Read, "Primitive Accumulation"; Tosel, "Les aléas du matérialisme aléatoire dans la dernière philosophie de Louis Althusser"; Morfino, "Escatologia à la cantonade"; and Fourtounis, "El materialismo tardío de Althusser y el corte epistemológico."

3 Althusser, "The Underground Current of the Materialism of the Encounter," 166.

4 Ibid., 179–80.

5 Ibid., 176, 204.

6 Ibid., 176, 177.

7 Macherey, *Introduction à l'éthique de Spinoza*, 73.

8 Spinoza, *Ethics* II, proposition 7, scholium.

9 Matheron, "The Recurrence of the Void in Louis Althusser"; Morfino, "An Althusserian Lexicon."

10 Althusser, "The Underground Current of the Materialism of the Encounter," 171, 174–75.

11 Althusser, *Philosophy and the Spontaneous Philosophy of the Scientists and Other Essays*, 25–26, 116.

12 Althusser, "The Underground Current of the Materialism of the Encounter," 188.

13 Althusser, *Philosophy and the Spontaneous Philosophy of the Scientists and Other Essays*, 82.

14 Althusser, "The Underground Current of the Materialism of the Encounter," 171, 181.

15 Ibid., 184, 186.

16 Althusser, *Philosophy of the Encounter*, 188.

17 Ibid., 188, 197; see Goshgarian, introduction to *Philosophy of the Encounter*.

18 Althusser, "The Underground Current of the Materialism of the Encounter," 197.

19 See Goshgarian, introduction to *Philosophy of the Encounter*.

20 Althusser, "The Underground Current of the Materialism of the Encounter," 191, 174.

21 Althusser, "Correspondence about 'Philosophy and Marxism,'" 227, 237.

22 See Derrida, "My Chances/Mes chances."

23 Derrida, "My Chances/Mes chances," 4–5.

24 Lucretius, *De Rerum Natura*, 2: 83, 105, 109.

25 Althusser, "The Underground Current of the Materialism of the Encounter," 190.

26 Derrida, "My Chances/Mes chances," 9.

27 Althusser, "The Underground Current of the Materialism of the Encounter," 191, 170.

28 Heidegger, *Sein und Zeit*, 220.

29 Derrida, "My Chances/Mes chances," 9.

30 Althusser, "The Underground Current of the Materialism of the Encounter," 170, 190–91.

31 In the Yiddish translation of Ecclesiastes by the great poet Yehoash, "vanity" is translated with the Yiddish equivalent of *Nichtigkeit* (נישטיקייט).

32 Ecclesiastes, 12:6.

33 Althusser, "The Underground Current of the Materialism of the Encounter," 174.

34 Benjamin, *Illuminations*, 253–64.

35 Foucault, *Folie et déraison*, 5.

36 Althusser, "The Underground Current of the Materialism of the Encounter," 174.

37 Deleuze, "Lucretius and the Simulacrum," 268.

38 Althusser, *For Marx*, 163–218.

39 Ibid., 106.

40 Althusser, *For Marx*, 134 (translation modified), 135–36 (translation modified), 143.

41 Beckett, *Three Novels*, 241.

CHAPTER 10
The End of Destiny
Althusser before Althusser

1 See Althusser, "The International of Decent Feelings."

2 Althusser, "Portrait of the Materialist Philosopher," 290.

3 Macherey, "Soutenance," 27.

4 Matheron, introduction *The Spectre of Hegel*, 4.

5 Ibid., 14.

6 The apparent exceptions are Pascal and Malebranche, figures who occupy a liminal place between theology and philosophy. Althusser's relation to these figures remains to be examined in detail.

7 Macherey, *Histoires de dinosaure*, 39–40.

8 Ibid., 40–42.

9 Althusser, "The International of Decent Feelings," 21–22.

10 André Malraux quoted in Althusser, "The International of Decent Feelings," 21.

11 See Albert Camus's commentary on the bombing of Hiroshima, first published in *Combat* on August 8, 1945, reprinted in *Actuelles*, 81–84.

12 Althusser, "The International of Decent Feelings," 23.

13 Camus, *Actuelles*, 147–48.

14 Ibid., 141.

15 Camus quoted in Althusser, "The International of Decent Feelings," 24.

16 Althusser, "The International of Decent Feelings," 24.

17 Marcel, *Les hommes contre l'humain*, 32.

18 Althusser, "The International of Decent Feelings," 29.

19 Marcel, *Les hommes contre l'humain*, 22, 51.

20 Althusser, "The International of Decent Feelings," 23, 29.

21 Camus, *Actuelles*, 147.

22 Ibid., 178.

23 Marcel, *Les hommes contre l'humain*, 55.

24 Althusser, "The International of Decent Feelings," 27–28.

25 Althusser, "The International of Decent Feelings," 26–27; see Malraux, *L'espoir*.

26 Malraux, *L'espoir*, 26.

27 Ibid., 86, 155–56, 87.

28 Schmitt, *Nomos of the Earth*.

29 Ibid., 59–62.

30 Ibid., 60.

31 See Meztger, *Katechon*.

32 Tertullian, *Apologetics*, xxxii.1.

33 Althusser, "The International of Decent Feelings," 31, 26.

34 Derrida, *Specters of Marx*, 90. See also, Balibar, "Eschatology versus Teleology," 64–65. See Hegel, *The Spirit of Christianity and Its Fate*.

35 Hegel, *L'esprit du christianisme et son destin*. Note the translation of "Schicksal" as "destiny," rather than "fate."

36 Althusser, "The International of Decent Feelings," 21, 31.

37 Hegel, *The Spirit of Christianity and Its Fate*, 192 (translation modified).

38 Ibid., 231.

39 Ibid.

40 Althusser, "The International of Decent Feelings," 23–24.

41 Ibid., 26.

42 Ibid., 24, 25.

43 Camus, *Le mythe de Sisyphe*, 82.

44 Derrida, "D'un ton apocalyptique adopté naguère en philosophie," 446.

45 2 Corinthians 3:15–16.

46 Althusser, "The International of Decent Feelings," 25.

47 Ibid., 28.

48 Matthew 24:36.

49 Boer, "Althusser's Catholic Marxism," 471.

50 Beckett, *Three Novels*, 40.

51 Althusser, "The International of Decent Feelings," 25.

AFTERWORD

Epigraph: Louis Althusser, *Machiavelli and Us*, trans. Gregory Elliot (London: Verso, 1999), 3–4 (translation modified).

1 Althusser et al., *Reading Capital*, 15.

2 Althusser, *For Marx*, 151.

3 Althusser, "Rousseau," 159–60.

Bibliography

Althusser, Louis. "Contradiction and Overdetermination." In Althusser, *For Marx*, 87–128.

———. "Correspondence about 'Philosophy and Marxism.'" In Althusser, *Philosophy of the Encounter*, 208–50.

———. "Dossier sur Épicure et l'épicurisme." ALT2.58–04.01.

———. "Dr. Freud's Discovery." In Althusser, *Writings on Psychoanalysis*, 85–104.

———. "Elements in Self-Criticism." In Althusser, *Essays in Self-Criticism*, 100–161.

———. *Essays in Self-Criticism*. Translated by Grahame Lock. London: New Left Books, 1976.

———. Foreword to "Georges Canguilhem's Philosophy of Science: Epistemology and History of Science," by Macherey, *In a Materialist Way*, 161–65.

———. *For Marx*. Translated by Ben Brewster. London: Verso, 1969.

———. "Foucault et la problématique des origines." ALT2.A40–02.02.

———. "Freud and Lacan." In Althusser, *Writings on Psychoanalysis*, 7–32.

———. "The Humanist Controversy." In Althusser, *The Humanist Controversy and Other Writings*, 221–306. Originally published as "La querelle de l'humanisme," in *Ecrits philosophique et politique II*, ed. François Matheron (Paris: Stock/IMEC, 1996).

———. *The Humanist Controversy and Other Writings*. Edited by François Matheron. Translated by G. M. Goshgarian. London: Verso, 2003.

———. "Idéologie et appareils idéologique d'État (Notes pour une recherché)." *La pensée* 151 (June 1970): 3–38.

———. "Ideology and Ideological State Apparatuses." In *Lenin and Philosophy and Other Essays*, translated by Ben Brewster, 121–76. New York: Monthly Review Press, 1971.

———. "The International of Decent Feelings." In Althusser, *The Spectre of Hegel*, 21–35.

———. "Is It Simple to Be a Marxist in Philosophy?" In Althusser, *Essays in Self-Criticism*, 163–207.

———. "Lenin and Philosophy." In *Lenin and Philosophy and Other Essays*, translated by Ben Brewster, 23–68. New York: Monthly Review Press, 1971.

———. "Letter to the Central Committee of the PCF 18 March 1966." Translated by William Lewis. *Historical Materialism* 15 (2007): 153–72.

———. "Letters to D.: 1966." In Althusser, *Writings on Psychoanalysis*, 33–77.

———. *Lettres à Franca (1961–1973)*. Paris: Stock/Imec, 1998.

———. "Lévi-Strauss à la recherché de ses ancêtres putatifs." ALT2.A40–02.03.

———. *Machiavelli and Us*. Translated by Gregory Elliot. London: Verso, 1999.

———. "Marx and Humanism." In Althusser, *For Marx*, 219–47. Originally published as "Marxisme et humanisme," *Cahiers de l'institut de science économique appliqué*, no. 20 (June 1964): 109–33.

———. "Montesquieu: Politics and History." In Althusser, *Politics and History*, 13–111.

———. "Notes sur les ISAs." In Althusser, *Sur la reproduction*, 253–67.

———. "Notes sur Lucrèce." ALT2.58–02.16.

———. "On Content in the Thought of G. W. F. Hegel." In Althusser, *The Spectre of Hegel: The Early Writings*, 36–184.

———. "On Feuerbach." In Althusser, *The Humanist Controversy and Other Writings*, 85–154. London: Verso, 2003. Originally published as "Sur Feuerbach," *Ecrits philosophiques et politiques II*, ed. François Matheron (Paris: Stock/Imec, 1996).

———. "On Lévi-Strauss." In Althusser, *The Humanist Controversy and Other Writings*, 19–29.

———. "On Marx and Freud." In Althusser, *Writings on Psychoanalysis*, 79–123.

———. "On Marx's Relation to Hegel." In Althusser, *Politics and History*, 161–86.

———. "On the Materialist Dialectic." In Althusser, *For Marx*, 161–217.

———. "The Only Materialist Tradition." In *The New Spinoza*, edited by Warren Montag and Ted Stolze, translated by Ted Stolze, 3–21. Minneapolis: University of Minnesota Press, 1997.

———. "The Philosophical Conjuncture and Marxist Theoretical Research." In Althusser, *The Humanist Controversy and Other Writings*, 1–18.

———. "Philosophie et sciences humaines." *Revue de l'enseignement philosophique* 10, no. 6. (August–September 1963): 161–217.

———. *Philosophy and the Spontaneous Philosophy of the Scientists and Other Essays*. Edited by Gregory Elliott. Translated by Ben Brewster. London: Verso, 1990. Originally published as *Philosophie et la philosophie spontanée des savants* (Paris: Maspero, 1974).

———. *Philosophy of the Encounter: Later Writings, 1978–1987*. Edited by François Matheron. Translated by G. M. Goshgarian. New York: Verso, 2006.

———. *Politics and History: Montesquieu, Rousseau, Marx*. Translated by Ben Brewster. London: New Left Books, 1977.

———. "Portrait of the Materialist Philosopher." In Althusser, *Philosophy of the Encounter*, 290–91.

———. *Positions (1964–1975)*. Paris: Éditions Sociale, 1976.

———. *Psychanalyse et sciences humaines: Deux conferences*. Paris: Livre de Poche, 1996.

———. "Remark on the Category: Process without a Subject or Goal(s)." In Althusser, *Essays in Self-Criticism*, 94–99.

———. "Reply to John Lewis." In Althusser, *Essays in Self-Criticism*, 33–99.

———. "Rousseau: The Social Contract." In Althusser, *Politics and History*, 112–60.

———. *The Spectre of Hegel*. Edited by François Matheron. Translated by G. M. Goshgarian. London: Verso, 1997.

———. "Sur la genèse." September 22, 1966. ALT2.A11–02.01.

———. *Sur la reproduction*. Edited by Jacques Bidet. Paris: Presses Universitaires de France, 1995.

———. "Sur l'objectivité de l'histoire. Lettre à Paul Ricouer (1955)." In *Solitude de Machiavel*, edited by Yves Sintomer, 17–31. Paris: Presses Universitaires de France, 1998.

———. "Three Notes on the Theory of Discourses." In Althusser, *The Humanist Controversy and Other Writings*, 33–84.

———. "The Underground Current of the Materialism of the Encounter." In Althusser, *Philosophy of the Encounter*, 163–207.

———. *Writings on Psychoanalysis: Freud and Lacan*. Edited by Olivier Corpet and François Matheron. Translated by Jeffrey Mehlman. New York: Columbia University Press, 1996.

Althusser, Louis, et al. *Reading Capital*. Translated by Ben Brewster. London: New Left Books, 1975. Originally published as *Lire le Capital* (Paris: Presses Universitaires de France, 1996).

Avenas, Denise, et al. *Contre Althusser*. Paris: Union Général d'Editions, 1974.

Bachelard, Gaston. *L'activité rationaliste de la physique contemporaine*. Paris: Presses Universitaires de France, 1951.

Badiou, Alain. "Althusser: Subjectivity without a Subject." In *Metapolitics*, translated by Jason Barker, 586–87. London: Verso, 2005.

———. *The Concept of the Model: An Introduction to the Materialist Epistemology of Mathematics*. Edited and translated by Zacharay Luke Fraser and Tzuchien Tho. Melbourne, Australia: Re-Press, 2007. Originally published as *Le concept du modèle* (Paris: Maspero, 1969).

Balibar, Étienne. "Citizen Subject." In *Who Comes after the Subject?*, edited by Eduardo Cavada, Peter Connor, and Jean-Luc Nancy, 33–57. London: Routledge, 1991.

———. "Eschatology versus Teleology: The Suspended Dialogue Between

Derrida and Althusser." In *Derrida and the Time of the Political*, edited by Peng
Cheah and Suzanne Guerlac, 64–65. Durham, NC: Duke University Press,
2009.

———. "Structural Causality: Overdetermination and Antagonsim." In
Postmodern Materialism and the Future of Marxist Theory, edited by Antonio
Callari and David F. Ruccio, 109–20. Middletown, CT: Weslayan University
Press, 1996.

———. "Structuralism: A Destitution of the Subject?" *differences: A Journal of
Feminist Cultural Studies* 14, no. 1 (2003): 1–21.

Balibar, Étienne, and Alain de Libera. "Le sujet." In *Vocabulaire européen des
philosophies*, edited by Barbara Cassin, 1234–53. Paris: Editions du Seuil, 2004.

Bastide, Roger, ed. *Sens et usages du terme "structure" dans les sciences humaines et
sociales*. Paris: Mouton, 1962.

Beckett, Samuel. *Three Novels*. New York: Grove Press, 1991.

Benjamin, Walter. *Illuminations*. Edited by Hannah Arendt. Translated by Harry
Zohn. New York: Schocken, 1968.

Benton, Ted. *The Rise and Fall of Structural Marxism*. New York: St. Martin's Press,
1984.

Boer, Roland. "Althusser's Catholic Marxism." *Rethinking Marxism* 19, no. 4
(2007): 469–86.

Bourdin, Jean-Claude, ed. *Althusser: Une lecture de Marx*. Paris: PUF, 2008.

———. "The Uncertain Materialism of Louis Althusser." *Graduate Faculty
Philosophy Journal* 22, no. 1 (2000): 271–87.

Bourgeois, Bernard. "Althusser et Hegel." In *Althusser philosophe*, edited by Pierre
Raymond, 87–104. Paris: Presses Universitaires de France, 1997.

Butler, Judith. "'Conscience Doth Make Subjects of Us All': Althusser's
Subjection." In *The Psychic Life of Power: Theories in Subjection*, 106–31. Stanford,
CA: Stanford University Press, 1997.

Camus, Albert. "Editorial de *Combat* on August 8, 1945." Reprinted in *Actuelles:
Chroniques 1944–1948*, 81–84. Paris: Gallimard, 1950.

———. *Le mythe de Sisyphe*. Paris: Gallimard, 1942.

Canguilhem, Georges. "The Death of Man or the Exhaustion of the Cogito."
In *The Cambridge Companion to Foucault*, edited by Gary Gutting, 74–94.
Cambridge: Cambridge University Press, 2005.

———. *La formation du concept de réflexe aux XVII et XVIII siècles*. Paris: Vrin,
1955.

Cavaillès, Jean. "On Logic and the Theory of Science." In *Phenomenology and the
Natural Sciences*, edited by Joseph J. Kockelmans, translated by Theodore J.
Kisiel, 353–412. Evanston, IL: Northwestern University Press, 1970. Originally
published as *Sur la logique et la théorie de la science* (Paris: Presses Universitaires
de France, 1947).

Choi, Won. "From or toward the Symbolic: A Critique of Žižek's Sublime Object of Ideology." *Décalages* 1, no. 2 (2012), www.decalages.net.

de Gandillac, M., L. Goldmann, and J. Piaget, eds. *Entretiens sur les notions de genèse et de structure*. Paris: Mouton, 1965.

de Ipola, Emilio. *El infinito adios*. Buenos Aires: Siglo XXI, 2007.

Deleuze, Gilles. "À quoi reconnait-on le structuralisme?" Unpublished manuscript. ALT2.A8-03.02

———. *Difference and Repetition*. Translated by Paul Patton. New York: Columbia University Press, 1994.

———. "How Do We Recognize Structuralism?" In *Desert Islands and Other Texts: 1953–1974*, 170–92. Los Angeles: Semiotexte, 2002.

———. *The Logic of Sense*. Edited by Constantin V. Boundas. Translated by Mark Lester. New York: Columbia University Press, 1990.

———. "Lucrèce et le naturalisme." *Etudes philosophiques*, series 16, no 1. (Jan.-March 1961), 19–29:

———. "Lucretius and the Simulacrum." In Deleuze, *The Logic of Sense*, 266–79.

de Libera, Alain. *Archéologie du sujet, tome 1: naissance du sujet*. Paris: Vrin, 2007.

Derrida, Jacques. "D'un ton apocalyptique adopté naguère en philosophie." In *Les fins de l'homme: A partir du travail de Jacques Derrida*, edited by Philippe Lacoue-Labarthes and Jean-Luc Nancy, 445–86. Paris: Galilée, 1981.

———. *Edmund Husserl's Origin of Geometry: An Introduction*. Edited by David B. Allison. Translated by John P. Leavey Jr. Lincoln: University of Nebraska Press, 1989. Originally published as *Introduction à "L'origine de la géométrie" de Husserl* (Paris: Presses Universitaires de France, 1962).

———. "Genesis and Structure in Phenomenology." In *Writing and Difference*, translated by Alan Bass, 193–211. Chicago: Chicago University Press, 1978.

———. "My Chances/Mes chances: A Rendezvous with some Epicurean Stereophonies." In *Taking Chances: Derrida, Psychoanalysis and Literature*, edited by Joseph H. Smith and William Kerrigan, 1–32. Baltimore: Johns Hopkins University Press, 1984.

———. *Of Grammatology*. Translated by Gayatri Chakravorty Spivak. Baltimore: Johns Hopkins University Press, 1976.

———. *Specters of Marx: The State of Debt, the Work of Mourning, and the New International*. Translated by Peggy Kamuf. London: Routledge, 1994.

———. "Structure, Sign, and Play in the Discourse of the Human Sciences." In *Writing and Difference*, translated by Alan Bass, 278–94. Chicago: University of Chicago Press, 1978. Originally published as "La structure, le signe et le jeu dans les discours des scences humaines," in *L'écriture et la difference* (Paris: Editions du Seuil, 1967), 409–29.

Descartes, René. *Discourse on Method*. The Philosophical Writings of Descartes.

Trans. John Cottingham, Robert Stoothoff, Dugald Murdoch. 2 vols. Cambridge: Cambridge University Press, 1985. I:109–51.

———. *The Passions of the Soul*. The Philosophical Writings of Descartes. Trans. John Cottingham, Robert Stoothoff, Dugald Murdoch. 2 vols. Cambridge: Cambridge University Press, 1985, I: 325–404.

Dilthey, Wilhelm. *Introduction to the Human Sciences*. Princeton, NJ: Princeton University Press, 1989.

Dosse, François. *History of Structuralism*. 2 vols. Minneapolis: University of Minnesota Press, 1997.

Duranti, Alessandro. "Husserl, Intersubjectivity, and Anthropology." *Anthropological Theory* 10, nos. 1–2 (March 2010): 16–35.

Études phonologiques dédiées à la mémoire de M. le Prince Trubetskoy. Tuscaloosa: University of Alabama Press, 1964. Originally published as *Travaux du Cercle linguisque de Prague* 8 (1939).

Fischbach, Franck. "Les sujets marchent tout seul . . . Althusser et l'interprellation." In *Althusser: Une lecture de Marx*, edited by Jean-Claude Bourdin, 113–45. Paris: PUF, 2008.

Foucault, Michel. *The Archaeology of Knowledge*. Translated by Alan Sheridan. New York: Harper and Row, 1972.

———. *Discipline and Punish: The Birth of the Prison*. Translated by Alan Sheridan. New York: Vintage, 1979.

———. *Folie et déraison: L'histoire de la folie à l'âge classique*. Paris: Gallimard, 1961.

———. Introduction to *The Normal and the Pathological*, by Georges Canguilhem, 7–24. Translated by Carolyn R. Fawcett. New York: Zone Books, 1980.

Fougeyrollas, Pierre. *Contre Lévi-Strauss, Lacan et Althusser: Trois essays sur l'obscurantisme contemporaine*. Paris: Savelli, 1976.

Fourtounis, Giorgos. "El materialismo tardío de Althusser y el corte epistemológico." *Décalages* 1, no. 1 (2011).

Franchi, Stefano. "Les jeux anaclastiques de Lévi-Strauss." In *Le moment philosophique, 1960*, edited by Patrice Maniglier. Paris: PUF, 2011.

Giannotti, J. A. *Contra Althusser*. São Paulo: Cebrap, 1975.

Gillot, Pascale. *Althusser et la psychanalyse*. Paris: PUF, 2009.

Goldmann, Lucien. *The Hidden God: A Study of the Tragic Vision in the Pensées of Pascal and the Tragedies of Racine*. Translated by Philip Thody. London: Routledge, 1964.

Goshgarian, G. M. Introduction to *Philosophy of the Encounter*, in Althusser, *Philosophy of the Encounter*, xli–xliii.

———. Introduction to *The Humanist Controversy and Other Writings*, in Althusser, *The Humanist Controversy and Other Writings*, xi–lxii.

Hegel, G. W. F. *L'esprit du christianisme et son destin*. Translated by Jacques Martin. Paris: Vrin, 1948.

———. *Philosophy of Mind (Encyclopedia of the Philosophical Sciences)*. Translated by William Wallace. Oxford: Oxford University Press, 1971.

———. *The Philosophy of Right*. Translated by Thomas Malcom Knox. Oxford: Oxford University Press, 1967.

———. *The Spirit of Christianity and Its Fate*. In *Early Theological Writings*, translated by T. M. Knox, 182–308. Philadelphia: Penn State University Press, 1988.

Heidegger, Martin. *Sein und Zeit*. Tübingen: Max Niemeyer Verlag, 1960.

Herrick, Tim. "A Book Which Is No Longer Discussed Today: Tran Duc Thao, Jacques Derrida, and Maurice Merleau-Ponty." *Journal of the History of Ideas* 66, no. 1 (January 2005): 113–31.

Hitchens, Christopher. "Transgressing the Boundaries." *New York Times*, May 22, 2005.

Hobbes, Thomas. *De Cive*. http://www.unilibrary.com/ebooks/Hobbes,Thomas -DeCive.pdf.

Husserl, Edmund. *Logical Investigations*. 2 vols. Translated by John N. Findlay. London: Routledge, 1970.

———. "The Origin of Geometry." In *The Crisis of the European Sciences and Transcendental Phenomenology: An Introduction to Phenomenological Philosophy*, translated by David Carr, 353–78. Evanston, IL: Northwestern University Press, 1970.

———. "Philosophy as Rigorous Science." In *Phenomenology and the Crisis in Philosophy*, translated by Quentin Lauer, 69–147. New York: Harper and Row, 1965.

Hyppolite, Jean. *Studies on Marx and Hegel*. New York: Basic Books, 1969.

Jakobson, Roman. *Lectures on Sound and Meaning*. Cambridge: MIT Press, 1942.

———. *Main Trends in the Science of Language*. London: Allen and Unwin, 1973.

Jameson, Fredric. "Deleuze and Dualism." In *Valences of the Dialectic*, 181–200. London: Verso, 2009.

———. *The Prison-House of Language: A Critical Account of Structuralism and Russian Formalism*. Princeton, NJ: Princeton University Press, 1972.

Judt, Tony. *Reappraisals: Reflections on the Forgotten Twentieth Century*. London: Penguin, 2008.

Lawler, Leonard. *Derrida and Husserl: The Basic Problem of Phenomenology*. Bloomington: Indiana University Press, 2002.

Le Blanc, Guillaume. *Canguilhem et les norms*. Paris: PUF, 1998.

———. *La vie humaine: Anthropologie et biologie chez Georeges Canguilhem*. Paris: PUF, 2002.

Lebrun, Gérard. *La patience du concept: Essai sur le discours hégélien*. Paris: Gallimard, 1972.

Lecourt, Dominique. *Bachelard: La jour et la nuit*. Paris: Grasset, 1974.

———. *Pour une critique de l'épistemologie*. Paris: Maspero, 1972.

Lefort, Claude. "L'échange et la lutte des homes." *Les Temps Modernes* 64 (February 1951): 1400–17.

Lévi-Strauss, Claude. *The Savage Mind*. Chicago: University of Chicago Press, 1966. Originally published as *La pensée sauvage* (Paris: Plon, 1962).

———. *Structural Anthropology*. Translated by Claire Jacobson and Brooke Grundfest Schoepf. New York: Doubleday, 1963. Originally published as *Anthropologie strucutrale* (Paris: Plon, 1958).

Lilla, Mark. "Marx and Murder." *Times Literary Supplement*, September 25, 1992.

Lucretius, *De Rerum Natura*. Vol. 2. Translated by Cyril Bailey. Oxford: Clarendon Press, 1947.

Lyotard, Jean-François. *Phenomenology*. Translated by Brian Beakley. Albany: State University of New York Press, 1991. Originally published as *La phenomenology* (Paris: Presses Universitaires de France, 1954).

Macherey, Pierre. "Althusser et le jeune Marx." *Actuel Marx* 1, no. 31 (2002): 159–75.

———. "Georges Canguilhem's Philosophy of Science: Epistemology and History of Science." In Macherey, *In a Materialist Way*, 161–87. Originally published as "La philosophie de la science de G. Canguilhem." *La Pensés* 113 (February 1964): 62–74.

———. *Hegel ou Spinoza*. Paris: Maspero, 1979.

———. *Histoires de dinosaure: Faire de la Philosophie, 1965–1997*. Paris: Presses Universitaires de France, 1999.

———. *In a Materialist Way*. Edited by Warren Montag. Translated by Ted Stolze. London: Verso, 1998.

———. *Introduction à l'Éthique de Spinoza. La seconde partie: La réalité mentale*. Paris: Presses Universitaires de France 1997.

———. "Judith Butler and the Althusserian Theory of Subjection." *Décalages* 1, no. 2 (2012).

———. "L'analyse litterarire: Tombeau de structures," *Les Temps Modernes* 246 (1966): 907–28.

———. "Soutenance." In Macherey, *In a Materialist Way*, 17–27.

———. *A Theory of Literary Production*. Translated by Geoffrey Wall. London: Routledge, 1978. Originally published as "L'analyse litterarire: Tombeau de structures," *Les Temps Modernes* 246 (1966). Reprinted with revisions in *Pour une théorie de la production littéraire* (Paris: Maspero, 1966).

———. "Towards a Natural History of Norms." In *Michel Foucault, Philosopher*, translated by Timothy J. Armstrong, 176–91. London: Routledge, 1992.

Macksey, Richard, and Eugenio Donato, eds. *The Languages of Criticism and the Sciences of Man: The Structuralist Controversy*. Baltimore: Johns Hopkins University Press, 1970.

Malraux, André. *L'espoir*. Paris: Gallimard, 1937.

Mandel, Ernest. *Contra Althusser*. Translated by Jose Sarret Grau. Barcelona: Ediciones Mandrágora, 1975.

Maniglier, Patrice. "L'humanisme interminable." *Les Temps Modernes*, no. 609 (June–August 2000): 216–41.

Maniglier, Patrice, ed. *Le moment philosophique des annees 1960 en France*. Paris: PUF, 2011.

Marcel, Gabriel. *Les hommes contre l'humain*. Paris: Editions du Vieux Colobier, 1951.

Marx, Karl. *Capital*. vol. I. New York: Vintage, 1977.

Matheron, François. Introduction to *The Spectre of Hegel*, in Althusser, *The Spectre of Hegel*, 1–13.

———. "The Recurrence of the Void in Louis Althusser." *Rethinking Marxism* 10, no. 3 (1998): 22–37.

McCormick, Peter, and Frederick A. Elliston. "The Dilthey-Husserl Correspondence." In *Husserl: Shorter Works*, edited by Peter McCormick and Frederick A. Elliston, 203–9. Notre Dame, IN: Notre Dame University Press, 1981.

Merleau-Ponty, Maurice. *Phenomenology of Perception*. Translated by Colin Smith. London: Routledge, 1962. Originally published as *Phénomènologie de la perception* (Paris: Gallimard, 1945).

Meztger, Paul. *Katechon: II Thess 2, 1–12 im Horizont apokalyptischen Denkens*. Berlin: Walter de Gruyter, 2005.

Milner, Jean Claude. *Le periple structural: Figures et paradigme*. Paris: Editions du Seuil, 2002.

Morfino, Vittorio. "An Althusserian Lexicon." *Borderlands* 4, no. 2 (2005): 3–6. http://www.borderlands.net.au/vo14no2_2005/morfino_lexicon.htm.

———. "Escatologia à la cantonade: Althusser oltre Derrida." *Décalages* 1, no. 1 (2011). www.decalages.net.

Morgenstern, Oskar, and John von Neumann. *The Theory of Games and Economic Behavior*. Princeton, NJ: Princeton University Press, 1947.

Mury, Gilbert. "Matérialisme et hyperempiricisme." *La Pensée* 108 (April 1963): 38–51.

Ogilvie, Bertrand. *Lacan, la formation du concept de sujet, 1932–1949*. Paris: Presses Universitaires de France, 1987.

O'Neill, John. *For Marx against Althusser*. Lanham, MD: University Press of America, 1982.

Pêcheux, Michel. "The French Political Winter." In *Language, Semantics, Ideology*, 211–20. New York: St. Martin's Press, 1982.

Politzer, Georges. *Critique des fondements de la psychologie*. Paris: Editions Rieder, 1928.

Pos, Hendrik J. "Perspectives du structuralisme." In *Études phonologiques dédiées à la mémoire de M. le Prince Trubetskoy*, 71–78. Tuscaloosa: University of Alabama Press, 1964. Originally published in *Travaux du Cercle Linguistique de Prague* 8 (1939).

Pouillon, Jean. Introduction to special issue, *Les problèmes de structuralisme. Les Temps Modernes* 246 (1966): 769–90.

Rancière, Jacques. *La leçon d'Althusser*. Paris: Gallimard, 1975.

Raymond, Pierre. *De la combinatoire à la probabilité*. Paris: Maspero, 1975.

Read, Jason. "Primitive Accumulation: The Aleatory Foundations of Capitalism." *Rethinking Marxism* 14, no. 2 (2002): 24–49.

Resch, Robert. *Althusser and the Renewal of Social Theory*. Berkeley: University of California Press, 1992.

Ricoeur, Paul. *Lectures on Ideology and Utopia*. Translated by George H. Taylor. New York: Columbia University Press, 1986.

———. "Structure and Hermeneutics." In *The Conflict of Interpretations*, edited by Don Ihde, translated by Kathleen McLaughlin, 27–61. Evanston, IL: Northwestern University Press, 1974. Originally published as "Structure et hermeneutique," *Esprit* 31, no. 11 (1963): 628–53.

Rosman, Abraham, and Paula G. Rubel. "Structure and Exchange." In *The Cambridge Companion to Lévi-Strauss*, edited by Boris Wiseman, 59–79. Cambridge: Cambridge University Press, 2010.

Roudinesco, Elisabeth. *Jacques Lacan & Co.: A History of Psychoanalysis in France*. Chicago: University of Chicago Press, 1990.

Sartre, Jean-Paul. *The Imaginary: A Phenomenological Psychology of the Imagination*. Translated by Jonathan Webber. London: Routledge, 2004. Originally published as *L'imaginaire* (Paris: Gallimard, 1940).

Schaff, Adam. *A Philosophy of Man*. New York: Monthly Review Press, 1963.

Schmitt, Carl. *Nomos of the Earth*. New York: Telos Press, 2003.

Sebag, Lucien. *Marxisme et structuralisme*. Paris: Payot, 1964.

Sinaceur, Hourya. *Jean Cavaillès. Philosophie mathématique*. Paris: PUF, 1994.

Smith, Steven B. *Reading Althusser: An Essay on Structural Marxism*. Ithaca, NY: Cornell University Press, 1984.

Spiegelberg, Herbert. *The Phenomenological Movement: A Historical Introduction*. Dordrecht: Kluwer, 1982.

Spinoza, Baruch. *Complete Works*. Edited by Michael L. Morgan. Translated by Samuel Shirley. Indianapolis: Hackett Press, 2002.

Sprinker, Michael. *Imaginary Relations: Aesthetics and Ideology in the Theory of Historical Materialism*. London: Verso, 1987.

Stolze, Ted. "Deleuze and Althusser: Flirting with Structuralism." *Rethinking Marxism* 10, no. 3 (1998): 51–63.

Terray, Emmanuel. *Marxism and "Primitive" Societies*. New York: Monthly Review Press, 1969.

Thao, Tran Duc. *Phenomenology and Dialectical Materialism*. Edited by Robert S. Cohen. Translated by Daniel J. Herman and Donald V. Morano. Dordrecht: Reidel Publishing, 1971. Originally published as *Phénomenologie at matérialisme dialectique* (Paris: Minh Tan, 1951).

Thompson, E. P. *The Poverty of Theory: An Orrery of Errors*. New York: Monthly Review Press, 1978.

Tosel, André. "Les aléas du matérialisme aléatoire dans la dernière philosophie de Louis Althusser." In *Sartre, Lukács, Althusser: Des Marxistes en philosophie*, edited by Eustache Kouvélakis and Vincent Charbonier, 169–96. Paris: PUF, 2005.

Troubetzkoy, Nikolai. *Principles of Phonology*. Berkeley: University of California Press, 1969.

Wallon, Henri. *Les origines du caractère chez l'enfant*. Paris: Boisvin, 1934.

Zafiropolous, Markos. *Lacan and Lévi-Strauss, or, The Return to Freud (1951–1957)*. London: Carnac Books, 2010.

Index

Engels, Friedrich, 107

Epicurus, 10, 16, 175, 182–83, 215n6

eschatology, 12, 190–91, 197, 202; Althusser's early critique of, 192–93

essence, 63, 67, 85–86, 92; singular, 43, 51, 93

Feuerbach, Ludwig, 50, 135–36, 149

formalism, 41–42, 51, 85; in Lévi-Strauss, 68–69; and structuralism, 77, 84

Foucault, Michel, 8, 186; Althusser on, 23–24; on ideology, 161–70; on phenomenology, 50–51, 54; and structuralism, 20–21, 25

Fourtounis, Giorgos, 96

Freud, Anna, 123–24

Freud, Sigmund, 18, 81, 118–19, 123, 147

Fromm, Erich, 105

game theory, 59–60

genesis, 50, 77; and structure, 33–35

Goldmann, Lucien, 32–33

government: three types of, 26–28

Gramsci, Antonio, 145, 158

Hegel, G. W. F., 5, 11, 36–37, 61–62, 156; Althusser's readings of, 28–33; as basis for structuralism, 66, 93; on destiny, 202–4; and nothingness, 185; refusal of origin, 49–50. *See also* dialectic: Hegelian

Heidegger, Martin, 47, 175; Althusser on, 181–84

hermeneutics, 64, 69

historicism, 10, 32, 34, 37–38, 73, 99

history, 10–11, 32, 36–39, 48–49, 186; of the body, 165–66; human, 31, 34; and ideology, 146–47; Montesquieu's conception of, 26–28; of science, 43–46

Hitchens, Christopher, 2

Hobbes, Thomas, 17, 124, 126, 157, 175–76; Rousseau's critique of, 124, 179–80

humanism, 65; anti-, 31, 67; Marxist, 105–6

Husserl, Edmund, 20, 33–35; critique of Dilthey (*see* Dilthey, Wilhelm); debates in France, 39–42; on Lebenswelt, 114–16; Marxist readings of, 46–48; and structuralism, 54–56

Hyppolite, Jean, 30, 49, 185

idealism, 9, 67–68; vs. materialism, 193

Ideological State Apparatus (ISA), 144–46, 150–51, 160; vs. repressive state apparatus (RSA), 158, 164

ideology, 11, 50, 67–68, 103–4, 159–60; Althusser's early definition of, 107–13; Althusser's theses on, 146–50; as conceived in "Ideology," 143–47; and consciousness (*see* consciousness); and history (*see* history); material existence of, 152–57; and psychoanalysis, 118–19; vs. science (*see* science); and unconscious (*see* unconscious)

immanence, 86–87, 89–90, 155

interpellation, 137–40, 156–58, 165–68

Jakobson, Roman, 20, 54–55

Judt, Tony, 2

Kant, Immanuel, 38, 40, 114, 155

katechon, 200–201, 203–5

Kojève, Alexandre, 30

Kuhn, Thomas, 16

Lacan, Jacques, 20, 25, 57–58, 108; Althusser's reading of, 118–21, 124–25, 131–32; Spinoza and, 123

Lagache, Daniel, 125

law: and Judaism, 200–203; and Montesquieu, 26–28

Lebenswelt (lifeworld): Althusser's critique of, 113–14

Lefort, Claude, 47, 58–59

Lenin, Vladimir, 95

Lévi-Strauss, Claude, 16, 27, 32, 84, 100, 109, 122, 218n1; Althusser's reading of, 53–54, 61–65, 67–70; Derrida on, 70–72; influence of Roman Jakobson, 54–55; and structuralism, 19–20, 58–59

Lilla, Mark, 2

linguistic model, 19–20, 26, 32, 53–54

linguistics, 58, 67, 76, 107; and discourse, 132–34, 138; structural, 53–54, 68

literature: Macherey on, 76

Locke, John, 180; definition of consciousness, 169

Lucretius, 10, 15–16, 75–76, 96, 215n7; as

interpreted by Deleuze (*see* Deleuze, Gilles); and materialism of the encounter, 181–83

Lukacs, Georg, 66

Lyotard, Jean-Francois, 47–49, 56, 217n5

Macherey, Pierre, 83–84, 87, 89, 96–97, 163, 193, 214n15; on Canguilhem, 43–45; critique of structure, 73–79, 100; "Literary Analysis: Tomb of Structures," 75–76, 78, 97; on Spinoza, 90–93, 176–77

Machiavelli, Niccolo, 175, 178–79, 209–10

Madonia, Franca, 23, 79–80

Malraux, André, 194, 198–200

Marcel, Gabriel, 196, 198

Marx, Karl, 29, 84, 175; discussion of *Darstellung* (see *Darstellung*); on ideology, 107; and materialism of the encounter, 180; and reading, 81–82, 191; relation to Hegel, 29–30; theory of base/superstructure, 143–44; young, 105–6

Marxism, 5, 25, 51, 93, 161, 195; and phenomenology, 46–47; structural, 15–16, 64; and structuralism, 65–66

materialism, 10, 16, 48, 68; aleatory (*see* materialism of the encounter); dialectical, 103; historical, 68; vs. idealism, 193; and phenomenology, 46–47

materialism of the encounter, 16, 180–81; historical development of, 175–76; and void, 187–89

Matheron, François, 30, 174, 176, 182

Merleau-Ponty, Maurice, 46, 57–58, 108, 116, 122

messianism, 197; critique of, 194

Montesquieu, Charles-Louis de Secondat: Althusser's reading of, 26–28, 31, 61; and Hegel, 29

Morgenstern, Oskar, 59–60

Mury, Gilbert, 93

Nietzsche, Friedrich, 44, 81

nominalism, 56

nothingness: originary, 184–85, 187

origin, 12, 72, 84, 115; in Hegel, 49–50; Heidegger's conception of, 183–84; and

Husserlian phenomenology, 34–36, 42, 46–49; and subject, 125–26, 129–30, 157; and the void, 179–81, 185–87

overdetermination, 62, 96

Panopticon, 169–70

Pascal, Blaise, 153–54, 227n6

Paul, St., 200–201

Pêcheux, Michel, 25, 156

phenomenology, 41–42, 51–52, 68; Derrida on, 33–35; and Lévi-Strauss, 54–55, 58; and materialism. 46–48; relation to ideology, 108, 113

philosophy, 6–7, 73, 210; Althusser's conception of, 17; and the encounter (*see* encounter; materialism of the encounter); French, 4, 50; and science, 37–38, 40, 43, 51; vs. theology, 193, 227n6; and the void, 178–80, 184, 186. *See also* void

phonology, 20, 55, 57

Plato, 61, 100, 148–49

Politzer, Georges, 120–21

Pos, Hendrik J., 55–58

Pouillon, Jean, 76

power: Foucault's conception of, 162–64, 167–70, 224n36

practice, 46, 154; scientific, 44–45

proletariat: universal, 205

psychoanalysis: Althusser's critique of, 118–19; relation to phenomenology, 120–22; specificity of, 123

psychology, 120–21, 126; vs. psychoanalysis, 124–25

Rancière, Jacques, 2–3, 10, 23, 25, 213n6, 223n7, 224n36

Raymond, Pierre, 61

reading, 7, 18, 70, 96, 174, 209; and Biblical interpretation, 141–42; symptomatic, 9, 18, 80–83, 152

Repressive State Apparatus (RSA), 144, 158

reproduction, 143–44

revolution, 94, 161

Ricoeur, Paul, 38–39, 64–65, 113

Rousseau, Jean-Jacques, 124, 175, 178, 180, 210

Made in the USA
San Bernardino, CA
25 May 2020